THE
ENTREPRENEURIAL
EXPERIENCE

W. GIBB DYER, JR.

THE ENTREPRENEURIAL EXPERIENCE

CONFRONTING CAREER DILEMMAS OF THE START-UP EXECUTIVE

Jossey-Bass Publishers · San Francisco

For sales outside the United States contact Maxwell Macmillan International Publishing Group, 866 Third Avenue, New York, New York 10022

Printed on acid-free paper and manufactured in the United States of America

 The paper used in this book meets the state of California requirements for recycled paper (50 percent recycled waste, including 10
percent postconsumer waste), which are the strictest guidelines for
recycled paper currently in use in the United States.

Library of Congress Cataloging-in-Publication Data

Dyer, W. Gibb, date.
    The entrepreneurial experience : confronting career dilemmas of
the start-up executive / W. Gibb Dyer, Jr.
       p.   cm. — (The Jossey-Bass management series)
    Includes bibliographical references and index.
    ISBN 1-55542-417-1
    1. New business enterprises—Management. 2. Entrepreneurship.
3. Career development. I. Title. II. Series.
HD62.5.D94 1992
658.1'141—dc20   91-39474
                                                   CIP

FIRST EDITION
HB Printing   10 9 8 7 6 5 4 3 2 1   *Code 9233*

THE JOSSEY-BASS
MANAGEMENT SERIES

CONTENTS

PREFACE

The dream of many people today is to be an entrepreneur and own their own business. Some want to embark on an entrepreneurial career because they have become dissatisfied with oppressive conditions in the organizations where they work. Others want to express their creative talents and abilities. Still others want to reap the rewards of their labors and be acknowledged for their accomplishments. The dream of being one's own boss is becoming a reality as more and more people discover the entrepreneurial spirit.

Despite this interest, there is little information regarding what it takes to succeed as an entrepreneur. Numerous books and articles offer advice about how to start a business, or recount the stories of individual entrepreneurs who have succeeded, but few describe the more universal problems, issues, and concerns that entrepreneurs encounter over the span of their careers, from start-up through retirement. As a result, few who become entrepreneurs are well equipped to cope with the rigors of a self-made career. Many stumble and fail because they are ill prepared to manage the problems that owners of new businesses face, problems for which there are no easy answers. Businesses, families, and entrepreneurs themselves often suffer as they watch their dream turn into a nightmare. So while the rewards of entrepreneurship can be great, so can the costs.

As a consultant to entrepreneurs, I have found that start-up executives need to better understand and anticipate the dilemmas in their own careers and to develop successful strategies to deal with those dilemmas. Seeing this need has motivated me to write this book.

The Entrepreneurial Experience describes the common hopes and dreams that most entrepreneurs cultivate, as well as the pitfalls and crises that they most frequently encounter. It presents the personal, professional, and family dilemmas that entrepreneurs face at each stage of their careers and discusses strategies that can be used to manage such problems successfully. It also describes how those associated with entrepreneurs — family members, co-workers, and consultants — can help them manage the changes that occur throughout the entrepreneur's career. Thus, this book will provide, both for entrepreneurs and for those who share in their lives, greater insight into the nature of the entrepreneurial experience.

Background of the Book

My own interest in entrepreneurship began more than a decade ago, during the first major research project I worked on as a doctoral student at the Massachusetts Institute of Technology. The research site for the project was the headquarters of the Digital Equipment Corporation (DEC) in Maynard, Massachusetts. As I studied the company history, I was amazed that founder Kenneth Olsen and a handful of committed followers had been able to create an organization that employed tens of thousands of people and had helped to spark the computer revolution. As I interviewed employees who had been with DEC during the 1950s, when the company was struggling to survive, their stories of how they had solved perplexing technical and organizational problems and their accounts of personal and family sacrifices left an indelible impression on me.

Since that time, I have continued to be interested in how entrepreneurs start and build businesses and in what kinds of personal, professional, and family dilemmas they have to resolve to be successful. My own research and consulting work over the past ten years have reflected this interest. More recently, I created a course at Brigham Young University entitled "Managing Entrepreneurial Firms and Family-Owned Businesses."

The students who take the course are generally interested in running their own businesses or entering the family business. They often ask me, "What is it like to be an entrepreneur?" "What problems do entrepreneurs face?" "How can I prepare myself for an entrepreneurial career?" While I often invite entrepreneurs to speak to the class and address students' concerns, I have found these questions difficult to answer. Thus, another reason for researching this topic and writing the book was to help my students better understand the dynamics of an entrepreneur's career.

Research Procedures

Data used in *The Entrepreneurial Experience* were gathered over the past several years by a team of researchers at Brigham Young University. Besides me, the group included Gene Dalton (professor emeritus in the Department of Organizational Behavior), and research assistants Jean Brown, Frank Holdaway, Gordon Holland, and Roger Peay. (When I refer to "we" in reference to data collection and analysis, it is to this group that I am referring.)

The material presented here was generated from a number of sources. Our research team at Brigham Young University conducted thirty-five interviews with entrepreneurs during a three-year period, from 1988 to 1991. Fourteen of the interviews, which lasted between one and three hours, were taped and transcribed. (The questions asked in the interviews can be found in the Resource.) However, the questions served only as a general guide for the interviewer; the entrepreneurs were encouraged to tell their own stories and cover any subject that they deemed important.

From 1987 to 1991, I also had student research teams carry out research and consulting projects in entrepreneurial firms, often in conjunction with the university's Small Business Development Center. The students conducted approximately seventy case studies of entrepreneurial firms, interviewing the founders to understand their concerns and problems, analyzing the strategy, structure, and culture of the organizations, and reporting on their findings. To supplement those sources, we analyzed the biographies of eleven entrepreneurs — including Walt Disney, Levi Strauss, Willard Marriott, Trammel Crow, and Thomas Watson — using the questions found in the Resource.

From 1980 to 1989, I had the opportunity to study four entrepreneurial firms in depth. Each of the studies lasted for more than two years. I interviewed founders, venture capitalists, members of the entrepreneurs' families, and employees at all levels in their organizations. Portions of these studies have been reported in various forms.[1] I also used several dozen short cases found in books and in journals such as *Forbes* and *INC.* to supplement the data from the interviews and case studies. These short vignettes generally did not provide the broad background and context for the entrepreneurs' careers, but they were useful in highlighting some of their key career dilemmas.

From the interviews and case studies I developed a list of fifteen dilemmas to discuss with a group of entrepreneurs affiliated with Brigham Young University. I asked the group to comment on whether the dilemmas were consistent with their own experiences; I also discussed the issue with several entrepreneurs individually. I used their feedback to further modify and refine my treatment of the dilemmas presented in the book. Since the data on which this book is based were collected from a wide variety of sources and by different methods, it is difficult to make exact comparisons among cases. Thus, the book should not be viewed as the result of a strictly controlled research study. Rather, it is the result of an attempt to gather data regarding entrepreneurs and their careers from a variety of sources, to synthesize those data, and then to describe the issues and dilemmas that seem to be common to the entrepreneurial experience.

Overview of the Contents

The Entrepreneurial Experience is organized into four parts, following the introductory chapter. Parts One, Two, and Three focus respectively on the dilemmas of early, middle, and late career; within each part, chapters are specifically devoted to the personal, business, and family aspects of these dilemmas. Part Four

offers specific strategies that the entrepreneur's family, co-
workers, and consultants can employ to help the entrepreneur
manage a successful career. It also summarizes the key dilemmas
and outlines a general career strategy that will help entrepreneurs successfully manage dilemmas regardless of the career
stage they are in. Strategies offered throughout the book come
from my own experience, from the experiences of experts in the
field, and from those of the entrepreneurs we studied. Since each
entrepreneur's experience is unique, most of the strategies focus
on the general process and approach for solving a given dilemma,
rather than provide a specific answer. The approaches are de-
signed to be adapted by the reader to fit his or her individual
situation.

In Part One, which discusses early career dilemmas,
Chapter One describes the attributes of those who embark on
an entrepreneurial career. Chapter Two highlights the issues
surrounding getting resources to start a business, with an emphasis on the role of networking to obtain resources. In Chapter Three, the problems entrepreneurs face in working with partners and boards of directors are described. Chapter Four points
out the difficulties entrepreneurs encounter as they attempt to
grow a business while trying to meet family responsibilities.

Part Two, with its focus on midcareer issues, begins with
Chapter Five, which discusses the potential stress and loneliness of the entrepreneurial life-style and presents several strategies for coping with these problems. Since many entrepreneurs
feel that they lose control of their businesses as they begin to
grow rapidly, Chapter Six gives advice on how to maintain control of a growing enterprise. Chapter Seven explores the problems associated with trying to turn an entrepreneurial firm into
a professionally managed organization, while Chapter Eight
presents the dilemmas that accompany the hiring of family members into the business.

Part Three begins its discussion of late-career issues with
Chapter Nine, which describes the psychological dilemmas that
entrepreneurs must grapple with as they think about retirement.
Chapter Ten discusses how an entrepreneur can plan for succession and prepare the business for the future, while Chapter

Eleven focuses on how the entrepreneur can successfully transfer personal values and financial assets to his or her family.

Part Four begins with Chapter Twelve, which offers advice to those associated with entrepreneurs. This chapter presents
various strategies that can be used by the entrepreneur's family,
co-workers, and consultants to help entrepreneurs succeed in
their careers. The final chapter, Chapter Thirteen, discusses the
key attributes that will help entrepreneurs achieve career success and presents several strategies for developing these attributes.

Acknowledgments

I would like to thank K. Fred Skousen, dean of the Marriott
School of Management at Brigham Young University, and the
Marriott School's Center for Entrepreneurial Studies for their
support of this project. My colleagues in the Department of Organizational Behavior have also been very supportive of my
work. The book was greatly improved by the criticism of Bar-
bara Bird, Ernesto J. Poza, Edgar H. Schein, Max S. Wort-
man, Jr., and William Hicks of Jossey-Bass. Two highly successful entrepreneurs, Nyal McMullin and Roy Spiers, also
provided timely guidance. To them I am grateful.

In particular, I would like to thank my father and mentor, William G. Dyer, dean emeritus of the Marriott School of
Management, for his help in developing the book. He read each
chapter carefully and provided invaluable comments and insight;
I am particularly grateful for his contribution to Chapter Four.
Both he and my mother, Bonnie Hansen Dyer, have provided
me with a great deal of support in my academic pursuits throughout my life.

Finally, I would like to acknowledge the support of my
wife, Theresa, and our six children: Emily, Justin, Alison,
Mary, Christine, and Laura. Their encouragement has made
writing this book a much easier task.

Provo, Utah   W. Gibb Dyer, Jr.
February 1992

THE AUTHOR

W. Gibb Dyer, Jr., is an associate professor of organizational behavior at Brigham Young University. He received his B.S. degree (1977) in psychology and his M.B.A. degree (1979) at Brigham Young University, and his Ph.D. degree in management philosophy from the Massachusetts Institute of Technology. He has written widely in the areas of family business, entrepreneurship, organizational culture, and managing change in organizations. His articles have appeared in the *Academy of Management Review,* the *Journal of Small Business Management,* the *Family Business Review,* the *Sloan Management Review,* and *Organizational Dynamics.* He is the author of the award-winning book *Cultural Change in Family Firms: Anticipating and Managing Business and Family Transitions* (1986) and coauthor of *Managing by the Numbers: Absentee Owners and the Decline of American Industry* (1988, with C. Meek and W. Woodworth).

Dyer has served as a consultant to numerous organizations in a variety of industries. In 1990 he received the Leavy Award for Excellence in Private Enterprise Education by the Freedoms Foundation of Valley Forge, Pennsylvania.

THE
ENTREPRENEURIAL
EXPERIENCE

What Are the Dilemmas of an Entrepreneurial Career?

The latter part of the twentieth century might one day be called by historians "the age of the entrepreneur." Never in the history of the United States (nor of many other countries) has there been such a surge of interest in entrepreneurship and entrepreneurial activity. New business start-ups in the United States have increased dramatically in recent years. There were approximately 1.3 million new enterprises being started annually by 1990 — a 1,400 percent increase from forty years ago — and Steve Jobs (founder of Apple and NEXT Computers) and Sam Walton of Walmart had become household names.[1] Entrepreneurial organizations, networks, newsletters, and journals have spread like wildfire. Biographies and autobiographies of entrepreneurs and self-help books on launching a new business have come to dominate the business sections of many bookstores.

Although they have generally lagged behind the popular interest in entrepreneurship, many universities have now set up centers for "entrepreneurial studies," and courses on various facets of entrepreneurship are now being taught at virtually every major university. College students can even declare a major in entrepreneurship, and chairs in entrepreneurial studies are routinely being endowed at colleges around the country.

Why the interest in entrepreneurship? Part of it has to do with the decline in employment in the Fortune 500 firms in the latter part of the twentieth century. It is estimated that more than 500,000 jobs were lost during the 1980s, largely as a result of the decline in smokestack industries and the increasing number of imports.[2] With this new state of affairs, many people who can no longer rely on large companies for lifetime employment have felt compelled to start new ventures to gain their livelihood. Another reason for the interest in entrepreneurship is governmental encouragement. As the United States has lost much of its competitive edge in the global economy during recent years, the U.S. administration has deemed entrepreneurship and innovation to be the appropriate response and has gone to great lengths to encourage an economic climate in which entrepreneurs can flourish. Small business development centers and other small business "incubators" are just a few signs of the government's interest in stimulating new business activity.

Possibly the most important reason for the interest in entrepreneurship is the fabulous success stories told by entrepreneurs who have become celebrities and millionaires almost overnight. No longer were the "organization men" such as former chairman of General Motors Roger Smith the businessmen to emulate; it was now the risk takers, the movers and shakers in the business world, such as Steve Jobs, who were admired and esteemed. Indeed, these individuals seemed to embody the American dream that anyone can pull him- or herself up by his or her own bootstraps, and their success stories motivated many to strike out on their own. Much as during the frenzied days of the California gold rush, many began to seek their fortunes by starting their own businesses. From most reports, the lives of the successful entrepreneurs were idyllic, filled with wealth and power. By taking charge of their own destinies, they seemed to have overcome what Thoreau described as the "lives of quiet desperation" that afflict the mass of mankind.

Despite the rather rosy picture that has often been painted of entrepreneurship, many entrepreneurs lead rather troubled lives. Over the past ten years, I have had the opportunity to do extensive research and consulting with those who have embarked on entrepreneurial careers. While they report that their careers are often exciting and rewarding, they also describe many difficult dilemmas that they face at various points. Indeed, many of them lead lives of quiet desperation as they grapple with personal, family, and business problems. Because they generally are breaking new ground as they go through their careers, there is often little guidance to help them avoid the pitfalls. Moreover, entrepreneurs are often proud individuals who avoid showing weakness and thus are reluctant to seek out counsel and help regarding their more troublesome personal problems. Thus, they are left to exorcise their demons alone.

As I have worked with various entrepreneurs, they have presented me with some difficult and complex questions that have no easy answers. For example:

- Should I rehire my son, whom I just fired for stealing from the company?
- How should I deal with the loneliness I feel as the leader of this company?
- Should I hire professional managers to run my business? Can I trust them?
- Should I hire family members? If I do, how do I evaluate their performance?
- How do I develop rules and guidelines to make my business more efficient?
- Should I retire? If so, who should be my successor?
- How do I find the right partner?

Unfortunately, much that has been written about entrepreneurs and entrepreneurship has failed to deal with these kinds of questions. Most writers on entrepreneurship have focused on the personality of the entrepreneur or on the issues concerning the start-up phase of a business. Little attention has been paid to how entrepreneurs feel about their careers over time and how the dilemmas that they deal with change dramatically at different points during their lives. For example, entrepreneurs nearing the end of their careers and contemplating retirement deal with a set of issues very different from those confronting entrepreneurs struggling to start a business or experiencing rapid growth of their firms.

In the course of this book, we will explore the issues that are part of the experience of an entrepreneurial career, highlighting the personal, family, and business dilemmas that entrepreneurs face over the course of their careers and discussing the various options available to the entrepreneur confronting those dilemmas. Before proceeding further, however, we need to clearly define what is meant by an *entrepreneurial career* and then provide an overall framework for understanding the dilemmas facing entrepreneurs at the various stages of their careers.

What Is an Entrepreneurial Career?

As we begin our discussion of the dilemmas that entrepreneurs face over the course of their careers, we must develop working definitions of the terms *entrepreneur* and *career*. The meanings of these terms are rather elusive. The term *entrepreneur* comes from the twelfth-century French word *entreprendre*, which means "to undertake" or "to do something."[3] The term was often used to describe "merchant adventurers" during the Renaissance. In more recent times, the term *entrepreneur* has been popularized by the Harvard economist Joseph Schumpeter, who has argued that entrepreneurs develop "new combinations" that lead to the development of new markets, new products, new services, new production and distribution methods, and so forth. Other definitions of *entrepreneurship* are generally variations on Schumpeter's theme.[4]

The core attribute of entrepreneurs is their ability to found new enterprises. Indeed, the founding of new businesses is the essence of entrepreneurial activity. Thus, for the purposes of this book, the study of entrepreneurial careers will be confined to an analysis of the careers of those who create new enterprises.

The sociologist Erving Goffman defined *career* as "any social strand of any person's course through life."[5] That is, one's career is not merely what one does in the world of work but the total experience of one's life. In our study of entrepreneurial careers, we will use the term *career* in this broad sense as we explore the personal, family, and business issues and dilemmas that are integral to the life course of an entrepreneur.[6] Goffman also notes that the term is useful because of its "two-sidedness": "One side is linked to the internal matters held dearly and closely, such as image of self and felt identity; the other side concerns official position, jural relations, and the style of life and is part of a publicly accessible institutional complex. The concept of career, then, allows one to move back and forth between the personal and the public, between the self and its significant society."[7] In Goffman's view, one can study careers "objectively," in terms of their role and place in society (as when we study the careers of police officers, fire fighters, doctors, or college professors), as well as "subjectively," in terms of how a person feels and thinks about his or her career. In this book, we focus largely on the subjective side of the entrepreneurial career, describing how entrepreneurs interpret their worlds as they attempt to manage the dilemmas that confront them in their careers.

The Dynamics of an Entrepreneurial Career

Despite the renewed interest in entrepreneurship, little research has been done to examine how entrepreneurs manage their careers. For example, a recent anthology of research on careers virtually ignored the entrepreneur.[8] Much of the research in academia seems to focus on organizational and occupational careers, where individuals are attempting to adapt to the constraints imposed on them by an organization or occupation. The focus of such research is understanding how individuals move up in the occupational or organizational hierarchy.

In contrast, entrepreneurs have the ability to create the environment and context for their own careers. They do not have to move up in the organization since, by definition, they start at the top and, if successful, create an organizational hierarchy below them. Moreover, entrepreneurial careers seem to take many and varied paths, so that it is difficult to develop a general theory of what constitutes an entrepreneurial career. These difficulties seem to be reflected in the dearth of research on entrepreneurial careers.

Career Stages and Dilemmas

The dilemmas that entrepreneurs encounter in the course of their careers are rather specific to their life-style. Moreover, the kinds of dilemmas that they face differ according to the stages of their lives and the development of their businesses. There are three general career stages that entrepreneurs appear to go through. Most entrepreneurs begin their businesses in the period between their late twenties and late thirties. Midcareer dilemmas seem to emerge when they are in their forties to mid fifties, while late career dilemmas become more acute after age fifty-five. While there are certainly exceptions to this timetable, it is the most common temporal ordering of the stages. The common dilemmas found at each stage are listed in Table I.1.

Early Career Dilemmas. Those just embarking on an entrepreneurial career commonly experience four dilemmas. The first is finding their sense of identity as entrepreneurs. Most have doubts as to whether they can succeed and are uncertain about just what is needed for success. "Am I an entrepreneur?" is the initial question facing many who want to become entrepreneurs.

There are also two significant business dilemmas related to the starting of the new enterprise. One of these is finding the resources to get started. Most entrepreneurs need labor, capital,

Table I.1. The Dilemmas of an Entrepreneurial Career.

	Personal	*Business*	*Family*
Early career	Am I an entrepreneur?	How do I get started?	How do I balance work and family?
		How do I manage problems with partners and boards?	
Midcareer	Why is it so lonely at the top?	How do I stay in control of my business?	Should I employ family members?
		Should I hire professional managers?	
Late career	Should I retire?	How do I prepare my business for the future?	What should I leave to my family?

and raw materials to get their businesses started, and many fail because they are not able to obtain these resources. The other business dilemma concerns how the new enterprise is governed. Many entrepreneurs tell horror stories about their relationships with partners and boards of directors. Few feel that they have developed successful strategies for dealing with problem partners.

The final early career dilemma is balancing the needs of work and family. Most entrepreneurs start their families and their businesses at about the same time. Thus, they often feel pulled by the conflicting demands of business and family systems and frequently have feelings of guilt regarding their family life. As they reflect on their work-family relationships, many entrepreneurs in the later stages of their careers note that they managed the balancing act between the two systems quite poorly.

Midcareer Dilemmas. The dilemmas in midcareer are quite different from those in the early career stage. As the business grows, the problems are concerned more with sustaining and building it than with merely struggling to keep it alive. Four significant dilemmas are commonly encountered at this time. The first is the feelings of loneliness that often plague entrepreneurs in a growing business. As the business grows and the number of employees increases, the pressures and responsibilities also become greater. More people depend on the entrepreneur for their livelihoods. It is at this stage that many entrepreneurs report that they often feel isolated from their employees and even from their families and have few people to whom they can confide their fears and frustrations. If such feelings of loneliness are not dealt with, they can overwhelm the entrepreneur and turn the career from a satisfying experience into a terrible burden.

The second dilemma concerns the entrepreneur's ability to remain in control of a growing enterprise. While the new business is in its infancy, the entrepreneur can generally be aware of almost everything that is going on in it and closely supervise all business operations. As the business grows, however, the entrepreneur may suddenly realize that he or she no longer has intimate knowledge of or direct control over each area of the business. This can lead to a great deal of emotional pain and discomfort for entrepreneurs unless they can develop new ways to organize and control their businesses.

The third dilemma in midcareer is the issue of whether to bring in "professional managers" to run the business. Most entrepreneurs report that they need many of the skills of those trained in leading business schools in areas such as finance, market research, and production planning and yet feel uncomfortable with the values espoused by those with formal business training. Thus, the entrepreneur must develop some means to obtain these needed skills while remaining true to his or her own values and vision of the firm.

The fourth dilemma is the question of hiring family members. The children of entrepreneurs who are in midcareer are usually old enough to begin working in the business. But hiring children or other family members may pose significant challenges, since business and family norms and practices are often at odds with each other. If this dilemma is not handled skillfully, entrepreneurs may build successful businesses but at the same time destroy their families.

Late Career Dilemmas. Late career dilemmas involve disengaging from the entrepreneurial career and preparing oneself, one's family, and one's business for the future. The three dilemmas at this stage of the career are captured in the following questions: (1) Should I retire? (2) How should I prepare my business for the future? (3) What should I leave to my family? The answers to these questions depend on how the entrepreneur feels about retirement and succession. Most entrepreneurs would rather not think about these issues, yet avoiding them can create serious problems for the entrepreneurs themselves and for succeeding generations. Developing an estate plan, grooming a successor for the business, teaching values to the next generation, and developing new interests are activities that require attention by the entrepreneur in late career.

Variations on the Career Stages. Of course, in some cases, time becomes compressed, and issues that demand resolution at each career stage seem to overlap or may arise simultaneously. For example, a person with grown children who starts an entrepreneurial career in his or her late fifties may have all the early career dilemmas to deal with as well as the midcareer dilemma of deciding whether to hire family members. This entrepreneur may also need to begin thinking about late career issues such as estate planning and succession in the near future. In this situation, while the dilemmas still have a temporal ordering, they may need to be dealt with in rapid-fire succession.

Some entrepreneurs may never encounter some of the usual dilemmas. For example, if the entrepreneur's firm never really expands or grows, the issue of professional management may not arise. Moreover, because different entrepreneurs may see the world differently and have different skills, what might be a dilemma for one might not be a problem for another. However, among the entrepreneurs that we studied, most of whom were quite successful and had thriving businesses, these were the most common dilemmas that demanded their attention and proved difficult to resolve.

Influences of Race, Ethnic Background, and Gender

While this book attempts to describe the most common dilemmas experienced by entrepreneurs, the entrepreneur's race, ethnic background, and gender will influence how his or her career develops. For example, we find that the percentage of Asian Americans who own their own businesses is more than three times as high as that of African Americans.[9] Many of these differences can be traced to cultural norms supporting entrepreneurship, role models in the community, and community and institutional support for entrepreneurial activity. Thus, one must be aware of these kinds of differences when analyzing the careers of entrepreneurs.

Gender may also affect one's entrepreneurial experience. A recent review of the research on the differences between male and female entrepreneurs by Sue Birley, a noted researcher on entrepreneurship, revealed the following:

1. Men and women have similar motivations for starting an entrepreneurial career.

2. Male and female entrepreneurs are quite similar in terms of marital status and family backgrounds. However, women may feel more pressure to make a decision regarding whether to have children, since their "biological clocks" are ticking.
3. Both men and women have similar problems acquiring resources such as capital. Discrimination does not appear to be a significant barrier.
4. Women tend to emphasize the retail industry and the service sector more than men do.

Birley feels that the differences between men and women entrepreneurs are not particularly significant. In summarizing her review, she writes that "the profile of women entrepreneurs in the future . . . [will] move even closer to that of their male colleagues."[10]

    While it appears that race, ethnic background, and to a certain degree gender influence how one experiences an entrepreneurial career, my data base does not allow for an easy comparison of these groups. However, there did not appear to be any systematic differences in the kinds of dilemmas faced by the entrepreneurs that we studied based on race, ethnic background, and gender (although there was a relatively small number of minority entrepreneurs in the data base). What this book attempts to do is articulate the dilemmas that appear to be universal — for example, all entrepreneurs must acquire resources to get started — and describe the more common approaches to dealing with those dilemmas. However, the reader should keep in mind that the factors of race, ethnic background, and gender will influence how the individual entrepreneur copes with a given dilemma. When possible, I will alert the reader if these factors appear to make a significant difference in managing a particular career dilemma.

Conclusion

Armed with this overview of the dynamics of an entrepreneurial career, we will use the following chapters to develop a better understanding of each career dilemma and discuss strategies for successfully managing these dilemmas. To confront the dilemmas of an entrepreneurial career requires a great deal of self-insight, careful planning, and hard work; entrepreneurs often find that they need to make significant changes in their personal lives and develop new problem-solving skills in order to have a satisfying career. With this in mind, we will now embark on our study of the entrepreneurial experience.

PART ONE

EARLY
CAREER
DILEMMAS

ONE

AM I AN ENTREPRENEUR?

As we begin our journey to explore the dilemmas of an entrepreneurial career, we must develop a basic understanding of these people who are called entrepreneurs. While researchers and writers in this field want to know what their backgrounds and motivations for starting their careers are and how they see and define themselves, those contemplating an entrepreneurial career deal with a different set of issues. Their questions are: Should I start a new (and risky) venture? Can I do it? How do I begin? In this chapter, we deal with both sets of questions in greater detail by examining the backgrounds, motivations, and attributes of those attempting to start an entrepreneurial career and focus on the key psychological dilemma facing each potential entrepreneur: Do I have what it takes to succeed?

What Is an Entrepreneur?

An article by Peter Kilby published several years ago described the difficulties defining an entrepreneur. Kilby likened the entrepreneur to a "Heffalump," a fictional animal in A. A. Milne's Winnie-the-Pooh stories. Like the Heffalump, the entrepreneur "has been hunted by many individuals using various ingenious trapping devices, but no one so far has succeeded in capturing him. All who claim to have caught sight of him report that he is enormous, but they disagree on his particularities."[1]

Part of the problem of capturing the essence of entrepreneurship is the multifaceted nature of the entrepreneurial role. Entrepreneurs are often builders, creators, inventors, managers, and leaders, all at the same time. Furthermore, few individuals who are considered entrepreneurs have developed clear self-identities as entrepreneurs. Most see themselves as real estate developers, retailers, engineers, or investment bankers who hap-

15

pened to start a new enterprise. It is those in the academic community who have exploited the term *entrepreneur,* largely basing their arguments on the work of Joseph Schumpeter and attempting to study those individuals who seem to fit the Schumpeterian model.[2] At an academic conference on entrepreneurship that I attended, a group of entrepreneurs and several professors were wrestling with the definition of entrepreneurship when one entrepreneur expressed his opinion that there were many different kinds of entrepreneurs and that a single definition did not make sense. Most of the group agreed, and they began to describe the kinds of entrepreneurs that they were acquainted with. The general categories were as described below.

Technical Entrepreneurs

These individuals have a strong technical orientation. They love inventing things and developing ideas for new products. Developing new markets and even new industries based on state-of-the-art technologies is generally the goal of those with this technical orientation, and the creation of an organization is merely the means to achieving their goals, not an end in itself. One such entrepreneur is David Evans, the founder of Evans and Sutherland, a computer modeling and simulation firm. Evans started his career as a professor doing teaching and research. Eventually, he and a colleague, Ivan Sutherland, began collaborating while on the faculty of the University of Utah. Their goal was to revolutionize computer-aided design and computer simulation. In the process of achieving his dream, David Evans has built an organization with annual sales of around $100 million. While this has brought with it a variety of organizational and business challenges that occupy much of his time, Evans's first love is the technology. He prefers discussing design problems with his engineers to analyzing balance sheets and income statements.

Organization Builders

Some entrepreneurs appear to start their own businesses because they like to build organizations. They enjoy seeing their businesses grow in terms of both profits and people. As one entrepreneur we interviewed noted, "I enjoy building and managing a business. It's exciting to take a company from a small one to a large one." These organization builders, such as Thomas Watson of IBM, do have certain business skills, such as marketing, but their primary ability is in developing people, systems, and structures that serve to achieve the goals of the organization. Such entrepreneurs also generally enjoy working with people and wielding power and influence, in contrast to the technical entrepreneur, who often prefers working alone and dislikes "playing politics."

Deal Makers

The third type of entrepreneur described at the conference was labeled a "deal maker." Deal makers enjoy the excitement of negotiating a new agreement or arrangement. In the 1980s, for example, Donald Trump built his career on the art of deal making (although, as we have seen in the 1990s, some of his deals have come back to haunt him). Deal makers enjoy making the initial deal to start a new venture and often enjoy some of the start-up activities. However, unlike organization builders, they dislike having to manage and commit themselves to an organization over the long run. This orientation is best exemplified by an entrepreneur who had started several businesses. He observed, "I enjoy creating a new business, but I hate to manage them. I never get married to any business that I start. You should be ready to dump an idea or business at any time if it doesn't fit." Another deal maker said, "My rule is: Never fall in love with a business. You might have to sell it the next day."

While there may be other orientations to an entrepreneurial career, these three categories seem to encompass most entrepreneurs, and such a typology helps us understand why it is so difficult to define an entrepreneur using a single definition. We will now turn our attention to outlining some of the basic characteristics of entrepreneurs.

What It Takes to Succeed as an Entrepreneur

In our in-depth interviews with entrepreneurs, we were interested in discovering what they felt were the attributes of any successful entrepreneur, regardless of orientation. We rarely had to ask them about this directly, since most of them had developed their own sets of characteristics of the successful entrepreneur and were eager to share their views. The following nine characteristics summarize what the entrepreneurs felt were most important in starting and maintaining a successful entrepreneurial career.

The Ability to Take Risks

While entrepreneurs are often known as risk takers, the entrepreneurs we studied seemed to be careful to take only calculated risks. My research associates Gene Dalton and Frank Holdaway describe entrepreneurial risk taking this way:

> Many of the entrepreneurs that we talked to described themselves as "very high risk takers." One of the people who we interviewed said that being an entrepreneur is similar to being the recent Olympic ski-jumper who, after his take off, looked down and discovered that his skis had fallen off. But as we questioned these people further, we found that the type of risks that they typically take are perhaps more analogous to a ski-jumper who carefully checks his or her own equipment, inquires into the weather and snow conditions, practices for countless hours, and then jumps, feeling confident that the skis will not fall off.[3]

Many entrepreneurs emphasized that they are not gamblers. For example, one said that he would bet on his own horses but not on others, since he had a great deal of confidence in and knowledge about his own horses but did not have that information regarding other horses. Entrepreneurs attempt to reduce risk by doing their homework and retaining as much control of the outcomes as they can. Like the basketball player who takes the final shot that either wins or loses the game, the entrepreneur wants to be that person who designs the final play and takes the last shot. In such a risky win-lose situation, entrepreneurs want to gain as much control as possible to reduce risk and to take credit for the outcome, whether good or bad. They also tend to have a backup plan in case of failure.

The Desire to Compete

Entrepreneurs have a competitive spirit. They enjoy the challenge of starting a new enterprise and competing in the marketplace. As one entrepreneur stated, "I like to win playing Pictionary. I like to win. I try to be a good sport, but I am a poor loser. It drives my wife crazy. She asked me, 'Haven't you ever played a game just to play the game?' [I replied] 'Sorry, it's not in me. It's just not me.'" This competitive spirit helps entrepreneurs overcome the obstacles inherent in starting a new venture.

The Ability to Handle Stress

One common thread running through most of the entrepreneurs that we studied was the amount of stress that they feel at various times during their careers. The weight of decision making, the people (and jobs) that they are responsible for, the long hours, and the endless negotiations with customers and suppliers all can take their toll. Entrepreneurs who have developed ways to deal with the stress over the course of the career seem to be much more effective than those who succumb to the pressure.

The Ability to Make Work Fun

Several entrepreneurs described how much fun it was to be an entrepreneur. One said, "Work is play, and play is work." Another stated, "I don't work for money. I work because I enjoy it!" Successful entrepreneurs seem to get a great deal of enjoyment out of their work. They are excited about going to work. Some said they could not believe that they actually got paid for what they were doing. Others mentioned that they felt they were still like kids, since they were able to "play games" that were exciting to them even though they were now grown up. Such an ability to make work enjoyable may serve the entrepreneur well during difficult and stressful times, especially during the early phases of the career.

The Ability to Creatively Solve Problems

A number of entrepreneurs mentioned that the reason for their success was their ability to solve problems in creative ways. In some cases, it was not just the ability to solve problems but the ability to identify a given problem and then solve it. Entrepreneurs are not only good problem solvers but good "problem finders" as well. The nature of the problem, be it a technical problem, a marketing problem, or a people problem, was not as important as was the entrepreneur's interest in getting to the heart of the problem and solving it. In many ways, entrepreneurs seem to display most of their creativity and innovation as they engage in problem solving.

The Ability to Recognize Opportunities

Harvard professor Howard Stevenson defines an entrepreneur as one who defines value, creates value, or distributes value.[4] In other words, entrepreneurs can tell us what is valuable or important, can create something we value, or can help us acquire those things that we desire. All of this assumes that the entrepreneur is able to understand what others need — even if those others do not yet know that they need it — and then is able to fulfill that need. Kenneth Olsen, founder of Digital Equipment, created a whole new market when he envisioned a future where the need of engineers or businesspeople was not a large mainframe computer but a smaller, less costly computer that would help them solve their problems. Entrepreneurs seem to be able to anticipate trends and recognize opportunities that others are unable to see.

Commitment to the Business

The successful entrepreneur is seen as someone who "lives, eats, and sleeps the business." While this can cause certain problems, as we will see in the following chapters, their commitment to success can help them succeed when others fail. The likelihood of success for new ventures is not great; the commitment and determination of the entrepreneur can be the key ingredient in determining success or failure.

Goal Orientation

One of the most common features of our interviews with entrepreneurs was their emphasis on the importance of having and achieving goals. As one entrepreneur said, "Success is arriving at a goal and achieving that goal, and I don't care how big or small." Entrepreneurs tend to focus more on the ends that they are seeking—a new shopping center, a new computer, a new service—than on the details of the means to those ends. Most of the entrepreneurs whom we interviewed said that their goals helped to focus their energy and attention and gave them something to shoot for.

Realistic Optimism

Those who start a business can become paralyzed by a fear of failure, given that the vast majority of new businesses do fail. Thus, a sense of optimism—and a sense of humor—are often necessary, according to the entrepreneurs we studied. In a recent survey of 2,994 entrepreneurs who had been in business for an average of one year, 81 percent of the entrepreneurs said that their chances of success were seven in ten or better, and one-third said that their chances of success were 100 percent.[5] While this survey suggests that most entrepreneurs are optimistic, some may not be realistic. They may not spot certain flaws or problems that can undermine their business. Thus, optimism and faith in oneself seem to be essential to success as an entrepreneur, but such faith should be tempered by realistic expectations.

Summary

While these nine factors were deemed to be fundamental to career success by the entrepreneurs that we interviewed, they also pointed out that external factors, such as luck and timing, play a role as well. To get a deeper understanding of the entrepreneur's psyche, we now turn our attention to analyzing the motives behind starting a new venture.

Motivations for Starting an Entrepreneurial Career

Several studies have examined the initial decision to start an entrepreneurial career. A study of 200 entrepreneurs conducted at Babson College indicated that 80 percent had not started their careers as entrepreneurs and that 55 percent did not choose their first jobs to prepare to be entrepreneurs.[6] Robert Ronstadt, the author of the study and an entrepreneur himself, noted that "most [entrepreneurs] had no idea at the time that they would pursue an entrepreneurial career."[7] However, he noted that those who chose an entrepreneurial career early in life or took their first jobs to prepare for an entrepreneurial career had the longest (and presumably most successful) careers. Ronstadt also reported that more than 90 percent of the entrepreneurs he studied started their careers before age forty. After forty, there was a great reluctance to start a new venture. Moreover, those who tried starting later in life tended to fail more often than those who had started in their twenties or thirties. With this in mind, we will now explore the five most common factors that encourage someone to be an entrepreneur: early childhood experiences; the need to gain control over an uncertain world; frustrations with traditional organizational careers; challenge and excitement; and role models.

Early Childhood Experiences

Various studies of entrepreneurs note the impact of their early childhood experiences. About half of the entrepreneurs that we interviewed had grown up or worked on farms where hard work was the norm. One entrepreneur said that at age thirteen he would "get up before daylight and would harness a team of four horses before I was really able to reach the top of the horse." Willard Marriott's biography is filled with stories of his accomplishing difficult tasks at an early age.[8] For example, he drove a herd of cattle from Utah to California when he was in his early teens. Others reported going to work at an early age to support their families.

In addition to the theme of hard work, themes of self-reliance, a determination to succeed, and a knack for finding and developing opportunities are often found. The following excerpt from one interview is quite typical:

> My dad was a very busy and influential man from when I was a baby. He had important positions in the church and was, of course, a businessman. He was also on various civic boards and committees. He was a very active individual, very busy, always gone. We really didn't have much of a relationship when I was growing up, he was gone all of the time. He had meetings every night of the week. About the only time that I ever saw him was occasionally on a Saturday. . . . I think it led to a very successful partnership once we got in business together because it was more of a business relationship than a father-and-son relationship. Since that time, we have grown very close. I guess I have always been a born trader. I can remember when I was a little kid in first or second grade, I had a shoe box, and I would gather anything that I could find and go to school with my shoe box and convince the other kids to bring things to trade with me. I loved to trade and try to improve my position. I had two or three different spots around the house where I stored all my loot, and I had one place where I could pull the drawer out and underneath it was an area that nobody knew about. I would keep all of my treasures in that. . . . So I have always liked to save

things that I felt had some value to them. I've always had a desire to earn money since I was a little
kid. We lived on four acres of fruit trees, and my
dad let me clean the ditch, irrigate, and then he
let me sell the fruit. I set myself up a fruit stand
in front of the house, and I . . . really enjoyed it.
I had a paper route, but I did not enjoy the paper
route, because I didn't feel like I could make enough
money at it. I found at an early age that I didn't
enjoy having somebody standing right over the top
of me. I enjoyed being independent.

Such a description of childhood is typical of entrepreneurs. They
learn at an early age that they can succeed by acting in "entrepreneurial" ways.

The Need for Control

Some psychologists have argued that entrepreneurs spring from
childhoods of desertion, death, neglect, and poverty, with the
father usually emerging as the "villain."[9] Thus, the development
of an entrepreneurial life-style becomes a rebellion against an
environment that is perceived as dangerous and uncontrollable. Indeed, entrepreneurial behavior is an attempt to gain control over one's world. According to Manfred Kets de Vries, a
psychoanalyst and management theorist, the result of such a
childhood is an entrepreneur who is "a loner, isolated and rather
remote from even his closest relatives. This type of person gives
the impression of a 'reject,' a marginal man, a perception certainly not lessened by his often conflicting relationship(s) with
family members . . . we are dealing with an individual often inconsistent and confused about his motives, desires, and wishes,
a person under a lot of stress who often upsets us by his seem-
ingly 'irrational,' impulsive activities."[10] He concludes that "re-
jection, dissatisfaction, and a sense of failure follow the entrepreneur like an inseparable shadow."[11] Some studies seem to
support this view by showing that entrepreneurs score higher
on scales of "neuroticism" than do general managers.[12]

Some entrepreneurs that I have worked with seem to fit the pattern described by Kets de Vries. They are anxious and frustrated, have difficulty developing healthy relationships, and are quite unpredictable. They are not satisfied with their successes, believing that there must be some catch and that eventually they will lose it all. However, others seem to be quite well adjusted, with no apparent difficulties. They seem quite at peace with themselves and with others. A survey of more than seventy entrepreneurs that Roger Peay and I conducted revealed that 95 percent were either fairly satisfied, quite satisfied, or very satisfied with their careers and 96.2 percent were generally satisfied with their lives. This finding is consistent with other studies as well.[13] This raises the question, If entrepreneurs are by nature somewhat neurotic, why they are so happy? Can it be that they are so neurotic that they just think that they are happy, while those who must associate with them are miserable?

While it is probably impossible to answer these questions fully, my own experience in working with entrepreneurs leads me to believe that the reason that entrepreneurs are relatively happy — regardless of whether they are neurotic — is that they do have some control over their working lives. In interview after interview, case after case, entrepreneurs described how exhilarating it is to be one's own boss, to be in control of one's destiny. This appears to be the overriding factor that makes life bearable and even exciting for the entrepreneur, despite all the problems that such a career entails. Moreover, the need for control motivates the entrepreneur to accept the risks of such a career. To further illustrate this point, one woman we interviewed described her childhood as one of poverty. She had to put herself through school and work long hours, often holding down two or three jobs, to support her family. After marrying, she also continued to work to help make ends meet. When she learned that a cousin had died and she wanted to attend the funeral, her husband told her that there was no money to pay for her transportation. She said that this event was a turning point in her life, and she resolved never again to be unable to do the things that were important to her. To gain this independence, she started a cosmetics business that has become quite successful. Now she has the money and power that allow her the freedom and control that she desires.

Frustration with Traditional Careers

A third factor that influences someone to start an entrepreneurial career is dissatisfaction with traditional careers that involve working for someone else, often in a large organization. Slow career progress, the inability to effect quick changes within the organization, low wages, and office politics are just some of the reasons cited for this dissatisfaction. One survey of entrepreneurs revealed that 70 percent of them had started their businesses because they were dissatisfied with their jobs, 13 percent because they had been fired from a previous job and so had to start a new career, and 17 percent simply because they wanted to seize a new business opportunity.[14] The following story is typical of those who became entrepreneurs because of their frustration with large organizations:

> I graduated with my bachelor's degree in electrical engineering and went to work for a large computer company. I was put into management early on in my career. I was the youngest manager at a plant site with 25,000 people, and I had a budget of about $3 million and 100 people reporting to me. I also ran a companywide committee for a project. As I got to dealing with big company politics and big company mentality, I got frustrated because nothing happened very fast. Everything was based on committee decision, and it took forever to get things done. I became increasingly frustrated with that kind of thing . . . I'm an impatient person anyhow. Finally, I decided that it was just too much of a frustration for me.

For this entrepreneur and others like him, the means of escape from what he calls "the lethargic nature of big companies" was to create their own organizations.

Challenge and Excitement

One cannot interview or work with entrepreneurs without sensing the excitement and enthusiasm that most feel about their careers and their businesses. Each day seems to bring new challenges, which they thrive on. A study of entrepreneurs who were affiliated with the Massachusetts Institute of Technology (MIT) found that 30 percent of them had started their ventures because doing so presented a new challenge for them (39 percent wanted to be their own boss, and 20 percent wanted more money).[15] David McClelland, a Harvard psychologist who has studied entrepreneurs for many years, believes that a fundamental "need for achievement" spurs entrepreneurs to succeed and that such a need is developed early in childhood.[16] While it was difficult to measure such needs in the entrepreneurs that I have studied and worked with, the goals, dreams, and aspirations that they described seem to be related to this achivement motive. Money does not seem to be their primary goal, although it is important. Entrepreneurs see money mainly as a way of "keeping score," a rough measure of how they are doing; the challenge and excitement of the career are what stimulate them.

Role Models

Entrepreneurs often describe being inspired to start their entrepreneurial career by another entrepreneur — a parent, a local businessperson, or a famous entrepreneur. Watching others' successes, they developed a desire to emulate them. For example, Thomas Watson of IBM learned much about how to create and build an organization from John H. Patterson, the founder of National Cash Register (NCR). Many aspects of the IBM culture — its conservative business suits, its focus on values and aggressive marketing, and many company slogans — are the result of Watson's experience at NCR.

Highly visible role models seem to stimulate entrepreneurial activity. Asian Americans' successes in entrepreneurial endeavors can be traced in part to the high percentage of successful entrepreneurs in their community. From their examples, they see that it can be done and therefore are more willing to start their own businesses. Success seems to breed success. In contrast, the lack of visible role models in African American communities — many successful entrepreneurs in these communities leave to live somewhere else — makes it more difficult for potential entrepreneurs to recognize that an entrepreneurial career is a viable option for them.[17]

Can I Succeed as an Entrepreneur?

Given the preceding discussion of the nature of entrepreneurs, their motivations for starting a business, and the kinds of attributes that help them succeed, we will now discuss how a person can determine whether he or she has what it takes to successfully launch an entrepreneurial career. The following are just a few suggestions for those who are grappling with this "identity dilemma."

Develop a Picture of Goals, Preferences, and Desires

The entrepreneurs whom we studied had fairly definite views regarding what they wanted to get out of life and what they wanted to achieve. Such self-insight helps them focus their energies and cope with the uncertainties associated with such a career. To gain such insight, those starting an entrepreneurial career might get a better picture of themselves by developing a list of the goals that they would like to achieve in life and then prioritize them. They might also list and rank order those things that they enjoy doing. After doing this, they should ask the following questions: Would an entrepreneurial career help me achieve these goals? Would I enjoy doing that kind of work? Do I enjoy making deals, running an organization, or developing new products? Can I go it alone against the ridicule of others? Do I enjoy being in control and responsible for what happens?

Writing a short life history could also be helpful in this regard. By focusing on the events, experiences, and people that have been influential and picking out some of the themes or preferences noted in the history, a person can get a better understanding of his or her desires and talents as well as some of the trade-offs entailed in an entrepreneurial career. For example, if people's histories indicate that they prefer jobs that are predictable and consistent or prefer to forget their work once they leave the job, an entrepreneurial career would not likely fit their preferences or goals.

Interview Several Entrepreneurs

An assignment that I often give to my students who are interested in entrepreneurial careers is to interview someone who has founded a business, asking questions such as these: How did you get started? What problems have you encountered? What do you like and dislike about your career? How has your career affected your family and you personally? By getting answers to these kinds of questions, the students gain deeper insights into the trade-offs that are associated with starting a new business and are better able to determine whether they are willing to make the kinds of sacrifices that are frequently required.

Take an Entrepreneurship Inventory

Another way to gain insight into one's ability to succeed as an entrepreneur is to take one of the various tests that have been developed to measure entrepreneurial orientation. Most colleges, universities, and job placement centers provide such inventories. One of the more widely recognized inventories for determining one's "career anchors"—the values and competencies that drive one's career—is the Career Anchors Inventory developed by Edgar H. Schein of MIT.[18] Another, rather simple way to gauge one's entrepreneurial orientation is to rank yourself as high, medium, or low on nine attributes discussed in this chapter:

1. The ability to take risks
2. The desire to compete
3. The ability to handle stress
4. The ability to make work fun
5. The ability to creatively solve problems

6. The ability to recognize opportunities
7. Commitment to the business
8. Goal orientation
9. Realistic optimism

If you have a majority of high rankings, you may have some of the key attributes that it takes to succeed. A majority of low rankings indicates that an entrepreneurial career might not be for you unless some other factors, such as your personal goals or expertise, carry greater weight in your decision to become an entrepreneur.

Develop Expertise and Broaden Knowledge

A final type of activity to consider when starting an entrepreneurial career is developing expertise in a particular area as well as broadening one's general knowledge. Entrepreneurs succeed because they know how to do something well, such as marketing, technical development, manufacturing, or finance. They also tend to have an intimate knowledge of a particular market or industry. The key for the prospective entrepreneur is to understand what he or she does particularly well. Such knowledge might be gained by interviewing former and current employers, co-workers, or classmates, past and present customers of one's services, or others who have knowledge of one's talents and abilities. I find that one's academic record may be somewhat related to one's skills and abilities but is more often related to one's interests.

   While specific skills are important, a broad knowledge of the world and of people is also important. For entrepreneurs to be innovative and effective, they must make connections with a broad range of ideas and a variety of people. Good judgment and good business sense are critical, and these require a broad knowledge of business areas such as finance, production, marketing, and human resources.

   A study by *INC.* magazine of the founders of the 500 fastest-growing private companies in the United States concluded, "Instead of swashbucklers, we found hardworking, experienced businesspeople . . . the creators of the INC. 500 companies are down-to-earth, practical-minded people for whom, more often than not, building a business was simply the next logical step in a career."[19] Thus, those thinking about an entrepreneurial career should see it as a natural progression in their personal and professional lives, rather than a leap of faith into the unknown.

Conclusion

In this chapter, we have explored what it takes to begin the entrepreneurial adventure. Entrepreneurs seem to come in various shapes and sizes, but they do appear to share some common characteristics, which have been outlined. The chapter has attempted to help budding entrepreneurs to better understand their motives, their goals, and their abilities — and hence some of the trade-offs involved in an entrepreneurial career — so that they will be better prepared to tackle the dilemmas discussed in the following chapters.

TWO

HOW DO I GET STARTED?

The excitement surrounding the tremendous growth in the number of entrepreneurial enterprises in recent years has to be tempered by the fact that few survive for more than a few years. Forty percent of all new businesses fail in the first year, 60 percent by the end of the second year, and 90 percent by the tenth year.[1] These gloomy statistics reflect the tenuous nature of a new enterprise and put great pressure on an already overburdened entrepreneur. In virtually every interview, case study, and biography included in our study, the entrepreneurs had difficulty obtaining resources to get their ventures started. One study of fledgling entrepreneurs uncovered some of the major problems entrepreneurs face as they begin the work of starting a new enterprise:[2]

Type of Problem	Percentage Responding
Obtaining financing from banks	33
Not knowing what I was doing	26
Lack of credibility	20
Lack of confidence	7
High risk	7
Lack of community support	7

The entrepreneurs in this study reported that some of their problems in getting started involved personal issues, such as confidence in knowing what to do and having credibility, while others were more related to the nature of the enterprise, such as getting funding and managing risks related to the new venture. Chapter One outlined many of the personal issues and concerns that must be confronted in starting a business. In this chapter, we focus on the problems related to getting the resources, such as labor and capital, that are needed to start any new venture. As entrepreneurs begin a new venture, they often face a catch-22 dilemma: how to get resources to start a business if they cannot demonstrate that they have a viable business that deserves more resources.

Starting a New Enterprise

To illustrate the kinds of issues that entrepreneurs face as they start a new business, we will use the case of Jack Sorenson, the founder of a bank (all names in this case are disguised). The following is Jack's story of how he got into the banking business:

> A friend of mine and I had talked for years about starting a bank. We were fishing one day in Mexico and got to talking about it. I said to myself, "When I go back, I'm going to do it." So I got back home, picked up the telephone, and called a friend of mine who is an attorney. I said, "I'm going to start a bank. Tell me the name of an attorney who knows about starting banks." My friend said, "I don't know any, but I'll call you back." He called me back and gave me the names of three attorneys and said, "These three guys do more bank start-ups than anybody else in the state. I know one of them. Give him a call." I called the guy up and said, "I understand you know something about starting up banks." He said, "Yeah, I've done a few." I said, "So-and-so told me to call you. I want to come down and see you." He said, "Okay, when do you want to come?" I set up an appointment and went down and saw him.
>
> I walked into his office, sat down, and said, "I'm going to start a bank." He said, "Oh? What kind of bank are you going to start?" I said, "A bank. What else is there?" "Well," he said, "number one, do you want to start a national bank or a state chartered bank?" I said, "Good question.

Why would I start one and not the other?" He said, "These are the advantages of a national bank, and these are the advantages of a state bank." I said okay and made some notes. I said, "What do you have to do to start a bank?" He told me some of the things I needed to do. I said, "How long is it going to take? How much money is it going to cost?" He said, "Better than that, let me give you this little packet. You take it home and read it. It's got all the information in there you'll need to know, and if you decide you want to do something, call me." I said, "I can handle that." So I took the packet home, sat down, and read the packet through.

I said to myself, "That's no problem. I could handle that real easily." I called my friend whom I had talked with about the bank and said, "George, I've got a lawyer coming to your office next week. He's going to sit down and talk to us about a bank." George said, "Are you really going to do that?" And I said, "You bet I am." So the next week we met the lawyer in George's office. I told George, "I've done all this research, and in my opinion we ought to start a nationally chartered bank and not a state bank. Here's what we need to do."

The lawyer sat there and listened to it all and said, "Yeah, yeah, yup, uh-huh, nope. Do that, do that, this that, and the other." I said, "Good. It's going to cost 350 grand." The lawyer said, "Yeah, and that's just starting." I said, "I can handle that. George, can you handle that?" George said, "Yeah, we can handle it." What we needed to do was to get a lot of our friends to put up 25 grand apiece until we got $350 thousand. So George got on the phone and I got on the phone and called friends. Some of our friends then called their friends. Seven days later, we had $350 thousand. So I called the attorney, and we did all the things necessary to start the bank. The group that provided the funding became the original board of directors. They elected me chairman of the board. It was not a bank yet, but it was under way.

One of the things we needed was to hire a banking man to be president, even at this formative stage. We knew we'd have to hire him and pay him, so we looked around. I said, "I know a real good guy at the First National Bank. His name is Tom Allen." Some of the guys said, "Yeah, I know Tom." I went to Allen and said, "Tom, you slob. You've been stuck in this bank all of your life. It's time you got out on your own and found out what the world was like. We're putting together a bank. Why don't you come over and be the president." He said, "Oh, man. I can't believe you're serious." I talked like a Dutch uncle but couldn't get him to move. So we talked to some other people and finally found a guy that would be president of the bank. He quit where he was — he was assistant to the vice president of another bank — and he came to work for us. One of the things you have to worry about in starting a bank is that you have to have a correspondent bank, because you can't handle the loans and all the paperwork initially. So eventually we found a correspondent bank to help us.

The bank has been in business five years and was sold last year. It was sold for two and a half times book value. When the bank was sold, all those guys who put money in got their money out of it and made a little. What they really made essentially was 5½ percent interest. They would have done better to have left their money in a CD [certificate of deposit]. So the guys got their money out, but they're not going to make any money.

The story of Jack Sorenson's venture into the banking industry points out several of the key resources that are needed to start a new venture.

Information

Entrepreneurs who begin an enterprise need information on a variety of topics, such as the potential market, start-up procedures, and government regulations. In Jack's case, he needed to have specific information regarding how to properly set up a national chartered bank.

Legal Counsel

Related to the need for information is the need for legal counsel to help the entrepreneur set up the business as a legal entity and point out any possible legal pitfalls. Legal counsel was crucial in helping Jack wade through the legal morass involved in starting a bank. Entrepreneurs who do not receive good counsel pay a price. One entrepreneur describing his legal counsel noted, "Had I been more selective and dug into the lawyer's background a little more, he wouldn't have been part of the operation at all. He had great qualities, a Harvard Law School graduate. He had good credentials and was supposed to be a good lawyer. I relied heavily on him as we put the corporation together. As it turns out, you get what you pay for. His advice was poor, and it has come back to haunt us."

Financing

Getting financing is often the entrepreneur's most pressing problem. In virtually every study of entrepreneurial ventures, researchers note that financing is one of the most important issues. For example, in a study of 127 high-tech start-ups, the inability to find sources of funding was the number one problem facing the founders of those enterprises — particularly if the business was in the early stages of development.[3] To obtain capital, entrepreneurs frequently take out second mortgages on their homes, solicit money from family and friends, obtain bank loans, or find financial partners. The major source of capital for most new ventures is the entrepreneur's personal resources. Lending institutions provide the next largest source of funding, while funds from friends and family, other investors, the government, and venture capitalists constitute a much smaller portion of the funding. Jack and George obtained financing fairly easily by relying on their contacts with friends.

Personnel

Because a new venture relies heavily on just a few individuals, their expertise and commitment are critical to success. However, entrepreneurs generally have difficulty in attracting people who are willing to accept the risk and uncertainty of an entrepreneurial firm. Since Jack did not have extensive experience in the banking industry, he had to find someone with the appropriate expertise to lead the bank. Jack was disappointed many times before he finally found someone to serve as bank president.

Operational Expertise

Once a new organization begins to function, it must effectively produce goods or services in order to survive. A fledgling organization does not generally have the kinds of experience and established organizational routines that its competitors have, and this can put it at a serious disadvantage. In Jack's case, he needed to find a correspondent bank to help solve some of the initial operational problems until his organization gained the requisite expertise and experience to handle the various functions on its own.

Planning the Entrepreneurial Venture

In addition to obtaining the kinds of resources just mentioned, the entrepreneur needs to do strategic and operational planning and develop a detailed business plan.

Strategic Planning

It appears that Jack missed a crucial step before starting the bank. To succeed with a new venture, the entrepreneur needs to analyze the marketplace and develop a strategy to compete successfully.[4] The entrepreneur needs to answer questions such as these:

- What business am I in? What is the mission of this new business?
- What spells the difference between success and failure in this business?
- Who are my major competitors? What are their strengths and weaknesses?
- What is my competitive advantage vis-à-vis my competitors? Is it cost, service, quality, or some combination of these or other factors?
- How should I use my competitive advantage?

One possible reason that Jack's bank was not very successful was his inability to fully answer these questions. Jack wanted to run a bank because he thought that it would be interesting and exciting, but he seemed to fail to answer the key questions regarding the market and competitors. The study of 127 high-tech firms mentioned previously noted that other than obtaining financing, developing accurate business forecasts and locating potential customers were the most important tasks that needed to be performed.[5] Moreover, most of those high-tech entrepreneurs felt that they were not performing those tasks very well. One venture capitalist said that he had interviewed hundreds of entrepreneurs who had good technical ideas, but very few of them had a clear understanding of the marketplace and had developed a well-thought-out strategic plan. Thus, only a very small percentage — less than 5 percent — ever received funding from his venture capital fund, because they could not translate their technical ideas into a concrete business plan that would yield results.

Two examples of people who started a new venture with a thorough understanding of the marketplace are Forrest and Nina Wood, founders of Ranger Boats. The story of how they got started is rather remarkable:

By 1966 the Woods had established a successful float trip business, they had an enviable construction operation, and in their "spare time" farmed and raised cattle. At this time some bass fishing boats were being built, but the industry was very much in its infancy. Forrest was just beginning to lay fiberglass over flat Jon boats and had already hired a fiberglass man and two helpers. Bass fishing tournaments were beginning to spring up. Forrest saw an opportunity and decided to become serious about building bass fishing boats. When their first boat was finished and ready for the water test, Forrest arrived from one of his construction jobs to find his three boat builders looking forlorn. After they put the boat back in the water, he quickly understood why they were so chagrined. "The boat ran with its nose in the water." In traditional Wood spirit, Forrest said, "Well, let's find out the problem," and they began experimenting and securing 2×4s at various positions and angles and eventually got the modified Jon boat to trim properly. That year, a bass tournament was held on Greers Ferry, a local lake, where Forrest introduced his odd looking Jon boat with the high powered name of "Ranger." "I liked the name because it commanded respect, like the Texas Rangers, whose stories tell of uncompromising pursuit of their prey." Forrest left the tournament with four boat orders in hand, and thus Ranger Boats was born.[6]

One reason that the Woods have been so successful is that they understood the growing needs of anglers in the United States, developed boats that met those needs, and found a way to market their boats through the various bass fishing competitions that are held each year. In just a few years, Ranger Boats' work force has grown to over 450 employees, and the Ranger boat is the leading bass fishing boat in terms of "sales, safety, efficiency, comfort, and hull design."[7] Successful entrepreneurs such as the Woods think strategically. They understand the market and their customers' needs and know how to fulfill those needs.

Operational Planning

Operational planning includes such things as financial planning, cash flow analysis, development of marketing programs, and production planning and scheduling. Entrepreneurs often make a serious mistake in the early stages of their businesses by failing to have enough working capital. There are often unforeseen production delays, and marketing plans are not always implemented successfully. Thus, the entrepreneur must be able not only to do broad strategic thinking but also to develop tactical plans for carrying out the routine day-to-day operations as effectively as possible.

Developing the Business Plan

The final result of strategic and operational planning is a well-defined business plan. In today's competitive environment, entrepreneurs must develop a well-thought-out business plan to obtain financing and other resources necessary for getting started. While there are different formats for business plans, most have the following nine sections.[8]

- *Executive summary.* This section is critical if the business plan is to be presented to venture capitalists. The executive summary should be presented in an interesting way and identify the most important aspects of the plan.
- *Description of the business.* The description should include information about the industry that the business is in, describe the product or service in terms of unique benefits to the customer, and clarify the goals of the company.
- *Marketing.* This section should include research and analysis to identify the target market. The entrepreneur needs to find out who will buy the product or service. Possible com-

petitors should also be discussed in this section. With this information, the entrepreneur can develop a marketing plan that includes marketing strategy, sales and distribution, pricing, advertising, promotion, and public relations.

- *Research, development, and design.* This section discusses the developmental research leading to the design of the product or service.
- *Location.* For a manufacturing firm, the right location is determined by the proximity to suppliers, availability of transportation, and the labor supply. A retail business should be located where it will attract the target customer.
- *Management.* The entrepreneur needs to identify a management team that will make the venture a success. No matter how good the product or service is, without good management, the venture will fail. This section should also outline the method of compensation for management.
- *Critical risks.* This section attempts to identify potential problems before they materialize. The idea is to anticipate risk and know how to control or overcome the risk.
- *Financial forecasting.* The financial section, including budgeting and forecasting, is often the most difficult section of the business plan to prepare. Important elements of financial forecasting are pro forma financial statements, such as forecasted statements of earnings, financial position, and cash flows. The projections should be conservative and realistic. The business can use these statements as a standard for evaluating the first several years of business activity.
- *Milestone schedule.* The entrepreneur should identify milestones to be reached in the first few years of business. This section forces the entrepreneur to determine the timing of business objectives.

The business plan may need to be modified frequently to respond to new opportunities or threats, but it should serve as a general guide for entrepreneurs and those who work for them. A few entrepreneurs that we studied paid thousands of dollars to consultants to help them write their business plans. One woman paid $10,000 for her plan, which she needed to get financing. Unfortunately, though she got the financing, she did not fully understand the plan or how to implement it, and her business failed. While entrepreneurs may need some assistance in developing a business plan, I find that those who are successful develop a plan that is their own, not someone else's, and feel confident that they can carry it out.

Ethical Issues in Starting a New Business

One often hears reports of entrepreneurs being caught in illegal or unethical activities. Because the pressure to succeed is great, there is often the temptation to "cook the books" to avoid taxes, misrepresent one's product or service, shortchange customers and suppliers, or do any number of other things to break or bend the law. Because a new organization is in a precarious position and entrepreneurs fear failure, they may rationalize their unethical or illegal activities by saying that "everyone else does it" or feel that the benefits of having the business succeed for themselves, their families, and their employees outweigh any negative outcomes of their improprieties. Entrepreneurs may feel caught between what they believe to be right and the pressure to succeed.

There are numerous ways to approach ethical problems. One entrepreneur said that he used the following questions to avoid ethical traps: Is it legal? Is it fair? Do I feel good about it? By answering these questions regarding any business transaction, this entrepreneur felt that he could avoid illegal activities, develop good relations with customers, suppliers, and business associates, and have a clear conscience. Another entrepreneur told a story about Gene Autry that helped shape his views about ethics:

> Gene told me of a deal one time years ago where he had sold a radio station. . . . After the deal was consummated, he was looking over the figures again and saw where his business people had given him the wrong figure. He made about $12,000 too much. He called the guy up and sent him over a check for $12,000. The guy was flabbergasted. He

said, "You know, Mr. Autry, you don't have to do this." Gene replied, "Well, I want to do it because I want to be happy and I want you to be happy." I have kind of followed that philosophy too. In a business arrangement, both parties should be happy with the deal or I just don't want to be involved in it—and I sleep better too!

One entrepreneur told of a different kind of ethical dilemma. He had contracted with a new company to pick fruit for a year in his orchards, sealing the agreement with just a handshake. Soon after hiring the company, he discovered that it was short-changing him. But he felt that he had made a promise that he had to keep: "I gave those guys my word that they could pick it for a year regardless—and I let them do it. I strongly believe in that. You don't become dishonest because somebody else has been dishonest. Why lower yourself to their standards? I got hurt on that, but I feel like it'll make me stronger next time around. I can promise you I won't get involved with them again."

To maintain their ethical standards, entrepreneurs need to be well informed. Good legal and accounting help is often necessary. Entrepreneurs also need to be clear about their own values: What is fair and what is not? How should I treat others? Where are the potential pitfalls in this business? John Ward of Loyola University, who has done a great deal of research and consulting work with entrepreneurs, has noted that many entrepreneurs later in their careers feel quite guilty about their past illegal or unethical behaviors.[9] To compensate for their past behavior, they sometimes turn their attention to worthy philanthropic causes. However, I believe that most would have been better off avoiding these ethical problems in the first place. And if they are caught, their reputations, their families, and their businesses can suffer irreparable damage.

Networking to Solve the Resource Dilemma

Entrepreneurs have a wide variety of approaches to acquiring resources. Which strategies will be most successful depends on the type of market and industry. For example, an entrepreneur starting a software company typically needs little start-up capital and few personnel but has a great need for knowledge of competitive products and distribution channels. In contrast, an entrepreneur attempting to develop a new kind of bicycle probably has a good knowledge of competitive products but needs a great deal of financing and expertise to develop, manufacture, and distribute the new bike. The kinds of resources needed by the software entrepreneur and by the bicycle entrepreneur are quite different, and their approaches to obtaining resources are also likely to be different.

Despite the differences in the kinds of resources needed by entrepreneurs as they start their enterprises, it is clear that successful entrepreneurs are more adept at obtaining resources than their less successful counterparts. Some of the more successful entrepreneurs we studied used the term *networking* to describe their approach to gaining funding, information, personnel, ideas, and other resources needed to help a venture succeed. One entrepreneur described his networking abilities as being grounded in his youthful experiences:

> My mother died when I was very young, and my father was often ill and not able to work, so I had to help out moneywise. I would go out in the neighborhood in the summertime and mow lawns and rake them. In the wintertime, I would shovel snow and keep the walks clear. I think I kind of started networking then. I would do a good job for one person, and they would introduce me to a neighbor. I would go from one to another. Through networking, by being friendly, by asking questions, I tried to make friends. So wherever I was, I was trying to do networking through associating with people in proper places. I have done a lot of research on networking after I found out what I was doing. I did not put it into that frame, but I just love meeting people.

This "love of networking" served this entrepreneur well as he launched a new real estate venture:

I was teaching school, and Bank of America was close to us. That is where I banked. So I went in and filled out a loan application to borrow money to buy this property. It was a lot of money. I took the loan papers home, filled them all out, and took them back in and turned them in to the loan officer. They said they would let me know in a day or two. Well, on a Friday afternoon after school was out, I went to the bank and met with the loan officer. She proceeded to tell me that the venture was not going to make any money and gave me 101 reasons why they would not loan me the money. . . . So I visited with her and said, "Okay, I will get it somewhere else." As I was leaving the bank, the bank president happened to see me. He said, "Phil, how are things going?" I said, "Well, they were fine until I walked in here." He said, "What are you talking about?" By networking, I had made sure I knew the bank president before, but I wanted to follow the channels and go through that way. I went into the bank president's office, and we sat down. Now the way I met him was I was teaching his son in school the year before. I made a point to know every parent of my students and what they did. . . . So he and I sat down. He asked to see the papers, and he looked at them. He said, "I don't see why we can't lend you the money." He called the office and said, "Give Phil a check for X amount of dollars," and they said okay. I told him to just put it in my checking account. So I left the bank that day with a loan, the balance of what I needed to go into business.

Another entrepreneur described how he uses his information networks to make decisions:

If I need information, I pick up a telephone and call someone that I know that either knows something about that or that I know has some other contact that might know something about it. I talk to people. I pick up the phone. I know enough people in a wide enough variety of areas that I could probably find out about a lot of things that a lot of people wouldn't think I could find out. I had a deal brought to me — an idea for extracting gold. The person who had the idea described it to me and told me of a patent that he had on another item he'd developed. I said, "Gee, that's really interesting. What was the name of the item that you patented?" He told me, and I wrote it down. I left and called a friend of mine who is an important person in the patent office in Washington, D.C. I said, "Pete, I'm possibly going to be involved in a business venture with a guy who says that he patented an item called this, and this is the patent number. Can you check on it?" Pete said, "Just a second." He turned to his computer and pulled it up. He said, "Yup, the guy's name is John Smith and he patented this product." Pete could not have helped me make the decision as to whether or not to put any money in the deal. Pete could have helped me to keep me from putting money in it if he had verified that the man was dishonest.

Not all entrepreneurs develop the political, financial, and social contacts that can help them achieve their goals. One entrepreneur that I interviewed had had an excellent idea for a new product and had even developed a limited market for it. However, he was having great difficulty gaining the confidence of banks to provide financing and had not been able to develop good rapport with his few customers. In fact, he noted that he was about to lose his biggest client to a competitor. It turned out that he had had problems in his family relationships and had been divorced. As I interviewed him, I noted that he had difficulty expressing himself and seemed to be uncomfortable dealing with me interpersonally, even though the interview was conducted in his home. He also saw the world as quite threatening and felt little support from potential stakeholders or his main constituencies. This entrepreneur apparently had been unable to develop an effective resource network, largely because of his inability to convey the vision of his business to others and his poor interpersonal skills. He was facing bankruptcy as a consequence of his inability to network.

Race and ethnic differences seem to make a difference in the ability of an entrepreneur to network. Asian Americans have better networks of support than do Hispanics or African Americans.[10] Asian Americans use their networks to promote business, develop dependable sources of labor, capital, and raw materials, and keep dollars circulating in the local economy. In contrast, dollars tend to leave African American communities to support outside businesses.

Research on the Importance of Networks

A number of studies have also noted the importance of networks in starting a business. To illustrate a resource network, Figure 2.1 depicts the relationships that have developed between the computer science department at Brigham Young University (BYU) and more than thirty companies as a result of connections with professors in the department. The most prominent of these companies is the WordPerfect Corporation, which had sales in 1990 of approximately $500 million.[11] The figure depicts a network involving resources such as ideas, expertise, personnel, and even funding. For example, Paul Sybrowsky, the founder of Dynix, a company that specializes in computerized library systems and has annual revenues of $25 million, gained funding for his venture through Eyring Research. The connection between Sybrowsky and Eyring was made through Sybrowsky's "home teacher" — a person in the Church of Jesus Christ of Latter-Day Saints who makes monthly visits to church members to determine and meet their needs. When Sybrowsky's home teacher, an employee at Eyring, found out that Sybrowsky needed capital to fund his struggling venture, he introduced him to the right people at Eyring. Through the funding provided by Eyring, the company, initially a division of Eyring, has been able to grow substantially and is now an independent corporation.

Figure 2.1. Utah Valley High-Tech Firm Linkages.

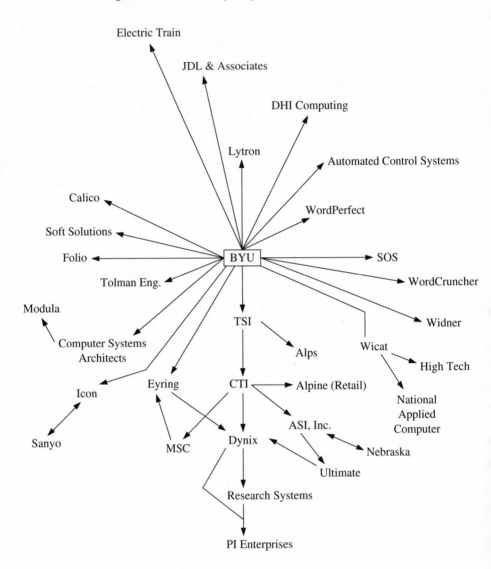

One study of resource networks and their impact on the profitability of new ventures found that "network variables (such as the amount of resources available to the entrepreneur, the accessibility of those resources, and the diversity of resources) had significant relationships with business foundings and profitability."[12] The study also found that maintaining the contacts in the network over time was one of the best predictors of early profitability and that entrepreneurs who are able to expand their networks are more likely than others to succeed.

Another study of entrepreneurial networks found that entrepreneurs who failed to expand their networks tended to be stymied in their efforts to gain resources.[13] Most of the entrepreneurs that participated in this study used only local, informal networks and did not take advantage of other potential contacts to gain resources. Broader contacts might be made through such forums as the chamber of commerce, local business colleges, trade associations, small business associations, and the small business development centers that are located across the United States. In many instances, however, the entrepreneur cannot rely on a formal forum to make key contacts but must take the initiative to make telephone calls and meet personally with those who might be able to provide the necessary resources. The *INC.* study of the founders of the most rapidly growing companies found that the success of these entrepreneurs could be attributed to the fact that they were "enmeshed and embedded in industries, with rich networks of contacts and colleagues they could draw on to help them build a business."[14]

Using an Entrepreneurial Team to Expand the Network

The need to develop a network of support can put enormous pressure and constraints on entrepreneurs. To help mitigate this pressure and expand the resource network, the entrepreneur might build a management team of people who bring with them their own networks, thus expanding the capacity to tap resources. A study of entrepreneurial teams noted that successful new ventures were started by teams that had the following qualities:[15] (1) The start-up was a team effort, not the product of one person.

(2) The members of the founding team had experience in starting up other ventures. (3) The team was balanced, with team members representing various functional areas, such as engineering, manufacturing, and marketing. (4) Members of the team were highly committed. They were persistent and tenacious in achieving their goals. Points two and three are particularly noteworthy. Team members who have been involved in other start-ups are likely to have developed numerous contacts. And a team whose members have different areas of expertise and interest is likely to have more diverse relationships and contacts than one whose members have similar backgrounds and experience. Such diversity naturally expands the resource network.

Avoiding the Pitfalls of Starting a New Venture

Several studies have looked at some of the major pitfalls that befall entrepreneurs as they begin a new venture. One study of 139 entrepreneurs asked them what was the most significant mistake that they had made in starting their businesses.[16] The results in rank order are as follows:

1. Inability to develop and implement a marketing plan
2. Failure to develop a well-thought-out strategic or business plan
3. Inability to find enough initial start-up capital
4. Failure to develop good production or operational planning
5. Hiring the wrong people
6. Failure to anticipate costs and demand
7. Wrong partners or cofounders

These results are very consistent with the kinds of mistakes that entrepreneurs mentioned in our own interviews and case studies.

One entrepreneur, Robert Ronstadt, thought when he began a new venture in the publishing business that he knew most of what there was to know about being an entrepreneur.[17] Now he says, "You don't really know what entrepreneurship is like until you have it all on the line."[18] Ronstadt found that there were more pitfalls in starting a business than he had imagined. After some initial successes, he found his company awash in red ink by 1989. As he reflected on his experience, Ronstadt, who has written several books on entrepreneurship, began thinking about what he might write in the future about the topic. He decided that he would add new chapters offering the following advice:

1. Go beyond obvious targets, such as wealthy people, to raise money. Do not expect to get venture capital; make sure that you have enough money to help raise more money.
2. Find team members who work well together, be open and honest with team members, and build some slack into the team by hiring an extra person or make sure that the team members can handle different responsibilities.
3. Do not hand your marketing over to an "expert" — stay close to the market.
4. Separate management control from ownership through a mechanism such as a voting trust. Expect investors to be anxious and to have goals different from your own.
5. Expect the unexpected; have more money than you need; and be prepared to wait for those you rely on, such as investors and suppliers.

Ronstadt's new chapters would also focus on the importance of networking. He stresses the importance of expanding contacts for funding, creating an effective team with broad skills, staying close to customers and suppliers, and building good relationships with investors.

Developing a Networking Strategy

The previous discussion should have convinced any budding entrepreneur of the need to expand his or her resource networks. This requires the entrepreneur to do the following:

1. List the key resources, such as funding, personnel, and raw materials, that are needed to help the business survive and thrive. Rank order these resources according to their importance.

2. List next to those resources the personal contacts useful in obtaining them. Note the nature of the relationship with the contact: long-term or short-term, good or bad.
3. Identify other potential contacts that could be solicited for resources. This might involve doing some investigative work and using some of the forums for contacts that have been mentioned here.
4. Identify contacts with whom problems are likely to occur that would lead them to withdraw or withhold resources.
5. Develop a plan for improving relationships with key contacts and developing contacts with other potential suppliers of resources, such as banks, venture capitalists, employment agencies, and legal counsel.

By periodically reviewing and improving the effectiveness of their resource network, entrepreneurs can help keep their businesses from joining the ranks of the many failures.

Conclusion

The start-up phase is one of the most difficult times during the entrepreneurial career. Finding money, people, information, and other resources is not easy and requires a great deal of dedication and patience, as well as attention to business ethics. The entrepreneurs who manage this resource dilemma successfully tend to be those with the ability to develop and utilize contacts that are a part of their social network. While there are many pitfalls to avoid, a well-developed resource network can help entrepreneurs overcome many of the obstacles that they face. Creating such a network will not be easy for the entrepreneur who favors going it alone. But the costs associated with failing to build and use a network far outweigh the time and effort required to develop key contacts that will enable the entrepreneur's business to survive.

THREE

How Do I
Manage Problems with
Partners and Boards?

As we have seen, successful entrepreneurs develop networking strategies to obtain the resources needed to keep their companies afloat. However, most entrepreneurs have few assets that they can use to attract the additional resources needed to get started. One asset that they can offer to those who do have resources is ownership in the new company through investment or partnership. Entrepreneurs often experience a variety of problems working with partners or other investors. When a portion of ownership is given up, the entrepreneur must develop a strategy to create a working relationship with the other owners. The strategy for managing partnership relationships involves setting up a governance structure—generally a board of directors—that will provide a forum for the various owners to resolve differences and provide direction for the company.

In this chapter, we explore some of the dilemmas that entrepreneurs face in working with partners and discuss the impact of entrepreneur-partner relationships on the business. Strategies for developing effective governance structures and partner relationships are also examined.

The Problem with Partners

To illustrate the problems that entrepreneurs have with partners, we present three case examples. The first is that of Illinois Computer Cable:

53

When Jim Eme walked into the building on Monday morning in July 1987, he was met by a roomful of empty desks and a pile of resignation letters thrust through the mail slot and fallen to the floor. Over the weekend, six of his eight salesmen had stolen into the company and cleaned out their desks while co-workers mingled at the company picnic. Gone, Eme says, were customer lists, price lists, and valuable parts diagrams that Illinois Computer Cable (ICC) had painstakingly assembled in five years of business. Even calculators and staplers had been swept off desks. The place was barren, as empty as the feeling in Eme's gut. The company he had founded was dead.[1]

One of the four founding partners, Bob Ohlson, had been ousted from the company several months earlier because he wanted more control than the other partners. After he left, he made the salespeople an offer that they could not refuse, and they left with him to start a new company, taking key information and skills that were needed to help ICC compete and survive. Regarding the impact of this experience, another founder, John Berst, said, "I tend to hold my thoughts in. I feel I have to be guarded about what I say and whom I say it to now. You're not sure who may be passing information to the other company or entertaining thoughts of doing something like this again. With Bob Ohlson I bared my soul. Now, I'm reluctant to totally confide in anyone."[2]

Another story of conflict is that of John Doran and Edward J. Lennon, Jr., the co-owners of T. J. Ronan Paint Company in the South Bronx section of New York City.[3] Conflicts between the two began as each came to feel that the other wanted too much power. As the conflict escalated, they began changing the locks on the doors of the company building to keep each other out. Lennon closed Ronan Paint's checking account and opened another one so that Doran would not have access to any company funds. Faced without any money to pay himself or his sons who worked in the business, Doran began to intercept checks from Ronan's customers and deposit them in his own checking account. On at least two occasions, the men came to blows:

> One secretary described a day in April 1979, when the postman approached Doran to hand him the mail. Lennon stepped forward and quickly grabbed it. When Doran objected, Lennon punched him in the face, breaking his glasses. Threatening to put a bullet through his partner's head, Lennon snatched a stapler and raised his arm to clobber Doran with it. His sons grabbed him. The Doran boys also interceded. Doran filed assault charges.[4]

Finally, Doran petitioned the court to have the company dissolved and the assets divided. In granting the petition, the presiding judge in the case wrote that "It appears that no one is interested in the settlement of this case to the detriment of the business."[5] As a result of their protracted legal battle, Lennon and Doran paid their lawyers a total of $1.5 million—equal to the company's annual revenues.

Our third example, from our own interviews, is that of an organization created to develop sophisticated computer technology. As the company grew from five employees (the founders) to more than thirty, the need for additional funding became evident. A Japanese company expressed interest and eventually provided several million dollars of funding in exchange for 65 percent ownership. The honeymoon between the Japanese investors and the American entrepreneurs was short-lived, however. The board of directors, composed of the five founders and four members of the Japanese company, was always in conflict and became virtually paralyzed. As the CEO, one of the original founders, noted,

> I got very little if any help from the board. The Japanese directors just weren't there. You can talk about how great the Japanese are, but as far as I'm concerned, they stink. They are really bad. As far

as I can tell, they never once helped us from a management standpoint. They had a negative influence. They insisted on all kinds of reports and were always here visiting us. I don't think in my six years as president of the company I went more than two weeks without a Japanese visitor I had to entertain. They require huge amounts of reporting. Finally, it got to the point where we told them no, we weren't going to do it. For a while we were amiable, because we wanted to build a relationship. [But] they were always around trying to find out things from middle management and professional people. It was such a negative influence. They didn't understand the market, and they didn't understand the technology. Basically, they were trying to recover their investment through selling us their expensive parts.

After several months of frustration and conflict, the CEO resigned. He now watches his company from the outside looking in. Other entrepreneurs have had similar experiences. One study reported that start-up companies go through an average of 2.7 chief executives before they go public.[6] This high turnover rate is largely due to the conflicts between partners or other investors.

Impact of Partner Relationships on Company Culture

As these three cases illustrate, partner relationships can be fraught with tension, anxiety, distrust, and anger. Such relationships exact a toll on the psyche of the entrepreneur. Furthermore, the interpersonal problems between partners can extend into the business as well. The relationships that develop between the entrepreneur and the other owners of the firm often determine its culture and can have a profound impact on organizational effectiveness. In particular, as the owners interact and enter into agreements, whether through formal legal documents or informal understandings, they develop a set of expectations regarding each other's behavior and such issues as who has power, what values are to be adopted, and who makes key decisions. These expectations seem to provide the context for the development of organizational norms, values, rituals, behavior patterns, and other key elements of the company culture. For example, distrust among the owners is likely to affect other relationships in the organization and permeate its culture. In the case of the T. J. Ronan Paint Company, the company culture was characterized by high conflict between the Doran family and the Lennon family, and that cultural pattern had great impact on the performance of the firm.

To illustrate how entrepreneurs and their relationships with other investors and owners can affect the culture of an organization, we will examine two high-technology firms that we studied over a number of years, which we will call Crystalazer, Inc. (CI), and Multi-Graphics, Inc. (MGI) (all names have been disguised).[7] Both companies had about a thousand employees and annual revenues of about $100 million. MGI was founded in 1968 and CI in 1980. In both companies, the founders had prominent ownership positions but venture capitalists provided significant funding and wielded a great deal of power. In the case of Crystalazer, the venture capitalists controlled more than 50 percent of the stock, and the ten-person team of founders controlled the rest. In the case of MGI, the ownership was divided more or less equally among the two founders, a number of early investors, and the venture capital firm. In both cases, the venture capitalists had a major voice in all key decisions, but their orientations toward the firms and their relationships with the founders were quite different.

While studying these firms, we gathered information from the founders, the venture capitalists who supplied the funds, key managers and engineers who participated in the development of major innovations, and lower-level managers and assembly workers and used archival data such as annual reports, newsletters, and financial data. Data were gathered over a three-year period at CI and a six-year period at MGI.

The Venture Capitalist's Orientations at Crystalazer and Multi-Graphics. These two cases illustrate how venture capitalists can view the entrepreneurial firms that they fund in very different ways. Some of the differences between the two firms may also reflect the different decades in which they were founded. In the 1960s, when MGI was founded, venture capital funds were relatively scarce. Indeed, the industry was relatively new, and those with capital were often interested primarily in the long-term development of a firm, a technology, or an industry. In the 1980s, when CI began, venture capital funds grew rapidly, with many investors wanting a high return on their investment in a short period of time.

If we look closely at the events surrounding the founding and funding of each of these two enterprises, we see quite different sets of assumptions of the key owners (the venture capitalists) in the two companies. Table 3.1 lists for each company the owners' assumptions about time, desired outcomes, the nature of people, and the role of the owners. The distinctions between the two companies are not quite as neat as the table suggests (for example, the venture capitalists in both companies pushed the founders to set specific goals), but it does illustrate some fundamental differences.

Table 3.1. Assumptions Underlying Venture
Capital–Founder Relationships at Two Firms.

	Multi-Graphics, Inc.	Crystalazer, Inc.
Time frame	The venture capitalists are committed to long-term company development.	The venture capitalists are committed to short-term profits.
Desired outcomes	The venture capitalists and founders are interested in technological development.	The venture capitalists want a quick return on investment.
Nature of people	The venture capitalists see people as resources to be developed.	The venture capitalists see people as assets to be managed—they are expendable.
Venture capitalists' role	The venture capitalists' role is to help train and develop founders.	The venture capitalists' role is to monitor performance and make needed changes.

At Crystalazer, the relationship was largely impersonal, based on a utilitarian logic. The venture capitalists saw the business as an asset to be managed and demanded a return on their investment. While the founders were also interested in developing a new technology, the demands of the venture capitalists received top priority, since they controlled the board of directors. The founder of MGI, Robert Graham, had quite a different relationship with those who funded his venture. While those venture capitalists also wanted a return on their investment, they were willing to wait a long time for that return and to endure company losses. They had faith in Graham's ability to develop the new technology, but they also felt that they needed to give him some "business sense" if he was to lead the firm effectively. With such an understanding between Graham and the venture capitalists, the company was able to invest significant amounts of money in research and development and to support projects that entailed relatively high risks — something that would not have been tolerated at Crystalazer.

Cultural Consequences of the Owners' Orientations. The orientation of the venture capitalists toward each company had significant implications for the kinds of cultures that developed. At Crystalazer, the employees were rewarded for meeting the numbers: deadlines, costs, sales, quotas, and so forth. Most of the activity in the company centered on meeting these goals. Indeed, company employees would cut corners to meet production and sales goals. For example, one executive reported that when he told company president Walter Smith that he was unable to meet a deadline for the development of a particular product, Smith refused to extend the deadline but offered the executive a sizable bonus if he met it. The deadline was met; the executive got the bonus; but, as he admitted, "We shipped a crap product."

The importance of meeting deadlines and quotas permeated the Crystalazer culture. At the end of the month or quarter, employees would work overtime to meet production goals or give large discounts to customers to meet their quotas. This would create slack periods at the first of the month or quarter. Thus, organizational activities were a race that started slowly but ended with frantic efforts toward reaching the finish line.

The Crystalazer culture valued short-term results and individual achievement. There was frequent political infighting between departments and a distinct lack of teamwork, since many employees saw other groups or individuals as enemies who could prevent them from achieving their personal goals. Moreover, the venture capitalists would quickly fire the CEO if their goals were not met—they had three CEOs during the first five years of operations. In describing why he fired one of the founders who was named as the first CEO, the president of the venture capital group said:

> None of the founders had any real management skills, but we felt that they should be able to get the product going, and then we would worry about the management as needs arose. I believed that Oscar [the CEO] could handle an engineering team, but he had an inability to set goals for functional groups, evaluate performance, and take remedial action. I was amazed by the pervasive inability to set standards of performance. You need to set standards on the first day the plant opens if you want to get good quality. One day I was there for a board meeting. There was a pile of papers and dirt on the factory floor—four or five square feet of it. Oscar didn't take immediate action with the vice president of manufacturing. He should have made it clear that it would not be tolerated. Dust is death for the kind of technology we were developing. I was incensed. I did not show it, but I knew then that Oscar could not remain the CEO.

As a result of this incident, Oscar was fired and the message made clear—either you meet the demands of the venture capitalists or you will be fired, even if you are one of the key founders of the business.

In contrast, the MGI culture rewarded those who developed new products. There were "technical geniuses" and "designated idea people" who held great power and influence. Much as in the university setting where Robert Graham was socialized, those who gained power and status were able to demonstrate the technical merit of their ideas. Moreover, engineers were encouraged to use 10 percent of their time to "bootleg" projects (develop projects that were not explicitly sanctioned by management) and pursue their own ideas. Much of the political activity in the company revolved around persuading the key engineers to support new ideas, in contrast to Crystalazer, where most of the politics centered on the achievement of production or sales goals. It was not that the venture capitalists and other investors did not want Graham to meet certain requirements and become profitable. In fact, Graham reported that he was "beaten up" many times by the venture capitalists in their attempt to teach him some business principles. However, the venture capitalists trusted Graham and relied on his experience and technical expertise. As a result, Graham was able to foster a technical culture at MGI, with a focus on product development, while Crystalazer had more of a production culture, with a focus on getting product out the door and to the customer. Again, the differences in the cultural patterns of these firms seem to be inextricably connected to the venture capitalists' orientation toward the founders of each company and their personal goals.

These cultural differences stemming from the relationships between the founders and the venture capitalists have had a definite impact on each firm. Six years after the founding of Crystalazer, the firm's stock was worth only one-tenth of what it had been a year earlier, and it has recovered only slightly since 1986. Sales and profits have also dropped substantially. Poor quality and the lack of new products have undermined the firm's ability to compete. Virtually all of CI's founders have resigned or been fired. At MGI, Graham has made some mistakes by pouring money into what have turned out to be unprofitable ventures, but the firm is still innovative, the stock price has remained relatively constant — about five times as high as Crystalazer's — and the future looks bright. Graham continues to lead the firm and receives recognition from local and national leaders for his contributions.

Governance Structures in an Entrepreneurial Firm

One of the first duties of those starting a new organization is to develop a governance structure to manage the kinds of problems previously described and to provide direction for the firm.

Types of Governance Structures

There are basically four types of governance forms.[8] In a *sole proprietorship* — typically reserved for very small companies — the entrepreneur is solely responsible for governing the business and personally assumes all the risks and liabilities associated with it. In a *partnership* structure, the entrepreneur may act as a general partner (with other, limited partners) and govern the organization with input from the other partners. As a general partner, the entrepreneur assumes most of the risk associated with the new venture. Some entrepreneurs decide to *incorporate* their businesses with either a C-corporate structure, which allows for unlimited shareholders and for profits to be taxed at the corporate rate, or an S-corporate structure, which limits the number of shareholders and in which profits can be taxed at the individual rate. With this governance structure, the corporation, rather than the entrepreneur, assumes the risks of doing business. Thus, if the corporation is sued, the entrepreneur's personal assets are protected. Incorporation requires the entrepreneur to set up a governing board of directors, generally with at least three members.

The fourth type of governance form is a *trust*. One entrepreneur whom I interviewed favored a business trust organization (BTO) as a governance form because of its flexibility. Such a trust has the following features: (1) Shareholders are anonymous. (2) The trust is controlled by a trustee (usually the entrepreneur). (3) Shareholders do not have a vote — control resides in the trustee. (4) There is no limit to the number of shareholders. (5) Profits may be taxed at the corporate rate or passed directly to the shareholders and taxed at the individual rate.

With a proprietorship, entrepreneurs do not have to account to anyone for their actions. With a partnership, the entrepreneur is accountable to the other partners. With a corporate structure, the entrepreneur is accountable not only to the board of directors but also to the other stockholders, whose interests should be represented by members of the board. With a trust, the entrepreneur is accountable to the trust's shareholders. Given that many entrepreneurs do not want to have their performance reviewed by others, the proprietorship might seem like a reasonable governance structure to use. However, the fact that the personal assets of the entrepreneur are at risk with this structure often makes this form of governance untenable. Another reason that a partnership, a trust, or a corporate structure may make more sense is the fact that entrepreneurs who enlist the help of partners or other investors tend to fare better than those who go it alone. A study of 2,000 businesses founded since 1960 found that companies that were started by partners were four times as likely to succeed as those that were started by individuals acting alone.[9] Even the smallest companies needed at least an "inside person" to organize product development and production and an "outside person" with expertise in marketing and sales. When partners are involved, discipline and accountability increase and, as we noted in Chapter Two, it is easier to expand one's resource network. Entrepreneurs who hope to build a large business need to find compatible partners and will generally need to incorporate. All entrepreneurs will find themselves attempting to meet the needs of a variety of constituencies and will need to manage relationships with these constituencies through some type of governing board or council.

How Boards Function in Entrepreneurial Firms

Several years ago, I did a study of board practices in a number of entrepreneurial firms and family-owned businesses.[10] The boards that I studied seemed to fall into four categories: paper boards, rubber-stamp boards, advisory boards, and overseer boards. I will briefly describe each in turn.

Paper Boards. A paper board is one that exists only on paper and only to meet the requirements of the law. This kind of board is generally composed of members of the entrepreneur's family and rarely if ever meets. Some entrepreneurs use Thanksgiving dinner or some other family occasion to let family members "vote" on any issues that require board approval. In most instances, however, decisions are made by the entrepreneur without input from the board. An example of a paper board is provided by the son of an entrepreneur who described how he became president of his father's company:

> [When] my father and mother came back from Florida, I used to pick them up at the airport and bring them home. [On one such occasion] it was late in the day, so they had dinner at our house. So over a cocktail my father said: "I think you ought to be president since you are doing it all." I said, "no." He said, "what do you mean, no!" I said, "well, there are two reasons: one is that I don't know enough about the job to do it right, and number two, all you are going to do is give me a title and not the authority." That took a little while to discuss. Anyway, he stayed the summer and then went back to Florida, and . . . the same thing happened the next year. The following year, however, he came back and said, "I'm sorry you missed the board meeting." And I said, "when was it?" and he said, "this morning." . . . I said, "well, what happened?" He said, "congratulations, you have been elected president." So that is how I became president.[11]

In this case, the board was composed of the founder, his wife, and the son. The founder and his wife had decided to appoint their son as president over breakfast that morning.

Entrepreneurs can run into difficulty if their board exists only on paper, for such a board may fail to meet the requirements of the law, such as holding annual meetings and keeping minutes of those meetings.

Rubber-Stamp Boards. A rubber-stamp board does exactly what the name implies — it rubber stamps decisions made by the entrepreneur. While this type of board tends to meet fairly regularly and may include some "outsiders," such as the family accountant or lawyer, the role of the board is to support the entrepreneur. The board may be asked to provide input regarding various decisions that the entrepreneur makes, but the entrepreneur does not want to be confronted or receive negative feedback during board meetings. Board members serve at the pleasure of the entrepreneur and can be dismissed if they fail to meet the entrepreneur's needs.

Advisory Boards. Advisory boards meet regularly, generally have some outside directors, and provide the entrepreneur with expertise and advice regarding key strategic and policy decisions, a sounding board for ideas, and regular performance evaluation. Board members may also be required to represent the interests of other investors.

Overseer Boards. With the first three types of boards, the entrepreneur generally has majority control of the firm's shares. When the entrepreneur controls 50 percent or fewer of the shares, with the remainder controlled by outside investors or partners, the firm will have an overseer board, whose members represent constituencies that may have widely differing goals for the business. This type of board meets regularly and is often a forum for conflict, since diverse interests are represented. Entrepreneurs who have taken their companies public often find themselves with overseer boards that they cannot control through the power of ownership but must influence through other means. Entrepreneurs who have high needs for secrecy, control, and predictability are quite uncomfortable in their relationship with an overseer board.

These four types of boards, to a large extent, reflect the different decision styles and power orientations of entrepreneurs. Those with high needs for control tend to rely on paper or rubber-stamp boards. Those who are more willing to be influenced and collaborate are more comfortable with advisory boards, and those who are willing to let others have a significant voice in determining the direction of the business tend to favor overseer boards. As one can see, problems begin to occur when entrepreneurs have assumptions that are different from those of other board members. For example, if the entrepreneur assumes that the board should perform a rubber-stamp role, while others feel that it should act as overseer and the entrepreneur should play a secondary role, serious conflicts are likely to occur.

A Survey of Board Practices

A survey of 147 boards in privately controlled companies gives us some insights regarding how entrepreneurs use their boards.[12] While not all the firms were led by entrepreneurs, 40 percent were identified as having "entrepreneurial ownership," 37 percent had "family ownership," and 23 percent were categorized as "investor owned." Of the 147 companies in the survey, 70 had some outsiders on the board, 51 had only family members or company employees on the board, and 26 had "token," or paper boards. Fifty-eight percent of the firms with "inside boards"— boards including only company employees or members of the founder's family — reported that the role of the board was to project a good public image and meet legal requirements. Only 31 percent of this group used the board for advice and direction. In contrast, 58 percent of the firms with "outside boards" — boards including individuals who did not work in the business — reported that the board's role was to give advice and direction, while only 17 percent said the board's purpose was simply to meet legal requirements or to enhance the company's public image.

The boards that functioned met an average of four times a year. The meetings lasted between two and four hours; in general, the larger the company, the longer the meeting. Forty-nine percent of the time at meetings was spent listening to various reports, 18 percent was spent on approving decisions, and only 33 percent was spent discussing critical issues, such as the firm's strategy or succession planning.

The CEOs of the firms with inside boards were less satisfied with the performance of their boards than the CEOs whose firms had outside boards. Thirty-nine percent of CEOs with inside boards felt that the board was either tremendously valuable or very valuable. In firms with outside boards, 67 percent of the CEOs saw their boards as tremendously valuable or very valuable. To improve board performance, a large percentage of CEOs felt that the number of outside board members should be increased and that they should be used more effectively.

The implications of this study are quite clear: entrepreneurs who wish to improve the performance of their boards must look outside their own families or organizations for directors. However, because of their needs for control and secrecy, many are unlikely to do this. And even if outsiders are found, there is no guarantee that the board will be effective. For example, the finding that only 33 percent of time in board meetings was used to discuss critical issues indicates that time in board meetings may not be well spent and that they could be conducted more effectively.

Managing the Governance Dilemma

To deal with the issues surrounding the governance of an entrepreneurial firm, the entrepreneur has several options. The first and perhaps most obvious option is to attempt to start the business without partners, financial or otherwise. In such cases, entrepreneurs can set up either paper boards or rubber-stamp boards that will allow them to exercise complete control of the business. Such an approach can succeed if there are few major capital costs associated with starting the business and the entrepreneur has the experience and expertise to run the business alone. In certain types of industries, such as consulting and computer software, this kind of approach can succeed. Even the large software company WordPerfect Corporation, with sales of more than $500 million, has not gone public, and the two founders, Alan Ashton and Bruce Bastian, control virtually all the stock. This is possible because initial capital costs did not require selling stock to gain resources.

This approach may have some long-term costs, however. Without outside partners, the entrepreneur may lack the skills and resources required to build the business and the capital needed to meet cash flow requirements. Finally, the synergy that can be created through debate and discussion between partners is often missing when there are no partners involved. If the entrepreneur has all the power, no one is likely to challenge the entrepreneur's authority or ideas. Thus, if the entrepreneur makes some wrong moves, there is no mechanism to provide for a course correction.

There is one strategy that can be used to mitigate against this problem: the creation of an advisory council to review operations and generate ideas that can help the firm survive.[13] The advisory council should not act as a board of directors, as it cannot set formal policy or vote on key business issues such as capital investment, but it can be a sounding board for the entrepreneur who needs guidance and support. Most entrepreneurs hire consultants to help them get started. Those consultants might constitute the advisory council, meeting several times a year to advise the entrepreneur. Another advantage of the advisory council is the fact that the entrepreneur will not need to carry liability insurance for the council members, since council members do not have the fiduciary responsibilities of elected directors. With increasing litigation, some directors have found themselves targets of lawsuits. Therefore, without adequate insurance, board members are unlikely to be willing to serve. Ward and Handy noted that the cost for such insurance averaged $24,111 in medium-sized private firms and $82,286 in larger ones.[14] Since few entrepreneurs have the ability to pay such fees as they begin a new venture, the advisory council is a reasonable option.

Working with Partners

Most entrepreneurs will find themselves working with partners. As we have seen, such relationships can be either a boon or a bust for the business. Entrepreneurs who have worked with partners as well as consultants who have helped entrepreneurs deal with partnership problems have made a number of suggestions regarding how to make a partnership work.[15] Some of those suggestions are detailed below.

Choose a Partner with Complementary Goals and Skills. Entrepreneurs should choose partners whose skills and experience are different from their own but with whom they can work well. They should avoid going into business with someone they do not know well, since they should have a good understanding of their partners' strengths and weaknesses. All partners should generally have the same long-term goals and objectives. Robert Graham of MGI went to great lengths to find the right financial partner. As one observer told us, "Robert Graham created a company because he thought it was the best way to realize his long-term vision. In his search for venture capital, he was most interested in finding someone who respected the technology and could see its long-term implications. He was not interested in maintaining control through equity in the company. Instead, he knew that if the venture capitalists would buy into his vision of an ultimate technology, then he could maintain technical control, because his vision extended beyond anyone else's." Indeed, this vision was shared by Graham's venture capitalists and has led to a very successful partnership.

Clarify Roles and Responsibilities. Accountability and authority for administrative and technical tasks should be distributed among the partners. As noted previously, it is helpful to have someone accountable for business operations and someone else responsible for marketing and other external issues and problems.

Create a Buy-Sell Agreement. This agreement should cover such events as the death or resignation of a partner. The partners must agree on a method of doing a valuation of the business if a buy-out takes place. Without such an agreement, estate claims could tie up a company's assets in court for years. Some consultants feel that every partnership needs a "shotgun" agreement — an agreement that if the partners cannot work together, one must buy out the other. This forces partners to either resolve their differences or part company.

Determine Where the Money Is Coming from. The partners must decide how money will be raised — whether they will use their own assets or find some other source. The partners must also decide how much compensation each will receive and how the compensation scheme will change over time once the business is established.

Set Up Lines of Communication. Many problems that partners have stem from their inability to effectively communicate with one another. Thus, partners should arrange for weekly meetings, memos, conference calls, or other types of forums to ensure that no partner is uninformed.

Develop Mechanisms to Handle Conflict. Conflicts are inevitable, and partners must develop ways to handle disagreements. Partners must trust one another and have open communication, and this is not easy. The entrepreneur and the other partners need to set up norms from the start that encourage open communication and make airing of disagreements as comfortable as possible. As one entrepreneur said, "The biggest mistake you can make is to let something bother you and keep quiet about it. We make sure that as soon as we see something wrong we express ourselves. We state our feelings and we live with whatever decision is made. It's hard, but you have to learn to be an adult."[16] If disagreements cannot be managed, an outside third party or a neutral board member might be asked to help mediate a dispute.

Decide How to Decide. One of the biggest problems partners have is determining how decisions are made. Early on in any partnership, it needs to be clear whether they are to be made by consensus, by majority vote, by the majority shareholder with input from others, or by some other method. To gain consensus requires a great deal more time and discussion than does decision making by one person. However, a decision made by consensus is likely to be more readily accepted and to be implemented with more commitment than one made by the entrepreneur acting alone. Taking this into account, the entrepreneur needs to determine with partners and the board what decisions require consensus and input and what decisions can be made by the entrepreneur alone. Without a clear understanding of the decision-making process, conflict is inevitable. Thus, the entrepreneur needs to clarify the decision-making process with partners as well as board members.

Determine Fairness of Time and Commitment. Partners need to decide how much time and energy each must devote to the business. Many conflicts occur when one partner feels that the others are not doing their fair share of the work. This breeds resentment and is one of the most common sources of conflict between partners.

Put It in Writing. Conflicts occur when expectations are violated. Thus, to avoid any ambiguity or miscommunication, most if not all of the items mentioned previously need to be set down in writing and reviewed periodically. Penalties for those who fail to follow the prescribed procedures should be outlined as well.

Get Appropriate Help. In most cases, the partners will need to work with a lawyer, accountant, or some other business adviser to work through their problems and set up agreements. Working through each of the items above under the guidance of a professional can help the entrepreneur avoid getting into a bad partnership. While keeping costs low is important, paying a professional to help navigate these minefields will pay great dividends over time.

Creating an Effective Board of Directors

Relationships with partners are often enhanced or undermined by the way the board of directors functions. There are a number of steps to be taken to create an effective board. First, find directors who can add value to the organization. During our interviews, an entrepreneur who had founded a cosmetics business said, "On the board I have one of the more powerful attorneys related to the cosmetics industry. I have a pharmacist who was involved in the manufacturing of products for many years. I also have a fellow that is very involved in the fragrance industry." These experts have helped to keep her business on firm footing. While directors with skills such as legal training can be very helpful, the most important criterion for selecting a director is good business judgment and common sense. While directors must understand financial reports, legal issues, and strategic issues, they must also have the ability to assimilate details and get at the heart of the problem. Moreover, having directors who have gone through the kinds of problems the business is facing allows the entrepreneur to better anticipate any pitfalls.

Good directors are not always easy to find. The local chamber of commerce, industry and trade associations, universities, or other forums may prove helpful. Speaking with other business owners about potential board members is often useful. To find good directors requires a great deal of detective work. Once a potential director is found, the entrepreneur, other partners, and key managers should have an opportunity to interview the prospective director to see whether there is a fit. Once chosen, the directors should recognize that they will need to spend several hours preparing before each board meeting and that they will be compensated for the time that they spend.

Board meetings should have clear agendas, and minutes should be taken at each meeting and distributed afterward. As noted earlier, much of the time in board meetings is spent listening to reports and approving decisions. While these are important, key strategic and policy questions should receive the most attention. The agenda and the time allotted for the various items should reflect the relative importance of the topics to be considered. Much as partners must do, the board needs to develop ways to communicate effectively, make decisions, and solve problems. If the board reaches an impasse, the entrepreneur should call in a third party to define the major problems and mediate the dispute. If some problems require more study or action, the board might appoint a subcommittee to focus on the problem or assign a board member to examine the problem and make recommendations at the next board meeting. By following these suggestions, entrepreneurs are more likely to get the help that they need to build their businesses.

Conclusion

Building successful relationships with partners and creating an effective board of directors can be two of the most difficult tasks facing an entrepreneur. Many of the entrepreneurs whom we studied had regrets regarding their relationships with partners. Others recognized that their boards were not effectively utilized. In a broader sense, the dilemma of whether to have partners is affected by the entrepreneur's need for control. Some entrepreneurs do not want to have to answer to others and be tied into a partnership relationship. If this is the case, the entrepreneur must develop a strategy for gaining resources without surrendering control. The use of an advisory board is one option for maintaining control. Entrepreneurs who are willing to engage in a partnership relationship must be skillful in finding the right partners and building on each other's strengths while covering each other's weaknesses. This is not easy, but it can spell the difference between success and failure.

FOUR

How Do I
Balance
Work and Family?

A dilemma that plagues most people is the trade-offs they face in dividing time and attention between work and family. Work and family are both important, yet we are faced with choices that tend to favor one at the expense of the other. Entrepreneurs often find making these choices extremely difficult because of the nature of their careers. Starting a new business takes a great deal of time and energy. Any new organization has a "liability of newness" and must establish customers, suppliers, or organizational routines for producing goods or services.

Given the time and emotional commitment that are needed to create a successful business, developing healthy family relationships can be extremely difficult. In a survey that I conducted of just over seventy entrepreneurs, while more than 90 percent reported that they were satisfied with their family lives, they were less satisfied with their family lives than with their personal lives and careers. A panel of entrepreneurs who had left the entrepreneurial career path to work for someone else reported that one of the major reasons they went back to a more conventional career was the lack of family support for their entrepreneurial life-style.[1] In this chapter, we discuss the work-family trade-offs facing entrepreneurs and suggest some ways to maintain a reasonable balance.

Difficulties Facing Entrepreneurial Families

Because of the nature of an entrepreneurial career, entrepreneurs and their families seem to have difficulties in the following four areas.

74

Finances

In most families, the parent who works has a fairly stable wage or salary and brings home a regular paycheck that the family can count on. At the beginning of an entrepreneurial career, scarce financial resources can be a special burden to the family. The entrepreneur, particularly in the early stages of the career, often must draw on family savings to start the business or finance new projects. This depletes the money available to the family, which does not have a regular, stable income to meet monthly expenses. Family members may have to give up such things as a new car, new furniture, or music lessons. Family members may overtly or covertly complain that the needs of the business seem to be more important than the needs of the family: "Why doesn't Dad get a regular job like everyone else?" If the new venture or business is a success, the entrepreneur will often try to make up for the lean years by lavishing material things on the family. This can cause problems of an entirely different nature, as we will see in later chapters.

Health

A number of entrepreneurs that we interviewed mentioned the fact that their lives were filled with a great deal of stress and anxiety. The precariousness of a new organization creates most of that stress; many entrepreneurs have to mortgage homes and take out loans to meet payrolls, which can be a huge financial burden. They also feel responsible for their employees and those who have invested in their companies. Such responsibility naturally introduces a lot of stress into the lives of entrepreneurs and exacts a physical toll. A study of 281 entrepreneurs conducted several years ago noted that 63 percent had insomnia, 62 percent had headaches, 58 percent had back problems, and 55 percent had impaired digestion at least once a week. One-third of this group experienced one or more of these symptoms at least twice a week. Since embarking on their entrepreneurial careers, 9 percent had increased their smoking and 18 percent had increased their alcohol consumption; 12 percent were undergoing psychiatric counseling.[2] Of course, other occupations (such as college professors and medical doctors) can create similar levels of stress and physical disorders; however, there is no question that the entrepreneurial life-style is highly stressful. One entrepreneur we interviewed said that the company investors "kept pressuring me more and more, and my health was deteriorating rapidly. Just prior to firing someone, I had peritonitis for a week before I realized I had it, so I was in the hospital. Just after that I had a heart attack over the stress. . . . I finally decided it just wasn't worth it, so I resigned as president and became chief scientist for the company." Another entrepreneur, who had left a large company that he had started to begin a smaller one, said, "My spiritual and family life suffered from the amount of time and energy I put into the company. I was physically depleted. If I had stayed with the company for six more months, I would have had serious health problems."

Even Walt Disney, who was known for his vitality and energy, suffered a nervous breakdown in 1931.[3] As financial pressures mounted in the early years of his career, Disney became increasingly irritable. A sudden disappointment would lead to crying spells. On the advice of his doctor, he took an extended vacation, which helped to restore his health. Upon returning to work, Disney started a new regimen of exercise and leisurely diversions, which served to reduce the stress in his life.

As these cases illustrate, the stress associated with an entrepreneurial career can sometimes overwhelm the entrepreneur both physically and psychologically. Some studies have shown that a high percentage of entrepreneurs (84 percent) are "Type A" personalities—they are hard-driving, competitive, impatient, and achievement-oriented and thus even more susceptible to the effects of stress than others.[4]

Setting Work-Family Priorities

Entrepreneurs are often aware that the demands of their careers have a negative effect on their families and find that setting priorities is extremely difficult. Here are just a few of their comments, most of them from our interviews:

I've always had a problem getting time for my family. I overdid it on the work side — I should have spent more time with my family.

Life is a balancing act, and I realized that life with my family was passing me by.[5]

I have been very adamant about spending time with my kids, and maybe that is because I missed a lot of that time with my dad. And yet, I had to admit that the first ten years . . . I was working eighty, ninety hours a week in the business, and so I didn't spend time with them. Fortunately, I got that behind me and got in a position where it freed my time up and I could spend more time with them. I really try to spend an awful lot of time with them. And I think there is a balance. There seems to be a balance in everything in life, and it's hard to get that balance. It is hard to know what your timing is in life. Is this when I work? Is this when I don't work?

My wife is very supportive but occasionally has to demand my attention. She gets fed up with me being gone all night and stuff, especially this spring, when I was traveling so much. It was very hard on her. It has been stressful in a lot of ways.

These comments reflect the difficulty that entrepreneurs have in sorting out work and family trade-offs and meeting the demands of both.

Outside Personal Interests

While this is an area where it is difficult to gather data, there are enough anecdotes to indicate that with the stresses of starting a new venture and conflicts that can arise between work and the family, some entrepreneurs are vulnerable to developing personal attachments outside the family that can be destructive to their marriages and to family life in general. They might find someone whose interests are more similar to their own, who "understands them better," offers only support and does not bombard them with questions regarding their family obligations. Several of the entrepreneurs we interviewed reported that their entrepreneur friends had been divorced or were experiencing marital difficulties as their own and their spouses' interests diverged.

Balancing Work and Family

There are a number of approaches that entrepreneurs have used to achieve a balance between work and family. One is reducing their family responsibilities. For example, some have decided not to marry or have children. Others have decided to defer marriage until they have achieved success in their careers. Helen Boehm, an entrepreneur who opted not to have children, describes her feelings about having a family:

> Many times I would be on the road nine months of the year, pushing Boehm art, and it was common for me to make ten calls a day on various buyers and stores. I remember one Christmas Eve, flying in a DC-3 over the snow capped mountains of Colorado. It was beautiful but my heart sank as I saw the little lights of the farm houses and I knew families were together for Christmas dinner. At one time we thought about adopting a young girl. We had her at the house on weekends. One weekend, I had to host an out of town buyer for dinner. I left Gloria for three hours with Ed, to return to find her crying for me. Gloria also had relatives nearby — what if they later wanted her back? I couldn't put us or Gloria through that and my travel schedule would have made it very difficult.[6]

To fill her need for family affiliation, Boehm became a foster parent for dozens of children, and she has received a great deal of satisfaction from taking them on field trips and other outings.

Another approach to achieving balance is trying to separate work and family into two different worlds. The entrepreneur attempts to avoid bringing the stresses of work home and sets aside a certain amount of time each week for the family and a certain amount for work. In effect, the attempt is to create two lives — one work, the other family — and buffer each system from the other. By creating these two lives, the entrepreneurs attempt to avoid feeling guilty when at work because they are not spending time with the family and feeling guilty when at home because they are not working. While creating such distinct worlds is not easy or even possible in most cases, it is one approach to making life more manageable for the entrepreneur.

A third approach to the family-work dilemma is to combine work and family. Entrepreneurs who take this approach often have their spouses and children work with them in the business, so that the world of work becomes an extension of family life. One entrepreneur who has tried this said, "All the kids have worked in the business. I think that I taught them to be honest, straightforward, hard-working, and fair to people. . . . One of the fun things about having your own business is that you can have your kids come work for you." By working with his children, this entrepreneur also fulfills his role as a father in teaching them the values that he feels are important. Other children of entrepreneurs have told me how much they learned by going on business trips with their fathers. Peter Huntsman, the son of John Huntsman, a well-known entrepreneur in the petrochemical industry, commented to me how much he enjoyed going with his father to the various Huntsman-owned plants and meeting the company employees when he was very young. John would often ask Peter to say a few words to the employees as well. By their working together, John has been able to teach Peter what he feels is important and to prepare him for leadership in the firm. (Of course, working with family members can also entail problems, as we will see in Chapter Eight.) Other entrepreneurs, who give time to church, civic, or other service organizations (which they often see as part of their role as a community leader), have found that involving their families in these organizations as well can increase family unity. Regardless of which approach the entrepreneur decides to use to manage this dilemma — except avoiding family responsibilities altogether — the aim is to accomplish two goals: creating a successful business and building a strong family. We now turn our attention to outlining things that an entrepreneur can do to build a strong family.

Building a Strong Family

Some of the families of entrepreneurs that I have counseled have had a number of problems, such as poor communication, frequent conflicts, and a lack of trust. Others seemed to be able to develop supportive family relationships. While there is little evidence to suggest that the families of entrepreneurs have more problems than others, the challenges facing the entrepreneur make developing a successful family a daunting task. A study of more than 3,000 families by Nick Stinnett and John DeFrain helps us to better understand why developing an effective family is so difficult for entrepreneurs.[7] Stinnett and DeFrain noted that the "strong families" they studied had the following six qualities:

1.   *Commitment.* Members of strong families are dedicated to promoting each other's welfare and happiness. They value the unity of the family.
2.   *Appreciation.* Members of strong families show appreciation for each other a great deal.
3.   *Communication.* Members of strong families have good communication skills and spend a lot of time talking with each other.
4.   *Time.* Strong families spend time — quality time in large quantities — with each other.
5.   *Spiritual Wellness.* Whether they go to formal religious services or not, strong family members have a sense of a greater good or power in life, and that belief gives them strength and purpose.
6.   *Coping Ability.* Members of strong families are able to view stress or crises as an opportunity to grow.[8]

We will now discuss the challenges that entrepreneurs face developing each of these qualities in their families.

Commitment

Building a strong family requires high commitment to the family and its needs. In some cases, entrepreneurs feel that the time and energy that they spend on the business are a sacrifice that they are making for their families. Others feel that they can sacrifice time with the family early on in their careers and spend more time with them once the business is firmly established. Unfortunately, some end up sacrificing their families instead. The families that Stinnett and DeFrain studied reported instances of family members sacrificing for one another that demonstrated the importance of family relationships. For example, one man told of his mother diving in front of an automobile to rescue him from being run over. There was no uncertainty in his mind as to the commitment that his mother had made to him. While entrepreneurs need not jump in front of a car to show their devotion to their families, the way they spend their time and energy shows family members what is important.

Appreciation

I have known several entrepreneurs who have great difficulty expressing appreciation to others, whether family members or employees. For some reason, they cannot say "thank you" very well. In one entrepreneurial firm that I studied in depth, the managers reported that they frequently "beat each other up" verbally and rarely if ever praised one another or gave one other "positive strokes." Most employees said that this behavior was encouraged by the founder's management style. A number of sons of entrepreneurs have told me that their fathers rarely pay them compliments; most of the time, they find their fathers criticizing them for something they did or failed to do. This is particularly common when the son works directly with his entrepreneur father. Some entrepreneurs seem to assume that family members or employees should just be grateful to them for their employment and are not owed any expressions of appreciation. If this is how the entrepreneur views the world, expressing appreciation will be difficult, if not impossible.

Communication

Communication is essential in every family. In particular, discussing and solving problems as they arise is critical for the family to succeed. Time pressures or frequent travel may make it difficult for entrepreneurs to deal with family problems as they arise. In some families, such as the Binghams of Louisville, Kentucky, the children fail to carry on the dream of their parents because of their failure to develop open lines of communication. Mary Brenner, who studied the Binghams, writes that they were "camouflaging feelings with exquisite manners" and that "the Bingham children accepted this code unquestioningly, at least until everything fell apart and they stopped speaking to their parents and to one another."[9] As a result of the communication gap between family members, the father decided to sell his communications empire and informed his son, who wanted to take over the business, in a memo placed on a bulletin board at company headquarters. His son responded by writing a memo criticizing his father's actions, which was also displayed for all to see. While such a breakdown in communication is clearly extreme, entrepreneurs can experience similar problems if they fail to take the time to communicate with their spouses and children.

Time

Finding time for one's family is a constant challenge for the entrepreneur. A survey by Boyd and Gumpert[10] found that 82 percent of entrepreneurs who had been in their careers for five years or less, 70 percent of those who had been entrepreneurs for six to ten years, and 58 percent of those who had been in business more than ten years worked evenings. While the amount of time spent away from home seems to diminish over the course of the career, the time commitments are still great.

A major study of drug use in families reported that drug use was higher in families where the father was frequently absent.[11] The study noted that healthy families tended to have strong fathers and supportive mothers; mother-led families tended to have a variety of problems. This is not to say that all families with absent fathers are doomed to failure. However, the message is clear: if you fail to make time for your family, you run the risk of losing the loving and supporting relationships that a family can bring, and your spouse and children are likely to suffer.

Spiritual Wellness

Stinnett and DeFrain describe the dimension of spiritual wellness as "a unifying force, a caring center within each person that promotes sharing, love, and a compassion for others. It is a force that helps a person transcend self and become part of something larger."[12] A number of entrepreneurial families that we studied seemed to have this sense of spiritual wellness. These families had a set of goals and beliefs that went far beyond making money.

Some such families have developed a "creed" or "philosophy" that they attempt to inculcate into family members and even company employees. Some families have written down their "family values"; some talk about their "stewardships." They feel that they have been given much and need to give something back to society. Some have become heavily involved in philanthropic causes or other charitable work. Others devote much of their lives and financial support to a particular religion. John Huntsman, for example, left the company that he had started to serve a mission for his church for three years, during which time he focused all his energies in church service. Such actions showing commitment to a higher purpose provide meaning to the lives of individual family members and strengthen family ties.

Coping with Crisis and Stress

Psychiatrist Scott Peck begins his book *The Road Less Traveled* by stating that the first principle that we all must learn is that "Life is difficult."[13] Peck is indeed stating the obvious; all of us, entrepreneurs included, must face trials and tribulations in life. In my counseling and church responsibilities, I have had the opportunity to counsel hundreds of young people facing a variety of problems, including alcohol and drug abuse, eating disorders, emotional and sexual abuse, loneliness, and depression. I have come to the conclusion that we all have a particular "cross to bear" in this life. The issue is not whether we will have such trials or how to develop strategies to avoid them but how to prepare oneself and one's family to cope with them.

By the nature of their work, entrepreneurs are often faced with disappointment and frustrations, and it is easy for them to take these frustrations home. One son of an entrepreneur whom I interviewed mentioned that he hated Christmas. I was shocked, since Christmas has always been my favorite time of year. When I asked him why, he replied, "Ever since I was young, Christmas has been a very hectic time of year for my father's business. He was always anxious and upset during the Christmas season, which made life miserable for our family." To avoid such problems, the entrepreneur must be able to cope with such stress without letting it spill over into the family. Taking the time to help family members deal with their own disappointments and frustrations is also an essential part of developing a strong family.

Keeping the Entrepreneur in Balance: Assessing Family Needs

The entrepreneur can take a number of positive steps to keep an appropriate balance in life. First, it is important to get a clear fix on just what impact the entrepreneurial career is having on the family. Many entrepreneurs are honestly blind as to the state of the family — and some want to keep themselves blind to family problems. Getting information regarding the state of one's family is not easy. How do you find out what is really going on in your own home? A family team-building session might help. At such a session, each family member could be asked to respond to questions such as "What keeps us from being close as a family?" "What changes would you like to see made that would improve family relationships?" The parent-entrepreneur needs to talk frankly about the advantages and disadvantages of the business for the family. In a climate of openness and trust, family members can share honest feelings and begin to work out solutions.

A therapist or consultant may be needed if trust is low or there are severe problems that cannot be handled without a trained third party. However, there are often issues of the business that intrude on the entrepreneurial family, and many therapists and consultants have not learned to deal with these two systems simultaneously. If help is needed, seek out someone who has an understanding of both family and business systems.

If such team-building sessions are conducted, entrepreneurs must be willing to examine their own behaviors and to make changes. If they are not, the family will become disillusioned, for talk without action breeds cynicism. For example, would the entrepreneur be willing to abandon the new venture and go back to working for a stable salary? Would the entrepreneur be willing to hire more help or get more financial partners? The entrepreneur might even make a commitment to the family to move in a new career direction that better meets the needs of the family if the venture does not succeed in a year or two. Some smaller changes, such as spending a majority of evenings and weekends at home, reducing the number of business trips, or taking a vacation, might also be negotiated.

If the entrepreneur needs to spend more time with the family, what do they do together? For example, going to a movie, where little communication or interaction takes place, might not improve anything. It may take some personal insight and skill development to make the appropriate changes.

Improving Family Relationships

Good family relationships can help the entrepreneur weather the stresses of an entrepreneurial career. One study found that families whose members had strong bonds with each other and had developed good interpersonal skills were better able than others to cope with such stresses as the loss of a job, disability, or illness.[14] On the other hand, poor family relationships or a lack of support from the family can make the entrepreneurial career much more stressful. As one entrepreneur whom we interviewed said, "Some lose their health, their wives, and their families as entrepreneurs. Your biggest sale will be to your wife, who will go through the peaks and valleys with you. Once you've got her sold and she's on the team, then you can move forward." This entrepreneur intimated that he would not have succeeded as an entrepreneur without the support of his wife and family. And given the life-style of the entrepreneur — the long hours, the travel, the uncertainty — gaining that support is no easy task. While there are no magic formulas for building a strong family and gaining its support, there are several things that entrepreneurs might do.

Spend Quality Time with the Family

While entrepreneurs may not have a lot of time with the family, they must devote their full attention to the family when they are with them. I encourage entrepreneurs to go to work early, come home at a reasonable hour, and do not bring work home if that can be avoided. If work is brought home, the entrepreneur always feels torn and guilty because of competing family and work demands.

Have Regular Family Councils

A family council involves meeting together as a family and sharing ideas and concerns, solving problems, planning family outings or vacations, and discussing family values. A family team-building session might also be conducted at a family council meeting. The council meeting might end with a game or some type of refreshments for the younger children. Helping children understand what it means to be a family member — the responsibilities, the rights, and the privileges — is an important family task. Research on effective families by William Dyer and Philip Kunz showed that effective families have clear goals that all family members understand and accept.[15] These usually include getting an education, solid marriages, developing a good self-concept, having clear values, and becoming good citizens. A family council can be a setting for discussing such goals. Developing a family creed or values statement can help family members clarify what they believe in and support. The study by Dyer and Kunz noted that effective families maintain control more through strong expectations than through rules and punishment. Parents expect children to be responsible, get good grades, be on time, and meet commitments. Children understand these expectations and feel a personal sense of disappointment when they violate them. Effective families discuss how family chores will be done, how much money children will receive and whether they must work for it, how much television is watched, and how family members spend their time away from home. These are critical issues that can cause families to splinter if not handled well, and entrepreneurs often are not available for (or interested in) working out these basic family problems.

A family council is a good forum for the family to grapple with these issues. Entrepreneurs and their spouses should plan these meetings, set the agenda, and make assignments. While these family councils may last only twenty to thirty minutes, they should be held regularly to open communication channels and improve relationships.

Spend Individual Time with Family Members

While meeting as a family is important, spending time individually with one's spouse and children can be even more important. Some entrepreneurs take children or spouses on business trips. Others schedule time to take their children on special "dates" or outings. I have talked to several children of entrepreneurs who wish their fathers had spent more time with them individually when they were younger, and some would like to spend more time with them now even though they are married and are in their twenties and thirties.

Review the Attributes of a Strong Family

In this chapter, we have outlined some of the key attributes of a strong family. Entrepreneurs might occasionally ask themselves or their families how they are doing along each of these dimensions. If they are having difficulty showing appreciation, a letter or card expressing thanks might be appropriate. If there are communication breakdowns, the source of the problem needs to be discovered and corrected. As noted previously, counseling by a competent family therapist, member of the clergy, or psychologist is often the best option for families that are experiencing severe problems. Entrepreneurs by nature are frequently unwilling to admit that they are having problems in their families and invite others to help. However, the wise entrepreneur will recognize when help is needed and seek it out.

Develop Stress- and Time-Management Skills

Given the great stress of an entrepreneurial career, an entrepreneur will need to develop an active program of exercise, relaxation, and time management. I encourage the entrepreneurs with whom I work to set up a weekly exercise regimen and to find ways to relax each day in order to remain physically fit. I also advise them to use their time well by developing "to do" lists that rank the activities to be done each day in order of importance, to delegate those things that others can do, and to use effective meeting-management skills.[16] Through these activities, an entrepreneur can better cope with the strenuous demands of the career.

Conclusion

In this chapter, we have described some of the difficulties that entrepreneurs have in developing a balance between work and family. The stress of an entrepreneurial life-style makes achieving this balance a daunting task. However, if entrepreneurs understand the trade-offs involved and take appropriate steps to reduce stress and spend time with their families, they will not feel cheated at the end of their careers but will have experienced the joys of family life along with the business successes.

PART TWO

MIDCAREER
DILEMMAS

FIVE

WHY IS IT
SO LONELY AT THE TOP?

One hot summer afternoon, an entrepreneur and his wife, Fred and Sybil, were seated in my office (all names are disguised). They had come seeking counsel regarding a variety of problems that had plagued their relationship and their business. As we began discussing their problems, Sybil listed all of Fred's faults and failures that were, to her mind, contributing to the tension and anxiety in her life and "ruining the business." As I listened to her, I kept watching Fred out of the corner of my eye. His face became flushed, and I could see that he was becoming more and more agitated. Finally, he exploded: "Sybil! I know that you want me to take care of this thing and that thing. In fact, everybody seems to want something from me. I'm supposed to be taking care of the family and the business, but answer me this question: Who's taking care of *me*? Who's looking out for *me*?"

Fred's response is not unlike those of many other entrepreneurs. They are under great pressure and feel that they are all alone in dealing with their problems, with no one to talk to or confide in. A study of 156 entrepreneurs conducted several years ago found that 54 percent experienced a recurrent sense of loneliness and isolation.[1] The study's authors also indicated that the feelings of loneliness seemed to remain rather constant over an entrepreneur's career and that it was a significant cause of unhappiness. I have found that such feelings tend to intensify as entrepreneurs' families begin to mature and place more demands on them and as the business begins to grow, which also imposes more demands and strains.

While all of us experience loneliness at some point in our lives, entrepreneurs, by the nature of the roles that they play, often feel such loneliness acutely. Forrest Wood, the founder of a successful boat-manufacturing business, described the problem of loneliness this way: "You know, the entrepreneur is really a lonely breed, but Nina [my wife] and I have had each other, which has made it easier and has built a strong marriage. Most entrepreneurs are not necessarily happy because of the loneliness."[2] Nina describes the loneliness as stemming from the weight of decision making that falls on entrepreneurs: "There's a great responsibility for our people and sometimes the burdens of our decisions are very heavy, like when we decided to 'bet the farm' and sell the guide business . . . we worked so hard for over fourteen years . . . to provide jobs for our neighbors."[3]

In this chapter, we explore the dilemma of "loneliness at the top" and describe some of the problems that these feelings can cause for the entrepreneur. This sense of loneliness appears to be related to three major problems that confront entrepreneurs as their businesses and families grow and mature: difficulties in communicating effectively; inability to build a team; and the use of inappropriate change strategies, which result in the alienation of employees and sometimes the entrepreneur's family.

Communication Problems

The loneliness that many entrepreneurs feel seems to stem from their inability to communicate effectively with others. This is not to say that they do not know how to give orders — for they generally do that well — but they often do not know how to share their feelings, hopes, fears, and anxieties. Furthermore, they may find it difficult to carefully listen to others' problems and concerns when they have so many of their own. They may feel that no one can truly empathize with them and their problems since they play a unique role. Following are some of the reasons for this lack of communication.

The Power of Secrecy

Most of the entrepreneurs that I have studied or consulted with over the years have been very secretive about the inner workings of their businesses and their personal finances. Of course, there are several good reasons for this, but such secrecy tends to isolate the entrepreneur. Some entrepreneurs seem to run their businesses with a "need-to-know" communication strategy: company employees should be given only the information about company strategy, future plans, financial status of the business, and so on that they need to do their specific jobs. Elaborating on a subject or giving additional information regarding other aspects of the business is deemed unnecessary. The entrepreneurs tell themselves that the only ones who need to know everything are themselves. One example of such secrecy was found in the Haas family in the early days at Levi Strauss and Company. The family had learned from the business's founder, Levi Strauss, and from subsequent family leaders the importance of keeping information closely held. Each year, to meet the requirements of the law, the family had to share its annual report with shareholders, who were mostly company employees. David Beronio, a trusted family adviser, would bring one copy of the report to the shareholders' meeting, carry it around the room, and allow each stockholder a brief glance at it. After each shareholder had seen the report, it was locked safely away in Beronio's desk. In later years, as the number of shareholders multiplied, each shareholder was given a single numbered copy of the report at the annual meeting; at the end of the meeting, the reports were all collected and stored away from prying eyes.[4]

Such an approach to sharing information with shareholders or employees tends to compartmentalize the information in the business so that few people other than the founder are able to see the big picture. Employees sometimes become frustrated and resentful because the entrepreneur appears to be withholding information that would help them function more effectively. The perception that the entrepreneur does not trust them discourages them from attempting to develop a deeper relationship with the entrepreneur. The entrepreneur can often detect this resentment and may withdraw or isolate him- or herself from others in the firm or from family members. This vicious cycle of distrust leading to secrecy leading to withdrawal, which results in more distrust, can further intensify the entrepreneur's

94 The Entrepreneurial Experience

sense of loneliness. One might ask: Why do entrepreneurs not share more information? The answer, in most cases, seems rather clear: information is one of the entrepreneur's most significant power bases; it is a way to maintain control. If no one but the entrepreneur has all the information, the entrepreneur becomes indispensable. The entrepreneur is always "one up" on everyone else in the business and can always use the excuse that "We can't do that — you don't have all the facts."

Getting Negative Feedback

Another communication problem facing entrepreneurs is their inability to accept and deal with negative feedback regarding their performance or management style. While none of us likes to be told that we are wrong or that we need to improve, entrepreneurs often interpret confrontation and questioning as a sign of disloyalty. Since they are at the top, they rarely get feedback from peers or those with higher status; it is much harder to accept feedback from a subordinate than from a superior or a peer. Moreover, entrepreneurs who have been successful in building a business from the ground up may believe that no one should have the right to question their decisions. While some entrepreneurs are willing to accept criticism, I have found that most react to negative feedback in one of two ways. First, they may lash out at the one who is giving the feedback. They get angry, they yell, they may even call into question the motives of the person giving the feedback. Second, they may listen quietly to the feedback and make little or no response. They withdraw during the confrontation and give few signals regarding how they are feeling. With either approach, the people giving the feedback are likely to feel punished for their actions. They get either an angry response or no response at all, which makes it unlikely that they will ever make such an effort at confrontation again. This inability to accept negative feedback then leads to further isolation of the entrepreneur.

Projecting a Successful Image

Another factor that leads to entrepreneurs' sense of loneliness is their need to project a successful image to their employees,

their families, and the business community at large. In starting
a new business, entrepreneurs feel that they are vulnerable and
that any sign of weakness may cripple their ability to raise capital, attract employees, or gain other resources. Some may also
want to create a larger-than-life image for themselves. While
demonstrating a command of oneself is important, the entrepreneur can take this to an extreme. One entrepreneur whom
I interviewed could not stop talking about himself and his accomplishments. He bragged about how much money he had
made and what smart deals he had concocted. After listening
to the tales of his exploits, I was completely turned off by him
and his demeanor and began feeling sorry for those who had
to work for such a boss. Just to make sure that I had not mis-
judged him, I had my research assistant interview him as well,
without telling her of my reaction to him. Her interview went
exactly the same way that mine did. She reported that he was
arrogant and oblivious to her needs as an interviewer, so she
cut the interview short. While some entrepreneurs, such as Kenneth Olsen at Digital Equipment Corporation and William
Hewlett at Hewlett/Packard, tend to downplay their accomplishments and are often seen as much like the "common person,"
great success can make it easy for entrepreneurs to lose their
humility and, with it, their ability to empathize with others and
communicate effectively.

Different Goals

A lack of common goals among entrepreneurs, their families,
and their employees can also be a source of communication
difficulties. As illustrated by Fred's statement quoted at the beginning of the chapter, founders may feel that others are merely
trying to get something from them or trying to take advantage
of them in some way. While the founder, who created the business, wants to protect it, build it, and make sure that it endures,
family members may be more interested in selling the business
or taking large dividends from it, and nonfamily employees may
feel that high salaries and job security are their most important
goals. Given these potential differences in goals and orientation
toward the business, founders often find discussing the business

with others quite difficult. As one entrepreneur explained, "I have a hard time understanding these people—they think like managers, not like owners. They don't have the entrepreneurial spirit."

Inability to Build a Team

Another reason for entrepreneurs' feelings of loneliness is their inability to build a management team from which to draw social support and help in achieving their goals. Some entrepreneurs have told me that they feel uncomfortable in a group setting, preferring one-on-one discussions with subordinates. One entrepreneur who came to me for advice indicated that he had a number of major organizational problems. In particular, he noted that he and his top managers had difficulty coordinating their activities and solving problems that affected the entire company. When I asked him his approach to solving such problems, he replied, "Each week I have individual interviews with all my key employees. We discuss their problems, and I try to help them. However, sometimes the problems seem to be related to what some of the other managers are doing." I asked him why he did not meet with his managers as a group to solve those problems that were of a group nature. He seemed rather stunned. It had never really occurred to him that he could use a team approach to solving some of the problems he was facing. Furthermore, he said that he felt uncomfortable leading a group discussion.

One of the reasons for not using a team is the entrepreneur's need to be in control. Group dynamics can be difficult to manage and often are time-consuming and unwieldy. For fast-paced entrepreneurs, using a team can seem like having a millstone around their necks. As one entrepreneur stated, "I have to control . . . that's the reason I don't do well in civic and church functions where there are big committees. They drive me nuts. Nobody can make a decision. Nobody wants to do anything. All they want to talk about is all this planning, and nothing happens. It just drives me crazy." Thus, the need for control, the lack of skills in developing a team, and the time it takes to develop and use a team are all reasons why the entrepreneur often favors going it alone.

Lack of Discipline in Team Building

As noted in Chapter Two, the effective development of a team with the right mix of skills can help ensure the survival of the business. However, to develop such a team requires skill, effort, and discipline. A number of entrepreneurs that we studied had a fairly loose management style and a distinct lack of awareness of what it takes to build a team. Technical entrepreneurs, for example, often relish the technical aspects of their careers but have a great disdain for managerial tasks and prefer to work alone. In addition, the sheer amount of work needed to establish the business often leaves little time to spend working on human or team issues. One entrepreneur that exemplified this loose managerial approach was Nolan Bushnell, the founder of Atari. The start-up phase of Atari has been described as one of "entrepreneurial craziness," with "plenty of marijuana and beer" at the management meetings.[5] When Warner Communications bought Atari, one Warner insider described Bushnell this way: "There's a difference between having fun and running a company. Nolan is a creator, a dreamer, a pie-in-the-sky thinker . . . he operated in a 'hey, man' kind of way."[6] Other entrepreneurs, such as Steven Jobs, have been criticized for having the same flaw: they could create a business, but to run a large business effectively, they needed to create a disciplined management team.

Insufficient Delegation

If a team is to function effectively, the entrepreneur must be willing to delegate to some degree. He or she cannot do all the work but must use a team to accomplish goals. The following comments reflect some entrepreneurs' views regarding delegation:

> Now there are lots of jobs that are mundane, routine kinds of jobs that you can hire out, but if you really want something done right, sooner or later

you end up doing it yourself. You either look over the shoulder of the guy that's doing it until he does it your way, which is the right way, or you end up by doing it yourself.

I've learned a few things about delegating. I give it up very selectively. The tough part of delegating is giving it up and accepting less than what you could do yourself. It's been tough for me, but I've had to accept that because you can't do everything, and that means you can spend your time doing other things.

I like to find somebody and give them the job parameters and say go get it done, don't bother me, I'm not going to look over your shoulder. I'm not going to put my nose in what you're doing, but I'm available. If you need me, come and see me. The only time you'll see me and the only time I'll bother you is if you don't hit those numbers — then we will have a serious conversation.

The viewpoints expressed here indicate two basic problems that entrepreneurs have in delegating. The first is a basic lack of trust in others to carry out an assigned task in the way that the entrepreneur would like it performed. This lack of trust can be manifested in ways other than the reluctance to delegate. For example, one entrepreneur located his office in the middle of all the other offices and kept his door open so that he could hear and see everything that was going on. In another case, the founder of a successful computer company had all the computer terminals linked to the computer in his office. Periodically, he would scan each engineer's terminal to see whether the engineer was doing the work that he was assigned to do. When there is a basic lack of trust (and in some cases employees probably should not be trusted), the entrepreneur will never be willing to delegate important tasks.

The second problem is the kind of punishment that is often meted out to those who fail to perform a given task. It often happens that the entrepreneur delegates a task that may require some ingenuity or creativity but the subordinate knows that if he or she deviates from the prescribed pattern, he or she is likely to be punished. Thus, the job is done routinely, and the entrepreneur then complains that he or she cannot get anyone to show initiative or creativity. This is the catch-22 in some entrepreneurial firms. Thomas Watson, the builder of IBM, was known for attempting to encourage "wild ducks"—employees who would be creative. However, one observer of Watson and IBM noted, "Watson likes wild ducks all right. As long as they are flying in formation."

To effectively delegate, entrepreneurs must be willing to show trust in their subordinates and to let the job be done in ways that might be different from their own. Forrest and Nina Wood espoused this kind of philosophy when they said, "You have to have the self-confidence to let go and give your people free reign, and we give them the authority to make decisions without reprisal."[7] As a result of this style, one of their employees remarked, "It always amazes me that Forrest and Nina never dictate, but they call us together and get our opinions. When the project is complete, I can see my part and the impact of others. Our opinions really count, and it gives us pride."[8]

Unintended Team Building

One interesting feature of some of the entrepreneurial firms that I have worked with is the presence of some excellent teamwork at the management levels below the entrepreneur. What often happens is that the managers who report to the entrepreneur recognize the need to collaborate with others to solve their problems and to cope with the uncertainties created by working in an entrepreneurial environment. Thus, these managers band together to support one another emotionally as well as helping each other solve business problems. Entrepreneurs who have difficulty building a team of which they are a member may do well to foster a climate in which those at the level below them cooperate with one another and act as a team. While this can result in some problems in communication between the team and the entrepreneur, it appears to help the business as it grows and matures and thus can be a fortunate unintended consequence of the entrepreneur's management style.

Inappropriate Change Strategies

The third common problem facing entrepreneurs that tends to isolate them concerns the change strategies that they employ. Researchers and practitioners who study the process of change generally outline the following steps as essential to any successful change effort:

1. Define the problem.
2. Gather data regarding the problem.
3. Analyze the data.
4. Develop alternatives for solving the problem.
5. Select a plan of action.
6. Implement the plan.
7. Evaluate the effectiveness of the plan. See whether the problem has been solved. If not, go back and repeat the steps in the change process.

Such a change process encourages people initiating change to adequately diagnose the problem or problems before any action is taken.[9] As part of the diagnosis, it is also important to understand how people feel about a specific change plan: Are they ready to change? Are they capable of carrying out the change plan?

Peter Block, a highly successful consultant, argues that to be successful in initiating change, one must develop "allies" to help in the change effort.[10] According to Block, the person interested in initiating the change must develop a clear vision regarding the goals of the change effort and get people to trust him or her and to agree with that vision. Negotiating trust and agreement with those whose help is needed to make a change successful is crucial to developing the support needed to ensure success.

Unfortunately, entrepreneurs tend to skip a number of key steps in the change process. First, they tend to see the cause of the problem as being fairly clear, often centered in the performance of individual employees, and assume that everyone else sees the problem in much the same way. Second, they assume that there is only one clear course of action to be taken, which generally means applying more pressure to employees or more closely monitoring their actions. Little is done to diagnose the key systems that may be causing the problem: the technical system, the administrative system, or the social system of the organization.[11] After making a "quick and dirty" diagnosis with little input from others, the entrepreneurs move directly to implementing the solution. Since they believe that employees should merely follow orders and not ask questions, they give little thought to how employees feel about particular solutions, and the "vision"—if there is one—is not shared. Since the employees do not share in the entrepreneur's thinking, an "us versus the boss" mentality can be created, and this serves to further isolate the entrepreneur from employees.

Rather than developing a change strategy that fits a given situation, some entrepreneurs seem to rely on a universal power strategy to initiate change: they assume that they can merely mandate a change by the power of their position. This generally results in a strategy whereby the entrepreneur scolds or browbeats employees to make changes. For example, while William Millard, the founder of Computerland, was traveling extensively to open new markets for his computers, he discovered that product quality was deteriorating and shipments were late. Back at headquarters, he ordered all the employees to assemble in the parking lot, where he stood on the edge of a planter box and berated them for their lack of effort and poor performance. However, unknown to Millard, many of the employees were making great sacrifices to improve product quality. They were greatly offended by Millard's speech, and their morale plummeted.[12]

A related change strategy often used is threatening employees with loss of their jobs. One entrepreneur is fond of saying, "If you don't like it here, you can quit. We can always find a replacement." Such an approach to change generally leaves employees feeling angry, demeaned, and frustrated and unwilling or unable to do what is necessary to make the needed improvements.

One of the best examples of someone who did not think through the implications of his change strategy is an entrepreneur whom I will call Frank. I have known Frank for several years and have helped him and his family work on a variety of problems. One day, Frank called me with some distressing news: one or more of his employees were making unauthorized phone calls to a "sex talk" hot line. Frank was furious. He felt that whoever was doing this was clearly stealing from the company and from him personally. He had asked some employees whether they knew anything about the calls, and all of them had pleaded ignorance. My experience with Frank had taught me that he would sometimes take action without understanding all the implications. I was leaving on vacation and encouraged him to continue to find out the facts but to take no drastic action. Upon my return, I called Frank to see how things were going. To my horror, Frank told me the following: "I decided that most of the people I was talking to were lying to me, so I called my friend who is a polygraph expert. He encouraged me to let him test those employees who I felt weren't telling the whole truth. So I checked with my lawyer and eventually decided it was the right thing to do. The first person who I had tested was my son-in-law who works in the business."

The polygraph tests, although conducted on only a couple of employees with inconclusive results, sent shock waves through the company. The son-in-law was so upset that he quit, and this has created a great strain in the family. Also, graffiti began to appear in the plant, aimed at Frank and his lack of confidence in his employees. I asked Frank, "What would you have done if the tests had shown that the employees were lying? Would you have fired them? How would you have used that information?" Frank replied, "I'm not sure what I could have done from a business or a legal standpoint." Thus, Frank had moved ahead with a plan of action to catch the offenders without understanding how that plan would affect his employees and his family. Although an employee who was not tested did confess several weeks later, the result has been the loss of a key employee, lower employee morale, and the disruption of family relationships, and Frank must now spend time and money appealing a large government fine (the son-in-law filed a grievance). While not all entrepreneurs are as impetuous as Frank, I have seen many with similar tendencies.

Managing the Loneliness Dilemma

There are three major steps that entrepreneurs can take to successfully manage the loneliness dilemma: (1) gaining insight into their own feelings and behavior, (2) acquiring needed skills, and (3) building a support system. We briefly discuss each of these areas.

Gaining Insight

To combat feelings of loneliness and avoid isolation, entrepreneurs often need to increase their awareness of what they do that contributes to the problem. I have found that opening up the communication channels between the entrepreneurs and their families and employees is one of the better ways to deal with the problem. To open these channels, entrepreneurs might invite others to give them feedback regarding their performance and actions. This might be started by initially "priming the pump." With hand water pumps, one has to pour a little water into the pump to get the water flowing freely. Similarly, entrepreneurs need to prepare others to give feedback that might be threatening. To prime the communication pump, the entrepreneur might say, "I feel that I have been doing some things that have tended to make me less accessible and less connected with what is going on in the business (or the family). What do you think? Can you give me some examples? What might I do to change?" This could be done individually with people that the entrepreneur trusts or with a small group. Another approach is an anonymous survey focusing on how effective the entrepreneur is in communicating, building a team, delegating, managing change, and so forth—those things that have been discussed in this chapter. In many cases, the tension and emotion around these issues can be handled only by bringing in a third party, often a consultant or trusted adviser, to interview the entrepreneur and his or her subordinates to gain a better picture of what is going on, share the information with the entrepreneur, and help develop a plan of action to solve the most pressing problems. Still another approach is participating in a personal development program, such as a T-group, in which members are encouraged to become more open about their feelings and receive feedback from others in the group about their communication style and interpersonal effectiveness.

Developing Skills

Even if entrepreneurs gain insights that tell them that they need to change their behavior, they may lack the skills needed to change. For example, they may not know how to communicate with others without causing conflict or how to delegate effectively. While attending a management training seminar can be helpful, I generally find that such seminars do not have lasting impact. After going away for a day or two for a seminar, entrepreneurs come back and try out a few of the ideas that they have learned. However, since their subordinates do not understand what the entrepreneurs are trying to do, they are suspicious and unable to support the entrepreneurs' newly discovered "skills." After a short time, the entrepreneurs' behavior reverts to what it was before the seminar.

As an alternative to seminars, I have encouraged entrepreneurs to set up in-house training programs for the entrepreneur and key managers. The sessions may be conducted by an in-house human resource person, by managers who can teach the needed skills, or by an outside consultant. In these sessions, skills such as team building and delegating are not only discussed and practiced but applied to real situations and problems that the business is facing. In this way, the skills learned are more likely to be transferred to the "real world" and incorporated into the entrepreneur's management style. Such training also can establish norms that encourage learning, innovation, and risk taking, which can also help to improve communication between entrepreneurs and their subordinates.

Developing a Support System

To avoid becoming isolated, entrepreneurs need to build a support network to help them diffuse much of the tension and anxiety that they face in their careers. Regular family counsels or top management meetings to discuss key problems and share concerns are certainly options. However, as we have noted previously, entrepreneurs are often reluctant to share their innermost thoughts with these people. Another option that has helped many entrepreneurs is joining civic or business groups where they can associate with entrepreneurs who have had similar problems to share their experiences and gain empathy and support. One such vehicle is the Dialog program sponsored by the Small Business Association of New England. Each Dialog group consists of approximately ten entrepreneurs. The group meets each month at a different member's home, where the host entrepreneur tells his or her story and gets feedback and advice. The group continues until each entrepreneur in the group has hosted a meeting and shared his or her story. Then each member has the option of joining another group.

The founder of the Dialog program, an entrepreneur herself, describes the program this way: "In my estimation, the value of groups such as this is not only to resolve business problems. It would actually serve as group therapy for pressured executives. The ability to discuss their business problems, and have nine knowledgeable people concerned for one day with these problems, could be a great release valve for excess pressure. Even if the executive is just able to put his problems into proper perspectives for a fresher outlook, the meeting would be invaluable."[13] One entrepreneur who attends Dialog meetings acknowledged their value in combating loneliness: "You really get to the point where you would like to have some feedback and some companionship . . . from contacts outside the business. In a small business,

I think one of the great danger[s] is that you become so immersed in what's going on in your own little world . . . you kind of lose track of a larger world."[14]

Whether in a Dialog group or some other forum, entrepreneurs who can find peers to talk to and discuss their problems with are much better off psychologically than those who are unable or unwilling to participate in such networks. As noted in Chapter Three, an effective board of directors may also play this sounding-board role for the entrepreneur. In any event, along with gaining personal insight and improving skills, entrepreneurs need to actively build this type of network, not only for their own sakes but to help their businesses as well.

Conclusion

In this chapter, we have described why it is so lonely at the top for many entrepreneurs. Such feelings of isolation seem to intensify as the founder moves into midcareer. Poor communication, the inability to build a team, and inappropriate change strategies all combine to further isolate the entrepreneur from family and co-workers. To combat this problem, entrepreneurs need to actively seek self-insight, improve their management skills, and develop a support system. Without such actions, this problem can undermine the entrepreneur's family and business and make an entrepreneurial career quite lonely and frustrating.

SIX

How Do I Stay in Control of My Business?

As we have seen in previous chapters, the issue of control is central to the dynamics of an entrepreneurial career. Some entrepreneurs start their businesses because they want to escape from situations where they are not in control. Others enjoy being able to control others and influence the direction of the organization. Over time, however, entrepreneurs may find themselves losing control of their growing businesses and unable to guide them effectively. One entrepreneur commented on the "traumas" that entrepreneurs face as their companies begin to grow: "The first trauma is finding yourself not capable of doing everything. The second is realizing that you don't even know what's going on. The third is hiring people more capable than yourself." This statement highlights the dilemma of maintaining control of a growing business. In this chapter, we explore this issue and offer suggestions for entrepreneurs who want to see their organizations grow but at the same time stay in control.

Mechanisms of Control

All entrepreneurs are concerned to some degree about the "problem of control," which is defined as the ability to predict or alter the behavior of others. Organizational theorists have been interested in the issue of control for many years and have identified a number of control mechanisms, several of which are outlined below.[1]

Control Through Charisma

At the turn of the twentieth century, Max Weber, the German sociologist, wrote about what he called "charismatic leaders." Through the force of their own personalities, these leaders were able to move their followers to conform to their every wish. Robert House, a noted organization theorist, writes that a charismatic leader has "extremely high levels of self confidence, dominance, and a strong conviction in the moral righteousness of his/her beliefs."[2] House also notes that charismatics are able to be effective role models, create impressions of competence and success, articulate ideological goals (a vision), communicate high expectations and express confidence in their followers, and motivate and stimulate their followers to act. Most entrepreneurs exhibit one or more of these characteristics. They are often able to convince others of the rightness of their convictions and influence them to help to achieve their goals. While the concept of charismatic leadership remains elusive, most people are aware of world and national leaders such as Mahatma Gandhi, Martin Luther King, Jr., and John F. Kennedy or entrepreneurs such as Thomas Watson of IBM, Kenneth Olsen of Digital Equipment, and Henry Ford who have exhibited these "magical" leadership qualities.

Control Through Close Supervision

A second form of control is close supervision of those who are assigned to perform a given task. By using this form of control, entrepreneurs can quickly correct employees who deviate from their assigned tasks and praise and reward those who follow orders. In Chapter Five, we gave some examples of how entrepreneurs use this form of control: one monitored his subordinates through a computer in his office; another placed his office adjacent to his subordinates so that he could watch their every move. Others maintain control through closely monitoring company finances. One entrepreneur would not allow any purchases over fifty dollars unless they were authorized by him. In this way, he was able to make sure that he had knowledge of virtually every financial transaction. However, the major drawback to this form of control is that it is very labor intensive — a great deal of time and effort must be expended by the entrepreneur to monitor the behavior of each employee. Such a task becomes virtually impossible as the business grows.

Control Through Standard Operating Procedures

Another form of control is providing employees with a set of written rules to guide their behavior. When performing a task or solving a problem, the employee need only follow the prescribed rules. Organizations typically develop voluminous policy and procedure manuals or booklets of standard operating procedures for employees to read and follow. Fixed rules and procedures help to reduce the need for close supervision, since the rule, not the supervisor, provides the guide for behavior. However, this form of control can be circumvented if employees fail to follow the rules or make mistakes that are not easily detected. It can also lead to a bureaucratic mind-set whereby employees follow rules blindly without thinking on their own.

Control Through Culture

A final form of control is control through culture. Stated simply, culture is a set of assumptions, beliefs, and values that serves as a guide for behavior. By being inculcated with a set of beliefs about what is right and what is wrong, employees come to learn acceptable behaviors and are rewarded for behavior consistent with the basic assumptions and values of the organization. Often these "cultural rules" are not written down but are passed on as a newcomer watches veteran employees, picks up new language, or listens to stories that illustrate what is considered appropriate behavior.

An example of this form of control can be seen in a highly successful high-tech organization founded by two entrepreneurs.[3] One story often told in this company concerns a manager stationed several thousand miles away from company headquarters. One day, he had a difficult problem to solve and was unable to contact anyone at company headquarters to provide him with direction. To solve this problem, he asked himself the following question: What would the founders do if they were in my place? After asking himself this question, his course of action became clear. Later, when he asked the founders whether he had behaved appropriately, they responded that they would have acted the same way if they had been in his shoes, for he had followed the spirit of their philosophy. By influencing the way in which employees think about their work and solve problems, these two entrepreneurs are able to control their employees without always resorting to close supervision or formal rules.

Entrepreneurs and Control

Entrepreneurs typically use the first two types of control, charisma and close supervision, more than the others. When they develop a personal relationship with their employees, they are able to influence their employees to conform and carry out their wishes. When they maintain close contact with their subordinates, they can reward or punish an employee on the basis of an intimate knowledge of the employee's performance.

Implicit in each form of control that has been discussed is the notion that employees are rewarded or punished according to their behavior. The rewards that an entrepreneur can mete out can be great. The possibility of acquiring stock in the company or important positions can be powerful "carrots" for employees in entrepreneurial firms. Millionaires can be made overnight when a small firm goes public. Thus, promises of stock, position, power, or money can exert a great deal of control. The potential loss of these rewards can turn employees into "yes-men," who are unwilling to confront the entrepreneur for fear of losing favor. And more than one entrepreneur has manipulated employees by promising to give them great rewards but failing to do so.

Like the hub of a wheel, which provides the support for the wheel's spokes, the entrepreneur is the focal point for action, directing and coordinating the activities of employees. While the founder's role as the controlling agent for the organization can serve to provide clear direction and help to resolve problems, such a role also has its drawbacks. One reason entrepreneurial firms are so vulnerable is that they are unable to function effectively without the coordinating efforts of the entrepreneur. An example of the problem of such overreliance on a founder for direction can be found in the story of the Spanish conquistador Pizarro and his conquest of the Incan empire. Pizarro was able to conquer the Incas and subjugate its hundreds of thousands of inhabitants with only 106 soldiers and 50 horses. How was he able to do it? When Pizarro learned that the Incas believed that their king was a descendant of the gods and that they must completely rely on him for directions, he kidnapped the king and forced him to follow his orders. Without clear direction from their king, the Incas were unable to organize effectively to thwart the Spanish. Like an arch that has lost its keystone, the Incan resistance crumbled. Like the Incas, employees in an entrepreneurial firm can also become lost if the entrepreneur is not there to direct them.

Hitting the Wall: Increasing Organizational Complexity

Like the marathon runners who "hit the wall" of fatigue at a certain point in the race and must overcome exhaustion to finish, some entrepreneurs describe a feeling of "hitting the wall" as their organizations begin to grow and become more complex. At some point in their company's development, they finally realize that they have created a business that they themselves do not fully understand and are unable fully to control. In my experience, this phenomenon seems to occur as an organization grows to have about twenty-five employees and sales of $1 to $3 million. Of course, there are exceptions to this rule, depending on the industry, product line, or company strategy and the entrepreneur's ability to deal with complexity. Still, it seems to be a threshold where the organization either continues to grow and develop or stagnates because the entrepreneur is unable to move to the next level. It appears to be much easier to go from $6 to $10 million in sales than from $1 to $5 million, even though the difference in each case is $4 million.

Once their companies reach the point where entrepreneurs feel that they are losing control, they may use several different strategies. First, some attempt to curtail growth. One entrepreneur deliberately kept his work force at 100 employees, since he felt that he could not supervise more than that. This made it impossible for his company to expand sales. Second, the entrepreneur might decide to sell out. Some entrepreneurs enjoy only the start-up phase of organization building and want to avoid the headaches of running an organization. By selling out, they can get their "sweat equity" out of the company and move on to something else. Third, the entrepreneur might decide to hire others who are more adept at running a large organization. One entrepreneur with such a strategy was William Durant, the founder of General Motors. One Durant biographer wrote, "To a man of Durant's temperament, the fact that the Durant-Dort Carriage Company [a forerunner of GM] was running smoothly and making great profits meant that it was becoming rather dull. Durant liked to create organizations. When they were going well, he would just as soon let someone else take over the details and look for a new challenge."[4] (Hiring professional managers to operate the business poses its own set of problems, as we will see in Chapter Seven.) A control system based on formal rules and standard operating procedures or a common culture might also be employed at this point.

Of course, an entrepreneur may want to use a number of these options, such as hiring professional managers, developing more formal standard operating procedures, and emphasizing a common set of values, simultaneously. In a growing organization, more formal procedures and a common culture are generally needed for the entrepreneur to maintain some degree of control. However, entrepreneurs often have difficulty in changing their management style to encourage the development of formal rules. They also may resist taking the time and effort to clearly identify their core beliefs and values or teach them to their employees. In the remainder of this chapter, we discuss how the entrepreneur might use these two forms of control to deal with the dilemma of control.

Overcoming Psychological Barriers
to Formal Rules and Policies

Entrepreneurs generally exhibit a great reluctance to develop formal policies and procedures, for such rules stifle creativity, promote red tape, and encourage bureaucracy. Entrepreneurs who started their businesses to get away from the rules and regulations of large organizations may see such rules as constituting an organizational straitjacket. But another, more subtle reason to avoid rule making is that once a rule is made, the entrepreneur, as well as employees, must abide by it. Much of what an entrepreneur does seems to break the rules and is quite unpredictable. Furthermore, entrepreneurs tend to keep their methods of doing work away from prying eyes, and such control of information is a source of power. Formal rules, job descriptions, and the like all serve to force the entrepreneur to become more predictable, to share information, and to become subject to rules like everyone else. Thus, the notion of formalizing their organizations can generate a great deal of resistance in entrepreneurs who fear that their power to act will be undermined by rule making.

One entrepreneur, whom we will call Roger, had great difficulty in coming to terms with the need of his own organization to become more structured and formalized. I was asked by Roger's son, who was the chief operating officer of the company, to do a study to see what they might do to improve the performance of the business as well as the functioning of their family. Roger's retail business had grown rapidly in the 1980s to include more than fifteen stores. Sales and the number of employees had also grown dramatically. To get a better picture of what was happening in the business, I interviewed all members of the family (most worked in the business) and several of the key nonfamily employees.

While Roger had little formal education, he had a wealth of experience and drive. As I interviewed him, he described how he had started from very humble beginnings and built an enterprise that encouraged his store managers to be entrepreneurs themselves. He gave his managers a great deal of autonomy if they met their assigned goals. The company had little in the way of a formal retirement package, benefits, or even a compensation system; each employee's salary was determined in negotiations with Roger, and employees were responsible for setting up their own retirement and benefits packages. Roger pointed with pride to the fact that his employees had worked for him for many years and had a great deal of trust in him.

In my interviews with Roger's family and the store managers, they reported that they enjoyed working for Roger and were highly committed to seeing the business succeed. However, they all felt that improvements could be made in the way the business was managed. The following list, from a report prepared for Roger, summarizes the suggestions that his store managers made:

1. There need to be clear reporting relationships and job descriptions. An organization chart would help.
2. Employee retirement plans and benefit programs need to be developed and standardized.
3. Employee training needs to be standardized. A manual might prove helpful.
4. Policies and procedures need to be standardized and communicated. A policy manual and quarterly store manager meetings would help.
5. The compensation package needs to be updated and possibly made uniform.
6. Employees need to be given positive as well as negative feedback.
7. All programs, such as advertising, need to be coordinated.
8. Quality control needs to be improved. This might involve getting new equipment or improving inspections.

After compiling this report, I met with Roger and his wife, Sarah, to discuss it with them. As I handed the report to Roger, I was sure that he would be pleased to see how many good suggestions for improvement his employees had made. I also felt that Roger would be amenable to these suggestions, since they were not a major indictment of Roger's management style but merely reflected the fact that there was a need to begin some formalizing of their business methods. As I began going over the eight items, I could see that I had been wrong. Roger's face became flushed. Sarah also began to squirm in her chair. As I finished reading the last item, Roger stood up, threw the report to the floor, and exclaimed, "That's what I think of policies and procedures. If that's what they want, I don't want any part of it." With that, he stomped out of the room. I was left sitting in stunned silence with Sarah, thinking of what to say next. I finally asked Sarah, "Is he going to come back?" "I think so," she replied. "He'll just need a few minutes to cool off." She was right. About twenty minutes later, Roger returned. He had calmed down considerably, and we were able to finish discussing the rest of the report.

Since that time, Roger and I have had several meetings. He still dislikes rules and regulations, but he recognizes that standardizing some practices and clarifying roles can help his business to function better. He recognizes that he lacks the needed expertise and is not willing to spend time to develop a new system of procedures, so he has delegated that responsibility to his son, Tom, who has an M.B.A. degree and is more comfortable with running a business in a more formal manner. So far, most of these eight suggestions have been implemented by Tom, and the results seem to be quite good. Communication has improved, everyone has a better understanding of the roles that they play and how their roles relate to others', and there is better coordination. Company profits are at an all-time high.

Formal Control Systems

If entrepreneurs are unable to overcome their resistance to formal procedures, little can be done. But entrepreneurs should realize that by properly developing some formal procedures, they can gain *more* control of their organizations and that such rules can help get work accomplished much more efficiently and effectively. With this in mind, we will now explore three aspects of formal systems that can help the entrepreneur stay in control: structure and design, information systems, and compensation and benefits.

Structure and Design

Several seminal studies of organizational structure were conducted a number of years ago by Paul Lawrence and Jay Lorsch of the Harvard Business School.[5] They noted that in designing organizations, two tasks need to be performed. The first task is to *differentiate* the types of work that need to be performed into distinct, specialized tasks and assign the different tasks to those who are trained to carry them out. This division of labor allows the organization to perform its functions more effectively. The second task for those designing organizations is to *integrate* the efforts of those working at the various jobs so that they will not be working at cross-purposes. Teamwork and cooperation between departments and specialists is essential for the organization to achieve optimal performance. Lawrence and Lorsch studied how organizations attempted to differentiate and integrate the various business functions — engineering, sales, production — in three different industries. They concluded that the companies that are both highly differentiated and highly integrated are the most effective.

In the beginning stages of the development of an organization, employees may each have to carry out a variety of different tasks, such as engineering, sales, production, and maintenance, so there are few pure specialists. With the founder providing direction, the various aspects of the business can be coordinated fairly easily. As the organization grows, however, the tasks to be performed become more complex, require more work, and are often more specialized. With this new set of conditions, more employees with specialized training begin to be needed, and coordination between these specialists becomes more difficult.

What often happens is that as the business grows and the need for specialization and coordination increases, the informal, personality-based form of entrepreneurial control begins to break down. The entrepreneur may not be able to personally integrate all the various functions as in the past. Employees may not have a clear understanding of their jobs as the pace of business accelerates. As new employees are hired, they and the older employees may have difficulty understanding each other's roles and how to work together.

A high-tech entrepreneurial firm that I studied for more than two years provides an example of the importance of structure and design. Founded primarily by engineers from IBM, the firm grew rapidly, and new employees were hired from such companies as Control Data, Honeywell, Digital Equipment, and Intel. Others came from diverse industries, such as real estate development and public accounting, that were not at all related to the computer industry. Given that all these new employees entered this company with different views about how work should be done, it is not surprising that I found a lack of cooperation among departments and levels. Of course, the differences in values among the employees contributed to the lack of cooperation, but another important reason for it was the lack of clear rules governing how the firm's departments would interact with one another and of clear job descriptions that would help employees within a department work more effectively together. To solve some of their integration problems, the departments began to set up cross-functional teams that met periodically to discuss interdepartmental problems. In particular, the manufacturing engineers began to spend time with the design engineers before any new product was moved into production. This helped to break down a number of the communication barriers between these groups, and a number of design problems were solved before the new products went into production.

To facilitate integration, entrepreneurs should be aware of the various integrating mechanisms, such as cross-functional teams, liaison roles, job rotation, and matrix structure, that can promote teamwork and cooperation.[6] One organization that I have worked with was having just the kinds of problems that have been mentioned: employees did not understand their jobs, there was a lack of coordination among sales, production, and the front office, the founder felt that he could not get employees to do what he thought they should do, and employees were resentful when the founder scolded them for not doing their jobs correctly. To remedy this problem, I met several times with the founder, his wife and son, who worked in the business, and his vice president of sales. I initially asked them who was responsible for the various departments. The founder responded, "Well, of course, I am." But as we got into a deeper discussion of the issues of authority and control, it emerged that there was some confusion regarding who was in charge at the level immediately below the founder. As we developed a simple organization chart, the founder began to see that by clarifying who was reporting to whom and who was responsible for what, he could more easily identify where the breakdowns were occurring. He also was forced to make some hard choices in assigning responsibility. The organization chart was later presented to the key employees in the company, and their input prompted a few modifications.

After developing the organization chart, we began a process to help clarify the roles that the key managers would play in this "new" organization. I asked each manager, including the founder, to write a description of his or her job. We then met as a group, and all the managers in turn described what they felt were the key features of their jobs and what they needed from each other to perform them more effectively. After hearing each job description, all the managers had an opportunity to say whether they felt that it was accurate and to suggest changes. This prompted a lively discussion as to what each manager's responsibilities actually were. There was some disagreement about jobs with overlapping responsibilities, so some negotiation took place. In the end, the managers had a clearer understanding of their own jobs and how they were related to others in the company. They decided to meet weekly to discuss coordination problems among departments and to continue to use the team—not just individuals—to solve problems.

This process of developing a basic organization chart, developing job descriptions, clarifying roles, and using cross-functional teams can be very helpful to the entrepreneur who wants to remain in control. However, there are two things that must be kept in mind when formalizing an organization. The first is to avoid the "that's not my job syndrome." In too many organizations, employees use the job description to avoid helping out in areas that are not specifically spelled out. They protect their own "turf" and are reluctant to cooperate. Thus, the job description should be used only as a general guide, and employees should realize that in a fast-growing organization, their job description may change frequently. Such changes need to be communicated to other employees to avoid confusion. On this point, the experience of Robert Mondavi, the wine magnate, proves instructive:

> In the early going, Mondavi was persuaded that job descriptions were necessary to define lines of authority and responsibility. Once this was done, he soon found that people began to feel "bound in" and were becoming possessive about their turf instead of being open and part of a team. Recognizing that some degree of discipline was necessary, Mondavi has kept the job descriptions, but has softened them with the mandate that common sense and flexibility must prevail. Thus each key employee can work relatively unencumbered while recognizing that he and all the others are working toward a common goal. For Mondavi Winery, individuality, personality, and creativity will not be lost as a result of formal job descriptions.[7]

A second problem to avoid is breaking jobs down into such specific and mundane tasks that they are not very stimulating or motivating. If jobs are simplified to provide clarity, they may become quite unrewarding, and the full potential of the employee will remain untapped. Richard Hackman of Harvard has studied the problem of job design for more than two decades.[8] He provides five good rules of thumb in designing jobs that will motivate employees:

1. Design jobs so that the employee has the opportunity to do an entire task. By completing an entire task, such as

assembling a radio or completing a stock transaction, employees can see how their work relates to the whole and can get the satisfaction of accomplishment.

2. Allow employees to use a variety of skills. Hackman notes that employees whose jobs are repetitive and require only limited skills tend not to be highly motivated; they could do more if given the chance.

3. Provide employees with meaningful work. Entrepreneurs often like to do the most interesting and exciting jobs themselves. To motivate employees, the entrepreneur must delegate not only some of the mundane tasks but some of the more exciting ones as well.

4. Allow employees to have autonomy. If employees are unable to exercise any discretion in carrying out a task, they will have difficulty patting themselves on the back for doing a good job. As discussed previously, this may be one of the most difficult issues for an entrepreneur to deal with.

5. Employees must have timely feedback regarding their performance. Without feedback on whether they do a good job or a poor one, employees will be unable to improve their performance.

Entrepreneurs should attempt to include as many of these elements as possible in the jobs that they are designing. Of course, some jobs are inherently boring and difficult to change, yet much can often be done to combine jobs or modify them in some way to make them more enjoyable and encourage better performance.

Information Systems

Another approach to gaining more control for the entrepreneur is developing better information systems. Data regarding costs, productivity, gross margins, cash flow, taxes, and so forth are essential if the entrepreneur is to make good decisions and help the business grow. Entrepreneurs are notorious for having abysmal information systems. For example, one founder had no accounting system and merely kept some disorganized receipts and journal entries in a large box. Another, the founder of a small grocery store, requested help from one of our student consulting teams to determine why he was so unprofitable. He was asked a simple question: "Do you know what the profit margin is on the items you sell?" "No," was his reply. Without a knowledge of whether the selling price covers one's costs, it is difficult to be profitable. Still others had only their bank balance as a rough guide to determine whether they could meet their cash flow requirements. Finally, information regarding markets, customers, suppliers, and competitors is often woefully lacking in a new business.

Dealing with the information gap that may plague the entrepreneur requires some skill and discipline. The entrepreneur who does not have the time or needed skills should hire a good professional with a feel for management information systems, even if only part time. To begin creating an effective information system, entrepreneurs might ask themselves: What are the key pieces of information that I need to operate this business? What decisions do I need to make that require more information? How might we go about collecting this information in a timely manner? What form should the data be put into so they can be easily accessed and used?

Good information can warn the entrepreneur of impending problems or signal that the firm is performing well. In either case, entrepreneurs can feel more in control if they have the right information. For example, earlier in this chapter, I described how Roger had a difficult time dealing with any kind of formal rules and had turned over that responsibility to his son, Tom. One of Roger's goals was to spend less time at the business and begin to develop more outside interests. Eventually, he wanted to get away completely from the day-to-day affairs of the firm and become semiretired as chairman of the board. Roger has been able to achieve this goal to some degree because Tom has installed a computer system that provides timely and accurate information regarding the firm's financial status. At a board meeting I attended, Tom presented Roger and the board with an up-to-date balance sheet and income statement and a statement of cash flows for the year. Roger remarked that this was the first time he had ever had such information so quickly. The information presented by Tom did raise some questions for Roger and the board, but they were able to solve most of the problems at the meeting. Roger remarked at the end of the meeting that he felt much more confident and relaxed knowing that he was now going to have the information he needed to keep abreast of the firm's performance. His motto has been "no surprises," and the new information system makes a bad surprise more unlikely. He is also more confident that, armed with better information, he can still oversee the business and achieve his personal goals as well.

Compensation and Benefits

A third approach to retaining control is developing a reward system that ties the employees' interests more closely to those of the entrepreneur. The following are just some of the pitfalls that entrepreneurs seem to fall into as they attempt to reward their employees.

Failing to Provide Any Benefits. Some entrepreneurs do not ever want to give employees something for nothing, and benefits are often seen in this light. They are seen as being costly, with little received in return. In some cases, the entrepreneur is not financially able to provide many benefits. However, in what will be an increasingly competitive labor market, entrepreneurs will need to move ahead of their more established competition to attract and keep valuable employees. And while benefits such as health insurance and retirement plans are only a small piece of the total compensation package, they can be the deciding factor in attracting a new employee.

Rewarding Individuals Rather Than Groups. An entrepreneur might choose to focus on rewarding individuals rather than a group through one of several gain-sharing plans, such as the Scanlon plan. While individual rewards are sometimes needed, they often serve to create a "me-first" mentality: cooperation is discouraged if an activity or assignment does not help the individual to achieve his or her own goals. Entrepreneurs may need to think more systemically in creating group incentives that would foster cooperation and teamwork. Doing so can give the entrepreneur more control over organizational outcomes.

Rewarding with Money Rather Than Equity. Entrepreneurs jealously guard the ownership of their businesses, for ownership means power and control. However, entrepreneurs could help to increase employee commitment and more closely align employee interests with their own by distributing some of the company's stock to key employees. Several years ago, a well-known venture capitalist from the San Francisco area attended one of my classes. During the class, we discussed the case of Jones Entertainment (presented in more detail in Chapter Seven). Jones, the entrepreneur, and Lewis, the professional manager, saw the world quite differently and were frequently in conflict with one another. I asked the venture capitalist, who had worked with scores of entrepreneurs, what advice he would give Jones. He said, "I would have told Jones to give Lewis some equity in the company. By getting some equity, Lewis would begin to see the world from an owner's point of view, would be more sympathetic to Jones, and be more committed to seeing the business succeed." In other cases as well, even a small equity position in the company seems to stimulate the employees to work harder, be more committed, and act more consistently with the entrepreneur's vision for the business.

There is no easy answer to what type of compensation system makes the most sense. Every system has its flaws. One consultant who has studied many compensation systems once told me, "Every compensation system eventually fails. Organizations just go along with one for a while until enough people get dissatisfied, and then they change it. This cycle continues every few years." Despite the fact that there is no perfect system, entrepreneurs need to think through the implications of their compensation systems carefully if they are to achieve the desired results.

Creating a Common Culture

As outlined earlier, culture is a set of basic assumptions and values that are manifested in the way people think and act. They help people to make sense out of their world and determine appropriate courses of action in certain situations. By fostering shared assumptions and values among their employees, entrepreneurs are able to orient their employees to act in ways consistent with those values. In this way, like the high-tech founders who had taught the manager far from headquarters the appropriate way to respond to a problem, entrepreneurs can gain some measure of control over the behavior of their employees. The following are just a few of the options for entrepreneurs who want to develop a common culture in their organizations.

Select the "Right" Employees

Just finding employees who are willing to join an entrepreneurial firm can be difficult, but hiring those who fit the organization is an important task for the entrepreneur. New hires not only must have the right skills but must also feel comfortable with the type of values that the entrepreneur is trying to foster. For example, a person who is individually oriented and a loner would not likely succeed in an organization that emphasizes teamwork. This is not to say that all new hires should be clones of each other, for diversity has its virtues. However, thoughtful entrepreneurs that I have known have potential employees go through many interviews and at times psychological testing to see whether they will fit in. Entrepreneurs cannot afford to hire employees who are not going to be productive or comfortable in their organizations. To improve selection, the entrepreneur must be able to answer two questions: What are the attributes of a successful employee? How can we determine whether someone has those attributes? To answer these questions, the entrepreneur needs to take the lead — or get help if needed — to select the right kind of employee.

Socialize Employees Properly

Beyond the technical training that is sometimes needed to perform a specific job, a new employee needs to be taught the basic values of the business and organizational procedures. Without such knowledge, a new employee is likely to flounder. Such socialization is not likely to occur during a one-hour or even a one-day orientation. Digital Equipment Corporation has developed a unique way to deal with this problem. Every so often it conducts "boot camps" for employees who have been with the organization a year or less. These boot camps are run by company old-timers, who spend several days with the new employees teaching them the ropes and answering their questions. The boot camps have been quite successful in breaking down barriers between old and new employees. Whether it is accomplished through boot camps, meetings with the entrepreneur, or some other type of mentoring system, the systematic socialization of new employees is critical to creating a common culture.

Articulate Basic Values

Mission and values statements have become a fad in recent years. In some cases, they have helped; in others, they have created cynicism. While distributing written statements of company values or philosophy to employees does help to emphasize what is important to the company, if the entrepreneur fails to act in ways consistent with those ideals, employees become cynical and discouraged. Statements of philosophy are a two-edged sword: they may serve to promote understanding and cooperation, or they may create negative feelings toward the entrepreneur and the company. Whether or not they have written statements, entrepreneurs need to express through word and deed what they believe in and what it means to be an employee in their company. Through informal conversations or by working side by side with employees, entrepreneurs can begin to share their views of the world.

Demonstrate Basic Values

Entrepreneurs who are successful in developing a common culture have the ability to dramatically demonstrate the importance of adhering to company values. John H. Patterson, the founder of National Cash Register, was a master at this. Patterson "was intolerant of careless work. Taking some of his friends through a plant one day, he stopped before a cash register and began to demonstrate its features. The machine failed to work properly. He tried again, with no better result. Without a word, the exasperated industrialist picked up a sledge and demolished the machine. 'That is how we take care of faulty merchandise,' he said, as he walked away."[9] On another occasion, a newspaper printed a story about a meeting where Patterson was assigning sales goals for the year. Many of the salespeople complained that the goals were too high and could not be achieved. At the end of the meeting, Patterson said to the salespeople, "You know, it would be harder for me to turn this room into a rose garden than it would for you to reach your goals." With that statement, the meeting ended. As the salespeople walked out the door, Patterson turned to his assistant and said, "I want a rose garden here tomorrow morning before the next sales meeting." That night, the building was demolished and removed, and roses were brought in and planted. As the salespeople arrived for the meeting early the next morning, they were astonished to see the rose garden. Patterson had made his point.

While an entrepreneur's behavior need not be as extreme as Patterson's, finding ways of highlighting the core values of the company in a memorable way is essential in passing on those values to employees.

Link Rewards to Company Values

Despite all of one's efforts to encourage employees to adhere to company values, employees will not conform without some type of reward. For example, in one entrepreneurial firm, the founders preached quality, but employees were rewarded for "making the numbers." Sales quotas and production goals were paramount. As a result, employees focused on the numbers, and quality declined. Moreover, the employees became cynical because the founders did not "walk their talk." The reward system must be tied directly to the values, and employees must be rewarded and praised for acting in ways consistent with those values.

Conclusion

In this chapter, we have described how entrepreneurs tend to lose control of their organizations. The central problem stems from the fact that the forms of control that work well in a small organization — personal association and close supervision — are not as feasible in a growing company. To solve the control dilemma, the entrepreneur should begin to explore other forms of control. Clarifying roles, developing better information and compensation systems, and creating a common culture can all serve to help the entrepreneur retain some control. Most entrepreneurs must change their management styles to move to this form of control. They must be willing to develop and abide by some formal rules and procedures. They must be willing to collaborate with others to build a team. They must be willing to share information. Moreover, they must share their vision and their values in a systematic way. Such changes will not be easy, for they require a different way of thinking about control and a different set of skills on the part of the entrepreneur.

SEVEN

SHOULD I HIRE PROFESSIONAL MANAGERS?

As entrepreneurs attempt to build and strengthen their organizations, they need more skills and expertise to cope with the complexities of a growing business. One solution to this problem is to bring in professional managers to run certain aspects of the business. The results of professionalizing an entrepreneurial firm seem to be quite mixed, according to the entrepreneurs who have tried it. In some cases, professional management has helped them immensely; in others, the professional managers have created all manner of problems. One entrepreneur went so far as to claim that the professional managers she hired almost "brought my company to its knees."

The key dilemma facing the entrepreneur regarding this issue is this: Should I bring in (or develop) professional managers who may not share my vision of the firm and my values, or should I try to survive in the marketplace without the talents of professional management? Many entrepreneurs distrust those with a formal education, viewing it as a waste of time and in some cases even counterproductive. John Patterson, the founder of National Cash Register, echoed the sentiments of many entrepreneurs regarding formal education when he discussed his experience at Dartmouth: "What I learned mostly was what not to do. They gave me Greek and Latin and algebra and higher mathematics and Edwards on the Will—all useless."[1] Given this orientation toward formal education, the thought of bringing

Note: This chapter is adapted from Dyer, W. G., Jr. "Integrating Professional Management into a Family Owned Business." *Family Business Review*, 1989, *2*(3), 221–235.

128

in professional management can be anathema to the entrepreneur. Still, most entrepreneurs who manage growing companies attempt to professionalize their organizations. This chapter explores some of the pitfalls and options available to entrepreneurs facing this dilemma.

The Rise of Professional Management

In recent years, historians of American business have documented the development of management science and the inexorable growth in the population of "professional managers."[2] While there is considerable debate regarding what constitutes their role, professional managers typically have received formal training in a business school in areas such as finance, production, accounting, and personnel.[3] This is not to say that all those who receive management training are necessarily professional managers. For example, some who receive management training but have a technical background may still view themselves as primarily technical experts rather than managers.

The professionalization of management in the United States started in 1891, when Joseph Wharton donated $100,000 to the University of Pennsylvania to create a school of commerce. Since that time, some 650 business schools and 600 M.B.A. programs have been created. Currently, business schools are producing about 70,000 M.B.A.s per year and graduating many more with undergraduate business degrees.[4]

Where do all these professional managers go? In increasing number, professional managers are finding their way into positions in entrepreneurial organizations. This is largely due to the downsizing trend in Fortune 500 companies and the growth of entrepreneurial firms and family-owned businesses. While there has been considerable debate as to whether professional managers have improved or stymied the effectiveness of organizations,[5] most organizations seem to benefit by utilizing principles of management science. For example, market research, financial planning, and more effective methods of production (such as statistical process control or just-in-time inventory systems — skills that are frequently taught in business schools) have helped numerous organizations maintain a competitive edge. Most critics of professional management do not fault the skills of professional managers but are concerned with their application, as well as the values espoused by those with professional training. Often cited are professional managers' lack of understanding of human issues in organizations and their short-term focus on financial performance.

Why Professionalize?

There are a number of reasons why entrepreneurs might want to bring in professional managers or to professionalize their current management team. One of the most common is a lack of management talent. Entrepreneurs or employers often have technical skills but lack management skills in areas such as marketing, finance, or accounting. As a business grows — particularly in a complex environment — it is increasingly unlikely that the entrepreneur and members of the founding team will have all the skills necessary for the business to survive. Therefore, entrepreneurs may, out of necessity, look outside for help or attempt to broaden the skills of their employees.

A second reason for professionalizing management is to change the norms and values of business operations.[6] Family values in entrepreneurial firms, such as unconditional love and concern, often conflict with business values of profitability and efficiency. Paternalistic entrepreneurs may be unwilling to fire or reprimand unproductive employees. Some entrepreneurs believe that the family's lack of professionalism or employees' lack of concern about profitability and efficiency can be changed by indoctrinating the current managers with values that are more consistent with organizational efficiency and higher profits. The entrepreneur may feel that moving to professional management will mean that unproductive employees can be let go, employee discipline strengthened, and stricter controls enforced. Entrepreneurs who have a paternalistic orientation toward their employees often are reluctant to make such changes themselves, so they bring in "hired guns" to make the painful changes.

A third reason for acquiring or developing management expertise is to prepare for leadership succession. The entrepreneur may want to retire in the near future and feel that family members or nonfamily employees need additional training before assuming the mantle of leadership, or the founder may feel that no one in the family is capable of running the business after he or she is gone. A search then might be made to find outside professionals who can be trusted with the future leadership of the firm.

Problems of Professionalization

Many of the problems that accompany the transition to professional management can be traced to differences between the training and values of the entrepreneur and those of the professional managers. Edgar Schein of MIT points out how founders and professional managers analyze problems differently, occupy different positions of authority, and relate to others in very different ways.[7] For example, founders tend to be driven by their particular vision of their product or service. They tend to be intuitive in their decision making, their power is based on ownership, and they motivate their followers through their charismatic behavior. Conversely, those trained as professional managers generally derive their power not from ownership but from positions of authority. They tend to base decisions more on logic and rational analysis than on intuition. These managers tend to be rather impersonal in their interactions with others, in contrast to the more personal style of the founder.

While not all founders and professional managers differ dramatically along these dimensions (I have seen instances where professional managers act more like founders than the professional managers described by Schein), numerous case studies of professional managers entering an entrepreneurial firm generally support Schein's analysis.[8] Professional managers often have world views and assumptions that differ from those of entrepreneurs. The organizational systems and methods of operation that are preferred by professional managers are often antithetical to those of founders, who are accustomed to a more informal, sometimes seat-of-the-pants management style.

The reasons for the differences between professional managers and those without such training who work in entrepreneurial businesses can often be traced to organizations and occupational socialization experiences.[9] Those "growing up" in the start-up company learn skills and practices that tend to be idiosyncratic to that organization and may have had little or no experience in other types of organizations. These employees learn the importance of the entrepreneur's values and the role of the entrepreneur and the firm in the community and recognize how to accommodate the needs of the entrepreneur and top management. Their training is often informal, individual, and technical (not managerial) and specific to the particular work they perform.

In contrast, professional managers are typically socialized collectively in the classroom, where the training is formal and generic skills are taught as though they could be applied to most if not all organizations.[10] The case method, which is an integral part of most management training classes, is generally biased toward the analysis of large, bureaucratic organizations with well-defined systems and processes. Much of management training is value-free, despite recent attempts to integrate the study of ethics into the curriculum of business schools. After graduation, many professionals go to work in large companies. They also tend to change jobs frequently and thus gain a broad range of organizational experiences.[11]

The case of Jones Entertainment, Inc., illustrates some of the differences in orientation between professional managers and entrepreneurs (all names have been disguised).[12] While there are certainly events and personalities unique to Jones Entertainment, the case is prototypical of many other cases involving the professionalization of an entrepreneurial firm.[13]

Greg Jones and his wife, Marsha, started a home entertainment business in the early 1980s that included marketing books and audio- and videotapes for children. Initially, the business was just a hobby, but it grew more rapidly than they could have imagined. Marsha provided much of the creative inspiration for new products, while Greg handled the financial and management side of the business. As the company continued to grow, Greg felt that it was becoming too complex and consuming too much of his time. He felt a need to retire in a few years and wanted to find someone to replace him. Marsha was support-

ive of Greg's desire to be less involved in the day-to-day operation of the business. While some of Marsha and Greg's children worked in the business, neither of them felt that the children were interested in assuming Greg's role or qualified to do so.

To find the right person to replace him, Greg called a
local "headhunter," Tom Wilson. Wilson did a national search
and found John Lewis, who seemed to fit Greg's needs. Lewis
had many years of experience working for a large retailer but
now wanted to work for and lead a smaller organization. After
interviewing Lewis, Jones felt that the fit between Lewis and
Jones Entertainment was a good one. Lewis was hired and began working for Jones in 1987.

After just a few weeks of working together, problems began to surface in the relationship between Jones and Lewis, and
the organization began to suffer as a result. As the tension
mounted between Jones and Lewis, they began to avoid each
other. Weeks sometimes went by without a meaningful conversation between them. Finally, they decided to bring in an outside consultant to help them analyze their differences and to
facilitate a resolution of the conflict. After interviewing Jones
and Lewis, the consultant identified seven issues on which Jones
and Lewis had different views and expectations. These differences are summarized in Table. 7.1. Not only did Jones and
Lewis differ about these issues, but they disagreed on their priority. Jones felt that improving distribution channels was the
most important problem facing the firm, while Lewis felt that
expanding the sales force should be the company's top priority.

The firm's employees also noticed several differences between the two men. The employees saw Lewis as a good moti-
vator, communicator, and trainer and felt that he worked well
with the company's distributors. Jones was seen as a rather
authoritarian manager who needed to check on all the details
of the business and had little time to deal with larger issues.
He did not delegate well or provide his employees with much
feedback on their performance. In addition, he did not relate
well in one-on-one situations with his distributors. Still, Jones
was seen as the visionary who had built the organization from
nothing and was acknowledged as the clear leader.

Table 7.1. Differences in Views and
Expectations of Jones and Lewis.

Issue	Jones	Lewis
Salary	Jones feels that he is paying Lewis an extremely high salary. As a result, he expects maximum time and effort with quick results.	Lewis realizes that he has a high salary, but it is a cut in pay for him. His performance in the past has been recognized and rewarded. He feels no need to change his work habits.
Results	Jones (and others) expected that the new high-salaried executive vice president would come in and make immediate, even dramatic improvements in sales and profits.	Lewis feels that it is unrealistic to expect any real changes immediately and that one should be given two or three years to make significant changes.
Time	Jones believes that Lewis should be spending a great deal of time every day, including weekends, learning the business and being on top of all issues of the business.	Lewis believes that he can get on top of the business by putting in a full regular day.
Detail	Jones recognizes that Lewis should work on broad areas but feels that he should also perform detail work. Jones is concerned that Lewis does not follow through.	Lewis does not think that detail work is a wise use of his time. He prefers broad-range thinking and has others do the detail work for him.
Level of commitment	Jones has a vision that the type of home entertainment he sells can positively affect all who use it. He feels that Lewis must have the same vision.	Lewis is excited about the product and wants the company to succeed but does not have the same sense of mission as Jones does.
Writing	Jones is not satisfied with Lewis's writing skills and rewrites many of Lewis's reports.	Lewis feels pressured to write as Jones writes and thinks that much of the rewriting that Jones does is not worth the time.
Expenses	Jones is very frugal with expenses. His motto is "Stay out of debt and pay as you go." He feels that every expenditure should pay off.	Lewis feels that one must invest in development and not expect an immediate return. He is accustomed to having his own budget to spend as he sees fit.

The differences between the two men reflect two distinctly different views of the world and the role of management. Lewis sees his role as one of a hired employee, with an accompanying utilitarian logic: he brings various skills and abilities to the workplace, puts in an eight-hour day, and in return is compensated for his work. According to Lewis, his role is to understand the big picture by analyzing the overall business situation and to avoid getting bogged down in details. Jones, on the other hand, is driven by the mission of his business: to provide wholesome entertainment to young people. As the founder, his name is on the company's products, and he thus feels a sense of responsibility for all aspects of the business. Moreover, he feels that each employee should be as dedicated as he is and should share his vision.

After working with the consultant and recognizing that there were significant differences in their views, Jones and Lewis came to the conclusion that there were basically three options: (1) Lewis could leave the company by choice or by being fired, (2) the men could develop a new working relationship, or (3) they could continue on as they were and hope that things would improve. Both Jones and Lewis felt that it was to their advantage to renegotiate the contract written when Lewis was hired. (Jones's first choice would have been to fire Lewis, but the contract required Jones to pay Lewis one year's salary in such an event, and Jones wanted to avoid such a payment.) They decided that Lewis would no longer be considered Jones's successor and that he would work on a commission basis. Lewis was confident that he could increase profits, and Jones was certainly willing to pay for any increase in profitability.

The case of Jones Entertainment highlights many of the issues that arise when an entrepreneur's values conflict with the values of professional managers. The entrepreneur has expectations regarding the function and role of professional management that often do not correspond with those of professionally trained managers. Conflict often ensues, resulting in uncertainty and confusion among company employees. Decision making is slowed down, priorities and goals become unclear, and new ideas and projects are delayed. In many cases, the firm begins to lose its competitive edge, and profitability declines. We will now turn to some alternatives available to mitigate such conflicts.

Options for Integrating Professional
Management into the Firm

There are three basic options available to entrepreneurs who wish to bring professional management skills into their organizations: (1) professionalize members of the entrepreneur's family, (2) professionalize nonfamily employees currently working in the business, or (3) bring in professional management talent. The first two options typically represent evolutionary and incremental changes in methods of doing business; that is, changes that will occur rather slowly over a number of years. With these options, the company culture will probably not change dramatically. The third option generally reflects a more revolutionary type of change effort, where significant changes in both methods of operation and company culture can occur rather quickly.

Professionalizing the Family

This option is most viable when the following four conditions exist: First, there must be family members who are willing and able to gain the necessary management skills and who want to work in the business. Second, the entrepreneur must feel that the family's values need to be perpetuated and that the family is best able to ensure the continuity of those values. Third, the family must wish to continue to both own and manage the business. Fourth, the strategic focus of the business should be unlikely to change in the near future — that is, there must be a relatively good fit between the organization's strategy and its environment.

   Under these conditions, the family is likely to be successful in developing its own talent. Creating a training and development program for family members is essential to this success, and leaders of family firms have used a variety of different methods to do so. At Levi Strauss, for example, the Haas family has encouraged family members to get a Harvard M.B.A. degree before working in the business. Another family firm requires that family members not only get a formal business education but also work at another company for at least two years before returning to the family business. To ensure that his children brought the right set of skills back to the business, one entrepreneur in Texas encouraged each of his four sons to get degrees in different areas. Each son came back to the firm with different expertise.

While business school education and work experience can help enhance a family member's management skills, additional training may be necessary once a family member enters the business. Executive management programs and seminars can be used to broaden skills. Affiliations with professional associations can help family members network and keep abreast of the latest developments in the business world. A mentoring system whereby highly respected nonfamily managers teach family members both management skills and company norms and values has also been successful in a number of family firms.[14] Finally, company-sponsored training and development programs can provide needed information and skills.

Choosing the family option to professionalize the business has drawbacks. Some children in the family may feel undue pressure to return to the family business, which can result in guilt feelings if they choose a career outside it. Moreover, feelings of resentment on the part of parents are common if the child follows a different career path. Sometimes the expectations of the family leaders and of the children are similar, but conflict may occur once the family member rejoins the business after completing his or her education. In one family firm, the son of the founder was sent to MIT to get a M.B.A. degree with the expectation that he would return to work in the business. After completing his degree and returning home, the son discovered that his father was not willing to listen to the new ideas that he had learned at business school. The son felt cheated and estranged from his father and family and soon left the family business, with bitter feelings.

Before choosing the family option, founders must understand the career aspirations of family members. This approach requires open communication among family members about career choices, with the option of career counseling, preferably by trained professionals, for potential family managers. The family must also recognize what future skills and abilities will be needed to make family members aware of business needs as they explore career options. For example, a business that once had needs for engineering talent may need personnel and marketing skills in the future. Thus, a family member who might not enjoy engineering but likes working with people could be encouraged to get training in personnel or marketing, with the understanding that there would likely be a future role for him or her in the business.

Professionalizing Nonfamily Employees

A second option is to give nonfamily employees the training and skills that will be needed by the organization in the future. This option makes sense if (1) few, if any, family members are interested in working in the firm; (2) nonfamily employees appear to have the necessary motivation and ability to improve their performance as managers; (3) the trust level between the entrepreneur and nonfamily employees is relatively high; and (4) the entrepreneur wants to perpetuate his or her values and continue the strategic focus of the business. In many firms where the entrepreneur's family is dominant, nonfamily employees are treated as second-class citizens and given little credit for the success of the business. These employees are often an overlooked and underutilized resource who may understand the business better than the entrepreneur realizes. They also have an appreciation for the values — and idiosyncrasies — of the entrepreneur and his or her family and thus can act in ways that will meet the family's expectations. These employees can play a significant role in developing the business if given the opportunity.

One firm that has attempted to improve the management skills of nonfamily employees is a large retail business in the Midwest. The two brothers who founded the business are in their mid sixties and would like to retire in the near future. While there are two family members working in the business, both are quite young, and the next generation of leadership will have to emerge from the pool of nonfamily managers. Although the current nonfamily employees generally have excellent technical skills, they have had little training in general management, particularly in the areas of strategic planning and finance. Moreover, they have spent little time developing their own subordinates — a critical management skill. These deficiencies are due, by and large, to the fact that the brothers have not given nonfamily managers experience in strategic planning and finance or spent time coaching them.

Recognizing the need to prepare the next generation of leaders, the brothers enlisted the aid of a consultant to help their human resource managers design an effective training and development program, which included the following:

1. Interviews by the consultant with the top twenty-five managers to better understand their career goals and aspirations.
2. An assessment of the management skills (planning, decision making, communication, team building, and so on) of the top sixty managers in the company. These assessments included feedback from each manager's superiors, peers, and subordinates. This feedback, which was confidential and given only to the manager, was used to help the manager set goals for improvement. These goals were then shared with the manager's boss, who reviewed the manager's progress in performance appraisal sessions.
3. Training sessions to help managers improve their skills in various areas.
4. A succession-planning process to ensure that each manager was preparing someone to replace him or her.
5. The opportunity for nonfamily managers to attend management seminars and conferences sponsored by professional associations.

So far, the results of this program have been quite favorable. This type of program, which encourages learning, has also created more open communication between the founders and nonfamily managers.

The example of this organization suggests a number of things that founders should consider if they wish to professionalize nonfamily employees. First, they must develop an appraisal system to identify nonfamily employees with the appropriate career aspirations and potential and then offer them career guidance and new career options. Second, they should provide incentives to encourage nonfamily employees to seek additional education. Tuition reimbursement and payment of fees for workshops and seminars are the most common ways to encourage the acquisition of additional skills outside the workplace. Inhouse training programs can also improve the performance of nonfamily employees. Third, the entrepreneur must be willing to treat nonfamily employees more or less as equals who can enjoy the benefits that may have been reserved for only the entrepreneur's family. To merely encourage education and personal development without a willingness to share the rewards creates cynicism and undermines morale.

A potential problem with training nonfamily managers is that they may be unwilling to try out their new skills or may accept training merely to please the entrepreneur, with little commitment to the education process. This is particularly true when the entrepreneur is paternalistic and has an autocratic management style. The entrepreneur can end up with highly trained employees who continue to follow company policies, procedures, and values blindly, failing to use their new knowledge and skills to improve company performance because they fear punishment or failure.

Bringing in Outside Professionals

The first two options are appropriate if the entrepreneur wishes to continue the firm's present strategy and wants to maintain traditional values. The third option, bringing in professional managers from outside, is generally deemed necessary when (1) there is little or no expertise, ability, or interest on the part of the family or nonfamily employees to manage the business, and (2) there may be a need to change business strategy or business values. Entrepreneurial firms that have failed to maintain a competitive advantage in the marketplace or that have been unable to effectively organize and coordinate the activities of the organization are often in need of an overhaul. Without outside help and new ideas, such changes cannot take place. As in the case of Jones Entertainment, the entry of professional managers is likely to create some tension within the organization as new skills and values are introduced.

The entrepreneur can take a number of positive steps to mitigate some of these problems. First, the entrepreneur can take the time to socialize the professional managers in the ways of the family and the business. Some professional managers see their role as "killing sacred cows"—that is, changing the business norms.[15] While some sacred cows may need to be killed, there are typically some values of commitment, loyalty, quality, and so forth that ought to be retained. Thus, the entrepreneur must communicate clearly those values that need to be upheld—and should focus on articulating ends rather than means. In other words, the entrepreneur should outline the ultimate goals to be achieved while allowing the professional managers some discretion to implement new ideas and new methods to achieve these goals. In the case cited previously, Jones spent little time trying to teach Lewis his goals and values. Instead, Jones relied on a headhunter to find the right person and then assumed that Lewis would follow his lead.

Another important approach is to tie the interests of the professional manager to the firm, which will influence his or her behavior to be more consistent with the entrepreneur's interests. As has been noted, one strategy is to offer ownership stock to key professional managers so that they will "think like owners" and not focus on parochial management interests. In addition, including key professional managers on the board of directors can be a good way to gain their input as well as teaching them how the founder feels about the business.

Professional managers should also be encouraged to become a part of the communities in which they work. Problems can arise when there is a lack of fit between community values and the values of professional managers. A number of studies have shown that professional managers often decide to live outside the communities in which they work because their interests are quite different from those of the indigenous work force.[16] When professionals live outside the community, communication barriers are often created between professional managers and local employees, and an "us versus them" mentality is created. Moreover, some family and nonfamily members may feel that their career goals and sense of self-worth are threatened if outsiders begin to occupy key management positions. This can intensify feelings of suspicion and distrust. In the firms that I have studied, such conflicts are common, and the result is lower morale, increased union activity, and eventually lower overall organizational effectiveness.

One such example is the Brown corporation, a medium-sized ($70 million sales) materials-handling firm located in a small town in the northeastern United States.[17] In 1974, the company faced a severe crisis, and the company president, John Brown, Jr., decided to bring in a professional manager, Reed Larson, to turn the company around. Larson took a number of steps to change the company. He implemented a more efficient inventory control system, set up financial controls, and fired a number of employees considered deadwood. Because of his tough, no-nonsense approach, he earned the nickname "Jaws." As a result of Larson's actions, sales and profits increased dramatically. However, after a few years, Brown began to recognize that Larson's values and orientation were undermining morale and that the workers were beginning to support a union movement. Furthermore, sales declined sharply in the early 1980s, and Larson laid off more than half of the work force to cut costs.

Conflict between Larson and Brown began to intensify as Brown saw the company's basic nature changing. As Brown attempted to find a way to change Larson or to fire him, Larson secretly lobbied for support from key managers and the board so that he could purchase the company and oust the Brown family. (The stock was publicly traded, with the Browns owning about one-third.) Brown found out that Larson was trying to "steal" the company from his family, and he eventually emerged the victor in the power struggle. Larson was fired, and a new professional manager was hired to replace him. The new manager, Phil Olsen, was also fired after only one year on the job. Although Olsen had an impressive track record at a large corporation, he too did not understand the family's values and was unable to develop any rapport with the work force. As one top executive explained, "Olsen brought in all new people and surrounded himself with those he knew at his former company. He used many consultants and had no confidence in the old-timers." Olsen viewed the local employees as "a small-town bunch of jerks." While not as tyrannical as Larson, Olsen was seen by employees as "more secretive and sneaky and less trustworthy."

During Olsen's tenure, sales rose but profitability declined as costs skyrocketed. Olsen had little feel for the company's product or how to organize effectively to improve productivity. Morale was extremely low, and union organizing continued. Finally, after hearing about Olsen's misdeeds from some company old-timers, John Brown, Jr., decided to fire Olsen in 1985.

Olsen's replacement, Brad Adams, has been much more successful than either Larson or Olsen. Adams, a long-time friend of Brown, was a successful distributor of the company's products. He knew the company and its problems and understood Brown and his family. After taking the position, Adams spent his first week on the job meeting with groups of employees. He made a conscious effort to be visible and accessible to employees, even to the point of visiting workers on the graveyard shift. He reinstated some of the employees who had been fired by the previous managers, which helped boost morale. Union organizing has virtually stopped, and the company's profits have improved in recent years. Adams's expertise in sales and marketing has helped strengthen the company, and his collaborative approach to solving the company's problems has received broad support.

The Brown case illustrates some ways to alleviate the problems associated with bringing in professional management. Entrepreneurs and professional managers must establish good communication with employees through group meetings, newsletters, informal lunches, and so on. Meetings to clarify roles and expectations and improve teamwork are also likely to be needed as professional management is introduced into the firm.[18] These actions can help reduce the ambiguity and uncertainty that naturally arise as people with different experiences and world views attempt to work together.

Conclusion

The issue of professionalizing an entrepreneurial business is one that many entrepreneurs must grapple with at some point in midcareer. How this issue is handled can often determine whether the firm will continue to function harmoniously and grow in the future. Three options for professionalizing the business have been outlined. They are not mutually exclusive and can be used in tandem. The key point, however, is that entrepreneurs must choose a strategy that makes sense to them and then communicate their expectations to family and nonfamily members alike.

EIGHT

SHOULD I EMPLOY
FAMILY MEMBERS?

L. S. Shoen, founder of U-Haul, watched the fortunes of his company sink to all-time lows in the 1980s.[1] Debt soared as profits dwindled. However, many of Shoen's problems were not related to the marketplace — they were a result of his family's involvement in the business. Over the years, his twelve children from three of his four marriages had been quarreling with each other. All of the children had worked in the business. Some of them supported the founder, while others wanted him out. At the end of 1986, two of Shoen's sons, Edward J. "Joe" Shoen and Samuel W. Shoen, forced their father into retirement. Since that time, the company's board meetings have been stormy, with family factions literally fighting it out with each other. One board meeting ended in fisticuffs. The following is the newspaper report of that meeting:

> A fistfight erupted at a recent U-Haul stockholders' meeting, punctuating a bitter family struggle over control of the rental empire. Witnesses said the fight Saturday involved the four sons of U-Haul founder Leonard Shoen, 73. . . . Two of the sons involved in the fight, Mike and Sam, support their father's position in the ownership struggle, while the other two, current board Chairman Joe and Mark, oppose it. . . . Hotel security guards quickly responded to the fight and broke it up. Sam Shoen, who was forced to hold an ice pack to his cheek afterward, said the fight occurred after the stockholders' meeting adjourned. "They ran it [the meeting] in the

145

most high-handed possible fashion even though they
knew they had the votes they needed to win," Sam
said. "They were not willing to allow discussion on
anything." . . . The elder Shoen contended that the
company has been devalued under Joe's leadership
and no longer adheres to its founding principles of
customer satisfaction. [L. S.] Shoen . . . appeared
visibly shaken by the brawl. "I created a monster,"
he said. . . . After Saturday's meeting, he said
the only way to defuse the situation is to sell the
company.[2]

Working with members of one's own family creates some
unique problems for the entrepreneur, as the case of L. S. Shoen
illustrates. The vast majority of entrepreneurs whom I have
worked with or studied employed family members or were planning to employ family members in the future. A few had decided
to deal with the "nepotism problem" by refusing to hire family
members. One entrepreneur with this view said, "I don't want
them. I wouldn't have my wife in the place. I wouldn't have
nobody that's related. The other people always figure that you
are favoring somebody."[3] This approach can create problems
as well, however, since family members may resent being left
out of creating the new venture and sharing in the rewards. In
this chapter, we focus on the dilemma of whether to hire family
members and provide some suggestions for those who wish to
employ family members but want to avoid the kinds of problems that have plagued the Shoen family.

Sources of Conflict: Family
Systems Versus Business Systems

To understand why conflicts occur when family members work
together, we need to analyze the norms that typically govern
family and business systems. Norms regarding goals, relationships, rules, evaluation, and succession are quite different in a
business and in a family.[4] Table 8.1 highlights those differences.

Table 8.1. A Comparison of Family and Business Systems.

Areas of Conflict	Family Systems	Business Systems
Goals	Development and support of family members	Profits, revenues, efficiency, growth
Relationships	Deeply personal, of primary importance	Semipersonal or impersonal, of secondary importance
Rules	Informal expectations ("That's how we've always done it")	Written and formal rules, often with rewards and punishment spelled out
Evaluation	Members rewarded for who they are; effort counts; unconditional love and support	Support conditional on performance and results; employees can be promoted or fired
Succession	Caused by death or divorce	Caused by retirement, promotion, or leaving

As the table indicates, there are a number of areas of conflict between the way a business operates and the way a family functions. In a business, goals are related to such things as profitability and efficiency, while a family is oriented toward providing support for each other and is focused on the personal development of family members. Relationships in a family are deeply personal and are generally the most important relationships that people have. Business relationships can be personal, but, by and large, they are rather impersonal and of secondary importance to most people.

Rules in a business are generally written down or spelled out quite clearly. Failure to follow those rules can result in a formal reprimand or even dismissal. A paper trail is often made to document various rules violations. In a family, informal expectations generally govern behavior, and informal sanctions—a frown, not speaking to the offender, being "grounded"—are applied to those who fail to meet those expectations.

Businesses reward people for their performance, and such rewards are conditional—those who succeed are rewarded; those

who fail get no reward and may even be punished. Families typically reward family members just because they are family members. Love and support are often unconditional, and family
members are rewarded for effort, not just performance. Take
a simple example from everyday life. In my own family, my
oldest daughter, Emily, plays the violin. She often plays at re-
citals, and I accompany her on the piano. Usually she plays well,
but at times she has made major mistakes. Regardless of how
she plays, my wife, Theresa, and I try as best we can to praise
her for her performance. Even if it was not the best performance,
at least she tried, we reason. Moreover, our own feelings of self-
worth and importance are inextricably tied to our children. If
they fail, we fail. If they succeed, we succeed. Thus, we tend
to discount the failures and emphasize the successes. Such an
approach to rewards is not often found in the business world.

Succession in a family takes place when a family leader
dies or a marriage dissolves and a new set of relationships is
created. In a business, succession takes place when someone re-
tires, is promoted, is fired, or decides to leave the firm for other
employment. Roles are more permanent in the family, and the
displacing of family members through succession is typically a
much longer and more difficult process than in a business.

While there are some commonalities between business systems and family systems — for example, authority and decision
making in both systems are generally centralized — the differences along these five dimensions are quite striking. Problems
and conflicts result when there is a clash between the norms of
these two systems, and family members or nonfamily employees
become confused as to what norms are operating at any given
time. Family members may wonder: Are we acting as a family, or are we acting as business associates?

Spillover Between Systems

Those who work in a family business interact with each other
in both business and family settings. Family members often
transfer feelings and emotions from one system to the other in
inappropriate ways. For example, a family member who is not

performing well on the job and is creating problems for family members at work may be ignored or criticized at a family gathering. Likewise, a family member whose behavior has created problems in the family system may be ostracized in the business system, even though he or she does the work well. Sibling rivalries, marital conflicts, differences with in-laws, and struggles for control between parents and children can be intensified when they are played out in both the family and the business.

In other cases, family members become confused with their overlapping roles. They are not sure whether they should be acting in their family role or their business role. There are numerous examples of this kind of problem. One entrepreneur, whom I will call John, founded a business with his brother Richard several years ago. As the two worked together over the years, John found himself feeling angry and hostile toward Richard. As he attempted to sort out his feelings, their source became clear to him: because Richard had been highly successful in local politics, he spent little time in the business and received much acclaim, while John labored in relative obscurity in the business. John felt that he was doing most of the work, but Richard was getting most of the rewards, which was unfair.

In another entrepreneurial firm, the founder found himself constantly criticizing his daughter for her performance in the business, even though she was performing quite well and meeting most of her goals. Their relationship slowly began to deteriorate. The source of the problem, however, was not related to the business but had to do with the daughter's boyfriend, whom the founder disliked. The relationship finally began to improve when the daughter broke up with her boyfriend. Another entrepreneur, whom I will call George, employed his son Tim in the hopes that one day he would take over the business. Tim was very bright and did his work well but had a fairly serious drug problem, which sometimes affected his work. George had known about this problem for several years but was afraid that confronting Tim would damage their father-son relationship. He also felt that such a confrontation might put too much pressure on Tim and thus exacerbate the problem. Thus, the problem was generally avoided in discussions between George and

Tim, and Tim has been protected from some of the consequences of his drug use.

Such spillovers between business and family create problems for the entrepreneur in terms of hiring and promotion, compensation, division of labor, distribution of equity, status incongruities, decision making, and emotional burdens. We will now discuss each of these areas.

Hiring and Promotion

The questions of whom to hire and whom to promote frequently create conflicts for the entrepreneur. Hiring and promotion involve some sort of evaluation, and, as we have seen, there are conflicts between the norms of evaluation in a business and the norms of evaluation in a family.

Entrepreneurs use a variety of criteria when hiring family members. Some entrepreneurs use the "interest" criterion to employ family members: those family members who show interest in the business are hired. This does ensure that family members who are hired have some interest in and commitment to the business, but it does not necessarily mean that the most competent family members will be employed. In some cases, the least competent family members show the most interest in the business, since they feel that they cannot get a job anywhere else. Another approach that entrepreneurs sometimes use is to set up a series of hurdles that must be overcome before a family member can be hired. Such hurdles might include acquiring a college degree, working for another company for a certain period of time, or some other type of vocational training. Such an approach tends to ensure that family members who are hired have some training and are motivated enough to acquire it. However, this approach may exclude family members who have little interest in education but might succeed if they went to work under the direct guidance of the entrepreneur. Still another approach is to use such criteria as age, sex, birth order, or relationship with the entrepreneur to determine who will be hired. While these criteria may make sense in some cases, the entrepreneur can be accused by family members of being unfair or playing favorites if they are used.

The issue of promotion poses many of the same problems that hiring does. Should family members be promoted on the basis of past performance, future potential, schooling, age, sex, or some other criteria? Should there be different promotion criteria for family members and nonfamily employees, or should they be treated the same? Some entrepreneurs use the "royalist model,"[5] which assumes that family members should have preference and that nonfamily employees are indeed second-class citizens. Another approach is to evaluate and promote family and nonfamily members on a more or less equal basis but give preference to family members if they are as competent as a non-family employee. Still other entrepreneurs try to treat everyone equally, regardless of family affiliation, and I have even seen a few entrepreneurs who seem to favor nonfamily employees at the expense of family members. For example, Henry Ford reportedly drove his son Edsel unmercifully. While we discuss how to deal with the problems of hiring and promotion later in this chapter, one can see the difficulties that can arise when using any of the above criteria.

Compensation

Among the entrepreneurs and their families with whom I work, the issue of compensation is often the critical stumbling block to improved business and family relationships. In the start-up phase of an entrepreneurial firm, family members may be asked to work for little or no compensation. Later on, if family members are not rewarded for such sacrifices, they may feel exploited by the entrepreneur, who also happens to be their mother, father, uncle, aunt, or some other family member. This can cause deep emotional traumas and schisms in the family. While money is certainly needed to meet expenses and maintain a certain standard of living, the amount of compensation also tends to be seen as an indication of importance and worth, not only as an employee of the business but as a family member as well. I have seen more than one family begin to disintegrate once family members and their spouses started to compare how much each was making in the business.

The case of the Peters family illustrates the compensation

problem well (all names have been changed). Bill, Joe, and Wilma Peters, brothers and sister, started a small business together in the early 1980s. The business was marginally successful, but over time, Bill and Joe felt that they could start another business that would have greater success. They left Wilma to run the original business and gave her one-third ownership in their new enterprise. In a very short time, the new business became a huge success. The brothers gained almost celebrity status. The original business was still struggling, so Wilma sold it and went to work with her brothers as personnel manager. Wilma's starting salary was less than half of what her brothers were making. This hurt her, for she felt that she had contributed to her brothers' success by running the original business so that they could leave and start the new venture; now she felt ignored and unappreciated. The brothers countered that Wilma had done little to create the new business, had no training or background for her current job in personnel, and, under the circumstances, was being paid quite well. They also reminded her that her stock in the company had already made her a millionaire. Her brothers' attitudes only fueled Wilma's anger.

I spent one afternoon with Bill, Joe, and Wilma attempting to help them resolve their differences. Wilma expressed her opinion that she was not appreciated and that she should be compensated with the same salary as her brothers, even though the brothers were vice presidents and she was a relatively low-level employee. The brothers repeated their position as well. A lot of tears, frustration, and anger came out of that meeting. I tried to help them find some common ground, but neither party would budge. Finally, Bill suggested that they sell the business, since this problem was just too exasperating to deal with. Neither Joe nor Wilma felt that that was a good idea. The three of them left still at odds with one another, with no clear solution in sight. This example underscores the need for the entrepreneur to anticipate such problems and develop a fair compensation system for family and nonfamily employees alike.

Division of Labor

If family members are hired, the entrepreneur must designate what kind of work they are to perform. A division of labor is needed for the firm to function effectively. However, even the act of assigning jobs can breed jealousy and distrust. As an entrepreneur who works with his wife and three children noted, "It's pretty hard to define roles within a family business. Some members see what other members are doing, and they tend to want to do that rather than what they are supposed to do."[6]

Some family members may feel that others are receiving the easier or more interesting jobs. This can cause family members to compete with one another in unhealthy ways for those favored positions. If there are conflicts between family members there is a tendency to place them in positions or departments where they will not have to interact with each other very often. This tends to delay rather than resolve conflicts and may undermine the effectiveness of the business, since family members may be placed in the wrong positions or be unable to collaborate with other family members to accomplish their tasks.

In other cases, the entrepreneur may not clearly spell out job assignments or develop clear job descriptions. This can result in conflicting expectations on the part of the entrepreneur and family members regarding the work to be performed. When job assignments are unclear, turf battles can erupt between family members who experience conflict in their roles.

Distribution of Equity

How the company's stock is distributed among family members can also be a source of frustration to entrepreneurs and their families. As with the problems accompanying compensation, some family members may feel that the distribution of stock is unfair. On the other hand, if family members are given equal shares, decision making can end up in a stalemate, since the power that ownership brings is divided equally among family members. Unlike the case of compensation, where one's salary can be raised or lowered quite easily, redistributing stock can be quite difficult, since it requires the cooperation of those who own it.

The problem of distributing equity to family members is illustrated in the case of the Williams family (all names are disguised). Frank Williams founded a very successful retail business and brought his three sons into the business to help him. The three boys worked hard, and Frank decided to leave the business to his sons when he died. Although Frank had two daughters, he did not see them as having any involvement in the business. Frank died unexpectedly at age fifty-nine, and his sons became joint owners of the business, each holding one-third of the stock. The business continued to prosper, and the brothers were able to build lavish homes, take exotic vacations, and acquire almost anything that money could buy. The sisters, however, married husbands who were not as successful as their brothers. They became the "poor in-laws" who lived in small homes in a less affluent section of town. This inequity created some resentment in the sisters and some embarrassment on the part of the brothers. While the brothers have been searching for some way to rectify this inequity, a good solution has not yet been found, and some of the ill will created by this inequitable division of stock continues. If Frank had only made some provision in his will to leave his daughters either stock or some other assets, many of the conflicts that have plagued the Williams family over the years could have been avoided.

Status Incongruities in the Business and the Family

Working with family members is often difficult because of the different status structures in the family and in the business. In a family, age and sometimes gender generally determine one's status. In a business, status is generally bestowed through formal positions. Given the different ways of bestowing status in these two systems, it is possible for a younger brother or sister to be giving orders to older siblings or making decisions without their input, which can cause hard feelings and conflict.

   In a class that I taught for executives, I asked each of them to describe the most difficult problem that they faced as managers. Some mentioned problems with decision making; others focused on communication problems and the like. Finally, it was the turn of the president of a small business. He had a rather different problem: "My biggest problem is that recently I had to fire my own mother, who was working in the business. Busi-

ness was slow, and there was simply no work for her to do."
The other executives gasped, except one who yelled, "Is she going
to invite you over for Thanksgiving dinner?" That remark high-
lighted the crux of the problem: should he have acted as a son
or as a boss? Entrepreneurs who work with family members are
constantly confronting the family-versus-business issue.

Decision Making

Decision making can also be negatively affected by family involvement in the business. In some cases, the family may turn
to the entrepreneurial father to make decisions and use the same
approach in the business as well. However, certain types of business decisions may require a more participative style, and the
authoritarian decision-making style of the entrepreneur and the
family may be transferred inappropriately to the business setting. One son of an entrepreneur said, "Whenever we reach an
impasse in decision making, we just turn to the Bible and follow the patriarchal order." Such a method for making decisions
may make sense when the entrepreneur has the right information to make a decision, but it may tend to stifle debate and
lead the family to depend too heavily on the entrepreneur for
guidance.

　　　In other cases, family members may have negative feelings toward other family members that are acted out as decisions are made. Rather than looking for the best decision, family members may end up competing with one another to see
whose idea will be deemed the best. Such a win-lose approach
to decision making inevitably leads to poor decisions.

Emotional Burdens

Significant emotional burdens can be carried by those working
in a family business. Some family members feel guilty if they
do not enter the family business but decide on a different career.
This is particularly true if entrepreneurs put pressure on their
children to join the business. Another type of guilt may be experienced by those who enter the business. If they are given

preference as family members, they may feel guilty for having such a favored position. They may feel guilty or disloyal if they disagree with the actions of other family members. Some family members develop feelings of jealousy and exploitation if their expectations are not met, and sibling rivalries can be acted out as family members work together. Others develop feelings of inadequacy or powerlessness if they are not allowed by the entrepreneur to exert some autonomy and independence. Many children who work for their fathers or mothers report that they are not given enough responsibility or credit for what they do. Thus, their self-esteem takes a battering day after day as they work in the business. Such emotional burdens can be the price that entrepreneurs and their families pay for working together.

Hiring Friends and Neighbors

Hiring friends and neighbors can present problems that are very similar to those that arise with family members. While the ties may not be as strong as those with family members, our friendships are an important source of satisfaction in our lives. Several entrepreneurs have described how some of their friendships had been destroyed by mixing business and friendship. For example, one entrepreneur ended up firing a close friend and next-door neighbor over a major difference of opinion. The friend and his family have undergone a number of financial trials since then. Still, the entrepreneur, his friend, and their wives see each other frequently in passing, their children play together, and they belong to the same church. This often places both families in some rather awkward situations. While the families remain civil to one another, the kind of personal relationship that they had in the past will probably never be regained. Thus, entrepreneurs must weigh the pros and cons if friends and neighbors are hired.

Managing the Employment Dilemma

While the preceding discussion has focused primarily on the problems that entrepreneurs face in working with family members, it is important to note that there can be some benefits from employing family members. Family members are often more committed to seeing the business succeed than are nonfamily employees, and such commitment is needed in a start-up company. Moreover, a family connection may facilitate relationships with customers and suppliers of the entrepreneurial firm, since key stakeholders may value relationships with members of the entrepreneur's family more than those with nonfamily employees. Thus, employing family members can make good business sense.

Family relationships can also be improved and strengthened by working together. Few families have the opportunity to get to know one another like families who work together on a daily basis. Some entrepreneurs feel that their relationships with their children and spouses actually improve as they work together in the business.

Family relationships can thrive in an entrepreneurial firm if the entrepreneur is aware of the conflicts involved and is able to manage them. In midcareer, the entrepreneur needs to continue to foster the attributes of an effective family that were described in Chapter Four. Furthermore, entrepreneurs must foster trust within the family, develop shared goals with family members, create mechanisms to resolve conflicts, and respond to family members' attempts to influence them and not always keep them in a dependent role. If this is done, the entrepreneur can look forward to building a successful business as well as a successful family.

When deciding whether to hire family members, entrepreneurs might begin by asking themselves the following questions:

1. Do I trust other members of my family?
2. Do other members of my family generally share the same goals?
3. Is my family able to handle disagreements and conflicts?
4. Do family members share their feelings and concerns rather than keeping them to themselves?
5. Can I make decisions *with* (rather than *for*) family members?
6. Do family members have knowledge, skills, or experience that will help the business?

If the answer to each of these questions is yes, the probability of succeeding as a family business is high. If one or more of the answers is no, then the entrepreneur must develop a strategy to overcome the weaknesses or choose not to employ family members.

Entrepreneurs who decide to employ family members after answering these questions need to be aware of a variety of strategies to help maintain harmony in the family and business. We will discuss five approaches to solving the kinds of problems that we have discussed in this chapter: developing clear expectations; use of asset management boards and family councils; use of third-party consultants; career counseling; and family therapy.

Developing Clear Expectations

Because of the overlapping of business and family systems, the possibility of role confusion for family members working together is great. To avoid this problem, the entrepreneur should take a number of steps, such as the four described here, to clarify roles and rules and delineate the boundaries between the two systems.

First, develop clear rules regarding which family members can be hired. One entrepreneur whom I interviewed favored hiring family members on a contract basis. After the contract expired, it could be renewed, or the family member could be encouraged to look elsewhere for a job. The advantage of the contract system is that it avoids the lifetime employment expectation that family members may have. Second, provide clear (perhaps written) job descriptions outlining the family members' duties, their compensation, and the criteria for evaluation and promotion. Third, conduct periodic performance reviews (preferably quarterly) of family members, not only to evaluate performance but also to clarify expectations or modify previous agreements that need updating. If the family member does not report to the entrepreneur, the family member's superior should conduct the review and report the outcome. Fourth, develop clear expectations regarding how the family is to relate to nonfamily employees. For example, are family members to be given preference? If so, under what conditions? Are all family members to be treated equally? If not, under what conditions will they be treated unequally?

These questions cannot be answered by the entrepreneur alone. Input from family members, board members, and nonfamily employees is generally required. A discussion with the family regarding the conflicting norms of the business and the family is needed to help clarify expectations. I have found that family businesses tend to be more successful if they develop a clear set of norms for business behavior that emphasizes competence and performance while also taking family goals and preferences into consideration. For example, a family might decide that family members should have the first chance at a promotion if they are qualified. One family that made this decision is the Haas family of Levi Strauss and Company. Younger family members have been given opportunities to become leaders in the business only after acquiring rigorous education. Many have received master's degrees in business administration from the Harvard Business School. Stanley Marcus, of Neiman-Marcus, used a different strategy with similar results. Marcus wanted his son Dick to eventually become president of the company but also wanted to avoid charges of nepotism. Dick started at the bottom and worked his way up through various functions, such as buying and merchandising. When the time came to select a new president, Stanley Marcus did not need to look beyond his own family. Dick was well prepared and had gained the confidence and respect of the nonfamily employees.

The entrepreneur should encourage family members to look at the big picture and attempt to be objective as they work through various problems. For example, the Peters family became hung up on the dollar amount of each other's salaries. If they had been able to look dispassionately at all of the factors, such as the amount of stock each one held, the kinds of work each was doing, the psychological needs of each family member, and how, in the long run, all family member's goals could be realized, it would have been much easier for them to resolve their issues. Trust is essential to working through these problems. If family members do not believe that there will be some kind of equal treatment in the long run, they will be unwilling to endure short-term inequities.

To avoid confusion, written rather than oral agreements regarding work assignments are preferable. Many conflicts seem to occur because each party remembers the employment contract a bit differently, and people become angry when they feel that the contract has been violated. For example, the son of one entrepreneur came to see me because he was angry that his father had not lived up to their agreement regarding his salary and job assignments. He complained that he was overworked and underpaid. When I spoke with the father, he gave a different version of the agreement. It was only after several hours of face-to-face negotiation between the father and the son (with myself as the intermediary) and the creation of a job description and employment contract that the dispute was finally resolved to the satisfaction of each.

Asset Management Boards and Family Business Councils

Another approach to solving problems is creating an asset management board.[7] An asset management board is composed of family members who own stock in the firm and meets periodically to make sure that the needs of family members are being met and to represent the positions of family members to the board of directors. The entrepreneur generally chairs such a board.

Another forum for resolving problems is the family business council, composed of family members who work in the family business. The entrepreneur generally chairs such a council, which meets periodically to discuss problems related to family involvement in the business. Family members can be encouraged to discuss how they feel about their roles and the roles of others. Common problems can be articulated and assignments given to develop strategies to solve those problems.

Third-Party Consultants

Some entrepreneurs make good use of third-party consultants to help the family work through business and family conflicts. For example, one entrepreneur regularly invites a business consultant with a background in family dynamics to attend meetings of the asset management board. The consultant helps the entrepreneur and his family clarify issues and develop agreements and then follows up to make sure that plans of action have been carried out. I often find myself in this role of referee or counselor to help family members develop a better working relationship.

Career Counseling and Career Development

Career counseling is often needed for young family members who are contemplating a career in the family business. Some children of entrepreneurs who have felt pressured to join the business when their real interests lie elsewhere come to resent working for their father or mother. To avoid this, young family members should be encouraged to take at least one of the occupational interest inventories offered during high school and college and discuss it with a counselor, a clergy member, professionals experienced in the particular fields of interest, or the entrepreneur. While these inventories do not necessarily tell a person what career he or she should choose, they can point to certain problems — or opportunities — that may be encountered if a person decides to work in the family business. Discussions of interests, abilities, and goals among entrepreneurs, their children, and counselors can help young family members make the best decisions regarding their careers.

Once a family member is hired, the next question is where they should start. Many entrepreneurs whose children have succeeded have started them in relatively low-level positions and let them work their way up in the organization. This can help the entrepreneur to avoid charges of nepotism. In addition, family members who start at the bottom have the opportunity to prove themselves over time and gain an appreciation of different facets of the business. The hard work required to achieve a top-level position will also help family members to remain humble and appreciate what they have earned. As they move up in the organization, they can also develop good relationships with nonfamily employees and networks of support at various levels as well. Some entrepreneurs assign a trusted nonfamily employee as an informal mentor for their children to help them overcome their weaknesses and to get a more objective view of the child's performance.

Family Therapy

Families experiencing serious problems may need to consult a family therapist or other trained counselors. The kinds of problems that may require therapy include severe role confusion, the inability of family members to develop distinct identities apart from the entrepreneur and the family, substance abuse, low trust among family members, coalitions within the family that are pitted against one another, feelings of powerlessness or experiences of discrimination on the part of family members, and the inability of the family to develop problem-solving mechanisms. To illustrate the kinds of problems that may require the help of therapists, Paul Rosenblatt and his colleagues, who often do family therapy, describe the following case:

> [One] couple . . . jointly owned and operated a business in which the husband spent virtually every waking moment. The business seemed well established and not in danger of failure were he to spend less time there. The wife came for therapy both depressed and angry. Her husband's unwillingness to be a companion away from the business, to participate in parenting of children, to help out with household chores, or to take her seriously was upsetting her. He was willing to join his wife in the therapist's office, but despite many attempts to negotiate differences he did not seem to take his wife's interests seriously. He seemed to think that things were as they had to be and that his wife's concerns were not matters in which she would continue to have strong feelings. However, she was uncompromising in her desire to have her husband

be more available in the ways that were important
to her, and her anger about their differences per-
sisted. In this example, it may be that long-existing
relationship issues came to a head through "symptoms" centering on the family business. She decided
to get a divorce. Even though one's ideal for therapy with a couple like that might be to resolve differences and to develop a strong marital relationship,
the divorce did lead to an ending of the wife's anger
and depression, while the husband continued to
have the business involvement he seemed to want.
In the divorce property settlement, the business was
divided, and each ex-spouse received and became
sole proprietor of a viable, separate business; his
absorbed all his waking hours and hers received
substantially less time commitment.[8]

While the marriage was not saved in this case, the therapist was
able to help the husband and wife to clarify their issues and see that
there were alternatives available to them. Because of their inability
to compromise, divorce turned out to be the best solution. This
case also illustrates another danger related to family problems. If
there is a divorce, the assets of the business often must be divided
between the husband and wife. Because it may not be easy to
divide such assets, the business may need to be sold; if the divorced
couple is still tied together by the business, conflicts can drag on
for years. Prenuptial agreements are one potential solution, but
even they can be challenged, which can lead to costly litigation
and bitter feelings. The optimal solution is for the entrepreneur
to anticipate problems, solve those problems as they arise, and
quickly seek out help if a problem cannot be resolved without
the benefit of an experienced counselor or therapist.

Conclusion

The conflicting norms of family and business can become a quag-
mire of confusion and conflict for the entrepreneur. Armed with

information presented in this chapter, entrepreneurs should be able to anticipate the kinds of problems that they are likely to face and take preventive action. Developing clear role expectations and ground rules is often the key to success. However, good communication, high trust, and problem-solving acumen are useful as well. Finally, the entrepreneur can use asset management boards and family business councils or consultants and therapists to help them cope with the more difficult family problems.

PART THREE

LATE
CAREER
DILEMMAS

NINE

SHOULD I RETIRE?

In the last stage of the entrepreneurial career, entrepreneurs begin to face the issue of retirement. As they get older, they come to realize that they do not have the energy that they once had. There are more aches and pains and visits to doctors as the aging process takes its toll. Despite the effects of age, many entrepreneurs who are well into their seventies and eighties have quick minds and good judgment. They still have goals that they would like to achieve and are enthusiastic about the challenges of an entrepreneurial career. They also recognize that they will not live forever and that they have a finite amount of time left. Early in their careers, they never thought about retirement and death. Now, in the last stage of life, the specter of death confronts them. The dilemma facing entrepreneurs as they grow older is embodied in the following question: Should I continue to run the business until I die and possibly miss out on some of the other pleasures of life during these golden years, or should I retire and possibly find myself with nothing to do? It is this dilemma that we address in this chapter.

Entrepreneurs' Views About Retirement

Entrepreneurs have various opinions about retirement. The following is typical:

Interviewer: Have you thought about retirement?

Entrepreneur: I haven't really thought about retirement. It's inevitable, but I haven't really thought about it.

Interviewer: So do you think that you will retire some day?

167

Entrepreneur: I'm sure I will.

Interviewer: When you see yourself in retirement, what do you see yourself doing?

Entrepreneur: Well, I am working on things right now that I can be doing in retirement. I've known a lot of people who have retired and are very sad. It's been a very difficult adjustment for them because they didn't prepare themselves for retirement. They found out when they finally retired that they didn't have anything to do.

Interviewer: Do you think that you will leave all of your involvement in business when you retire?

Entrepreneur: No, I don't think so. I think I will always have an interest there.

Interviewer: But retirement is not something that you are necessarily looking forward to?

Entrepreneur: No — I haven't even thought about it.

Another entrepreneur had this opinion:

> I enjoy living and I have seen too many people retire from their work and in two years they are dead because they not only retired from their job, they retired from living. They had no purpose to get up and go to work every day. Gene Autry is over eighty years old, and he gets up every day and gets dressed up as though he is going to fifteen board meetings that day. He may go out and have his breakfast at the country club or something and go by one of his offices and say hello to people and then go back home. But he is meeting friends all along the way and is working — that is a reason to live. So I have kind of patterned my thoughts after that, although I grew up in an area where the reason you work is so you can retire. I don't think that is right.

Levi Strauss, the founder of Levi Strauss and Company, saw retirement this way:

> I am a bachelor, and I fancy on that account that
> I need to work more, for my entire life is my busi-
> ness. I don't believe that a man who once forms the
> habit of being busy can retire and be contented. . . .
> My happiness lies in my routine work.[1]

Given these kinds of attitudes, it is not surprising that few entrepreneurs plan for retirement. A panel of 1,150 entrepreneurs who graduated from Harvard Business School were asked at what age they would like to retire. The results are as follows:

Preferred Age to Retire	Percentage
Under fifty-five	14.1
Fifty-six to sixty-four	13.8
Sixty-five or over	10.6
Never	48.9
Do not know	12.7

As this list shows, almost half of the entrepreneurs have no plans to retire.[2] If we add this group to those who do not know when they will retire and those who plan to retire sometime after age sixty-five, we see that nearly three-fourths of these entrepreneurs are likely to continue working until they die. There are several reasons why entrepreneurs prefer not to retire:

1. *A fear of death.* Entrepreneurs often equate retirement with death and point to several people they have known who died shortly after they retired. Some equate retirement with "building their own coffin."
2. *A strong work ethic.* Some entrepreneurs think retirement is at best wasteful and at worst immoral — one should continue to be productive throughout one's life.
3. *A need for meaning and satisfaction.* Much of the satisfaction

and meaning derived from life comes from the work that they perform. They enjoy work and see it as fun.

4. *Fear of loss of status.* Entrepreneurs fear that with retirement they may lose the prestige and status that they enjoy as leaders in the business community and heads of organizations.

5. *The need for money.* Some entrepreneurs do not retire because they need the income from their work. Most entrepreneurs are not independently wealthy, and some do not have the money to set up well-financed retirement plans. Thus, they must continue to work to make ends meet.

6. *A lack of alternatives.* Some entrepreneurs have been so engrossed in their work that they have taken little time to develop other interests. They have few hobbies, recreational activities, friendships, or family relationships to which they can devote their time and energies. In the absence of a good alternative, the entrepreneur will continue to work.

7. *Lack of a qualified replacement.* Some entrepreneurs continue working because they feel that there is no one qualified to take over their role. Others would like to sell out but cannot find a buyer. Entrepreneurs may feel trapped by the business if they have no one to trust to take over the leadership role.

Options for the Entrepreneur

There are basically three options available to entrepreneurs confronted with the retirement dilemma. First, they can continue working until they die or are incapacitated. This does help the entrepreneur to avoid many of the fears associated with retirement. However, without plans for retirement and succession, such an approach can leave the business and the entrepreneur's family in shambles, as we will see in more detail in the next two chapters.

Second, the entrepreneur may slow down over time and turn over some of the work to others. This strategy involves a conscious effort to delegate more authority and responsibility and to take some time to pursue outside interests. With such a strategy, the entrepreneur retains control of the business and continues to work but also spends time in other pursuits. One entrepreneur with this orientation said:

> I could care less about retiring. The guys that I know that are successful and do well are the ones who never retire — they just kind of slow down. They don't completely stop working. A good way of dying fast is going from being busy to doing nothing. I don't think I'll ever stop working. What I'd like to do, though, is slow down a little, because I do get really tired. Instead of working twelve hours a day, I'd like to go part-time and get someone else groomed. I'd come in three days a week or five afternoons or something like that. I'd rather have something to do to keep me busy. Otherwise, I'd go nuts. You can't just get in a rocking chair and waste your life away.

By slowing down, the entrepreneur can begin to prepare the next generation for leadership. However, moving slowly away from the business can create conflicts between the entrepreneur and potential successors regarding power and authority, since roles can easily become unclear and overlap. Such an approach requires good communication and clear expectations as entrepreneurs begin to define new roles for themselves and become less involved in the firm.

Third, the entrepreneur can formally retire and devote time and energy to other interests. Some entrepreneurs start their businesses with the idea of eventually selling them and becoming independently wealthy and thus able to retire. This option does require entrepreneurs to develop other interests and to recognize that it might be quite painful not to be directly involved in the business, although they might fill some oversight role on the board of directors. For example, one entrepreneur left a large corporation to start his own firm. After a few years, the new business became very successful, and the firm that he had previously worked for offered him a tremendous sum of money to buy his company. He agreed, and shortly thereafter he found himself very wealthy and unemployed. This caused a major crisis in his personal life, for he had not decided what to do with his life now that he had succeeded in fulfilling his dream. In some ways, the dream had become a nightmare. Without his business, his life had lost much of its meaning, and he had to search for new goals.

In the remainder of this chapter, we discuss the psychological, social, and financial barriers that prevent entrepreneurs from coping effectively with the retirement dilemma.

Overcoming Psychological Barriers to Retirement

As entrepreneurs begin to contemplate the prospect of retirement, they typically encounter great resistance within themselves that often deflects them from dealing with the issue. A Latin American entrepreneur who had built a highly successful insurance conglomerate describes his feelings regarding retirement and succession this way: "The basic dilemma is that succession planning by a founder is really . . . digging your own grave. It's preparing for your own death and it's very difficult to make contact with the concept of death emotionally. . . . [It's like] putting a dagger to your belly . . . and having someone behind you cut off your head. . . . That analogy sounds dramatic, but emotionally it's close to it. You're ripping yourself apart—your power, your significance, your leadership, your father role, your chief executive role, and your founder role."[3]

Psychological Stages

The graphic description equating retirement with a gruesome form of suicide points out the terrible psychological burden that an entrepreneur can carry when facing the prospect of retirement. The entrepreneurs that I have studied and worked with who were dealing with the issues of retirement and succession seemed to go through psychological stages similar to those of the terminally ill described by Elizabeth Kübler-Ross in her book *On Death and Dying.*[4] Kübler-Ross studied dozens of dying patients and noted that most tended to go through five psychological stages. I will describe each stage and show how each can be applied to the retirement dilemma facing an entrepreneur.

Stage 1: Denial. Initially, the entrepreneur would like the issue of retirement to just go away and would prefer not to think about it. For example, an executive who was the trusted aide of the founder of a large retail chain said that he had tried several times to get the founder to think about retirement and to plan for succession. Each time, he was met with a pained expression and silence. After a while, the executive gave up trying to get the founder to deal with the issue because he could see the pain that it caused him. Unfortunately, when the founder died, there was no succession plan and no clear successor, and the founder's family and the firm were thrown into great turmoil.

Stage 2: Anger. Once entrepreneurs recognize that the issue of retirement will not go away, they often become angry. Much of the anger expressed by Roger, described in Chapter Six, was not a response to the report that I gave him but a reaction to the realization that he could not retain complete control. It made him furious that much of what he had worked for and built would someday be turned over to people with values different from his own. In some sense, he was angry that death would prevent him from enjoying all the things that he had worked so hard for all of his life. Many entrepreneurs dealing with the retirement issue have some underlying feelings of anger and hostility.

Stage 3: Bargaining. Those facing death often begin to bargain with God, with some other deity, or with their doctors in an effort to stay alive. They may promise that if God removes the illness, they will devote their lives to his service. Similarly, some entrepreneurs attempt to reason with God, colleagues, board members, or even employees to find some way to remain in their role as founder. They want desperately to remain in control of their businesses and their lives and may be willing to trade anything to retain their roles.

Stage 4: Depression. After bargaining fails, it is not uncommon for entrepreneurs to have feelings of despair and depression. They are tortured by the fact that they cannot elude death and that retirement is inevitable. One entrepreneur noted that he "almost went crazy" when he tried to retire and let his son take over. Even visits with a renowned therapist could not alleviate his bouts of severe depression. He had lost his zest for life, and life had little meaning for him. Eventually, he came to the conclusion that he should go back to work, which he did. This created some problems for his son but helped relieve his depression.

Stage 5: Acceptance. After going through the previous four stages, mature entrepreneurs accept the fact that they must plan for the day when they will no longer be able to run the business. The entrepreneur who saw succession planning as a form of suicide also reported many days and nights of struggling with his own feelings of anger and despair. He said that he often played "psychological games" that helped to protect him against dealing with the succession issue. In time, however, he came to the realization that his life would eventually end and that he would need to find a successor. He also realized that there were still important things for him to accomplish. In accepting his fate, this founder has done a number of things to develop a succession plan and prepare his organization and family for the future without him. He also gets great enjoyment out of teaching at a local university and contributing to various social causes.

By listing these five stages, I do not mean to imply that all entrepreneurs go through all of them. Some entrepreneurs never get beyond the denial stage. Others never come to terms with their anger. Others remain depressed, and still others try to find a way to cheat death. Entrepreneurs who seem to cope well with the retirement dilemma are able to come to grips with these psychological issues and work through them and are, in some sense, refined by the process. They come to a better understanding of themselves and of life. The noted psychologist Erik Erikson believed that the key dilemma facing those at the end of their lives was whether they were able to leave a successful legacy to posterity and feel that their lives had had meaning, or whether they would become absorbed in their own problems.[5] Entrepreneurs who can deal with their feelings about retirement and channel their energies into passing on their legacy to the next generation are more likely to remain psychologically healthy than those who cannot.

Coping with Feelings Surrounding Retirement

To cope with feelings about retirement, the entrepreneur needs to gain self-insight and self-understanding to develop successful coping responses. Edgar H. Schein lists several questions that need to be answered to gain a better understanding of one's feelings:[6]

1. What feelings are being aroused: anger, frustration, despair, anxiety?
2. Given those feelings, what is the real problem? What choices can I make regarding my feelings?
3. Can I alter my feelings if they are getting in the way of dealing with the issue of retirement? Am I in enough control that I can get past my feelings of denial, anger, and so on?
4. Am I contributing to the way I feel by reacting inappropriately to people and external events? Can I do something about my reactions?
5. What options do I have for coping with these feelings? How do I feel about the various options? Do I have the skills and experience to try out new options? If not, how do I get them?

In answering these questions, entrepreneurs must try to be as open and honest as possible. They should identify the kinds of situations that bring on certain feelings. For example, one entrepreneur thinking about retirement began to have feelings of anger and resentment toward his son, whom he had designated as his successor, and his interactions with his son became increasingly uncomfortable. The answers to these questions are not likely to come easily. They require some time for reflection. Some entrepreneurs might enlist the help of a competent counselor to keep them honest and to help them uncover blind spots. In doing a self-assessment, the entrepreneur needs to realize that feelings of anger or depression are not unusual. The key concern is not that they have such feelings but whether they have coping mechanisms to deal with them.

Overcoming Social Barriers to Retirement

While entrepreneurs often have feelings that cause them to avoid grappling with the issue of retirement, those around them also can conspire to help them avoid dealing with the issue.[7] Family members may not want to upset the entrepreneur by talking about retirement. Moreover, they themselves may be unwilling to accept the mortality of the entrepreneur, particularly if the entrepreneur happens to be the mother or father in the family. Also, the family may want to keep the entrepreneur in power as long as possible in order to minimize family conflicts that might arise if the entrepreneur were to retire. While the entrepreneur has the leadership role, he or she is often able to quell conflicts and disputes between family members. Without such a stabilizing force, the harmony of the family could quickly be undermined.

Nonfamily managers who work for the entrepreneur may also be unwilling to let go of the entrepreneur. Like the family, nonfamily employees may not want to raise the issue of retirement with entrepreneurs for fear of upsetting them. Raising such an issue might also call into question their loyalty. In other instances, nonfamily employees may feel a great sense of loyalty to and dependence on the entrepreneur. They cannot envision themselves working for someone else, and their own positions of power may be undermined if the entrepreneur is not actively supporting them.

Other owners and business partners may also want the entrepreneur to continue to lead the firm indefinitely. The loss of the founder can create uncertainty. Since the success of many entrepreneurial firms depends on the founder's skills, ideas, and contacts with important stakeholders, the other owners and partners may not want to risk losing these key resources. Moreover, if the entrepreneur leaves the firm or sells out, the power structure can be altered dramatically. Thus, rather than risk a power struggle, the other partners may encourage the entrepreneur to stay on as long as possible.

Despite the resistance on the part of family members, nonfamily employees, and other owners to confront the issue of retirement, most entrepreneurs will need their support to help them work through this most difficult dilemma. There are several approaches to this.[8]

To mobilize their families to help them confront the issue of retirement, entrepreneurs must begin by getting support from their spouses or other key family members. This means that the entrepreneur must be willing to discuss the issue of retirement openly and begin planning for the future. Developing good communication with his or her spouse can provide the entrepreneur with much-needed support during this time. At times, a counselor may need to be called in to help the entrepreneur open lines of communication.

Once the entrepreneur has developed good communication with his or her spouse and done some preliminary planning for the future, a family council can be used to discuss a wide variety of issues and provide a forum for the family to ask questions and provide support. This also allows entrepreneurs to air their own feelings. As they express the fears and anxieties that they feel as they think about retirement, the family can help them work through the difficult psychological issues.

A special task force of top managers can also be created to help the entrepreneur plan for retirement. The managers on such a task force can be given the mandate to develop a management continuity plan, identifying a potential successor or successors and determining the training and development needs of future leaders. They might ask such questions as these: Do we have the right people inside the business to take it into the future, or do we need to look outside the firm? What skills and abilities will we need in the future? How are we developing our people for future leadership? What might we do now to better prepare them? By answering these questions, the task force can help the entrepreneur plan more effectively. It can also provide a forum for the entrepreneur to discuss succession issues, answer questions, and provide guidance.

To mobilize the owners to deal with the retirement question, the entrepreneur must use the board of directors. However, as we have seen, entrepreneurs are notorious for not utilizing their boards effectively. The entrepreneur should have the management task force report to the board regarding its activities to identify and develop future leaders. The board should oversee the search for a replacement for the entrepreneur and help the entrepreneur define a new role in the firm. Even if the entrepreneur moves away from day-to-day operations, it is generally a good idea to have the entrepreneur remain involved on the board of directors. Board members can help the entrepreneur develop a strategy for passing on key skills, contacts, and so forth to the next generation of leaders and to fulfill a new role as overseer and policy maker.

In mobilizing each of these three groups — the board, the management, and the family — to help the entrepreneur work through the retirement dilemma, entrepreneurs must create forums to discuss the issue of retirement. They must be willing to let others help them solve the succession problem and to share their concerns with others. Given that entrepreneurs often dislike working with committees, avoid depending on others for help, and tend to keep their innermost thoughts to themselves, mobilizing these three groups is not likely to be easy. In fact, most entrepreneurs fail to do it and end up suffering in silence.

Overcoming Financial Barriers to Retirement

One of the most difficult barriers to retirement is financial. Some entrepreneurs do not have the security of a pension or some other retirement program and must do their own financial planning for retirement. One entrepreneur, who was looking forward to retirement because he was tired and wanted to pursue some other interests, felt that he could not quit working because he and his wife needed his salary. I suggested to him that he could become chair of the board and pay himself a similar salary without working as hard. He replied, "There are only two problems with that. First, if those who take over the business run it into the ground, I'm stuck, for this company is my only source of income; second, I don't think this company should pay someone for not doing a full day's work. I wouldn't feel right about that." This statement points out how entrepreneurs can be chained to the business financially if they have not developed other sources of income to fund their retirement. To avoid this problem, the entrepreneur should begin to take several steps well before retirement.

First, the entrepreneur should enlist the aid of a competent financial planner to help set up a retirement program. Such a program generally consists of investing a certain amount of money each month to fund the retirement. A budget for retirement should be developed to determine how much money will be needed.

Second, with the help of legal counsel, the entrepreneur should create an estate plan that ensures that the assets left behind will be used in accordance with the entrepreneur's wishes. Such planning can serve to ease the entrepreneur's mind and help protect the interests of his or her spouse and family.

Third, if the entrepreneur needs to sell all or part of the business to fund the retirement, a plan needs to be developed to find potential buyers of the stock and, if the company is private, to determine the value of such stock. This approach could lead to the selling of the company to outside interests, to current partners, or to the employees themselves. Employee buyout programs have become increasingly popular in recent years.[9]

Finally, since there are significant tax implications for any type of retirement program, it is very important to get good counsel when developing a retirement plan. Entrepreneurs need to begin this planning process at least ten to fifteen years before retirement — the sooner the better.

Is There Life After Entrepreneurship?

Entrepreneurs will always be entrepreneurs, whether they formally retire or not. They have tremendous energy and want to make a contribution. The entrepreneurs who seem to cope the most effectively with retirement develop other interests as an outlet for their energies. Some get involved in philanthropic work; others devote their time to church service or social causes. Many entrepreneurs get great satisfaction from teaching or giving seminars to young people regarding starting and running a new business. They can also serve as advisers to budding entrepreneurs. Others decide to spend their time getting to know their families again. Since the long hours and nights away from home can turn family members into strangers, the entrepreneur may want to devote more time to better understanding each family member's needs, thoughts, and feelings. Recreation and hobbies can also be useful diversions, or the entrepreneur might want to develop some new talents and abilities.

In general, for entrepreneurs to successfully move into retirement, they must develop new ways to focus their entrepreneurial talents. Preferably, they will develop these interests well before retirement, so that retirement is just an extension of their normal life pattern. Developing these interests after retirement can prove to be quite difficult if a pattern has not already been established. Entrepreneurs can become frustrated and despondent as they frantically search for something to do. By giving back to their families and society their wisdom, their skills, and their enthusiasm, entrepreneurs can achieve an even higher sense of meaning and purpose to life.

Conclusion

As we have seen, most entrepreneurs do not want to retire. They would prefer to run their businesses forever. There are a number of psychological, social, and financial barriers that can deflect the entrepreneur from even thinking about retirement. However, most entrepreneurs do recognize the need to plan for retirement and succession. Through gaining self-insight, using family councils, management task forces, and boards of directors, and doing good financial planning, the entrepreneur can deal with the psychological traumas associated with retirement and receive the support necessary for making difficult decisions. Such planning is not easy for the entrepreneur, but it is necessary to protect the entrepreneur's legacy.

TEN

How Do I Prepare
My Business
for the Future?

As they prepare themselves for retirement, entrepreneurs must
also prepare their businesses for the time when they no longer
play the dominant role. Giving up the business that they have
created and nurtured to someone else can be one of the most
painful experiences that entrepreneurs can go through. The business is in a way the entrepreneur's own child. One entrepreneur believes that his business may even be more important than
his family:

> A man who starts his own business, an entrepre-
> neur, and has some success, this business becomes
> the most important thing in his life. He sees the busi-
> ness start, he loves it, he cherishes it. He always has
> quality time for that business. He goes home and
> is a father to his children and supposedly a good hus-
> band, but the love of his life is his business.

This statement illustrates the depth of feelings that some entrepreneurs can have toward their businesses. And this psychological attachment can deter them from engaging in succession
planning. The dilemma for the entrepreneur dealing with the
succession issue is this: How can I plan for succession and prepare my organization for the future and at the same time retain a meaningful role for myself? In this chapter, we outline
the approaches that entrepreneurs use to plan for succession and
offer some suggestions for dealing with this very difficult and
sensitive issue.

Approaches to Succession Planning

Entrepreneurs take a variety of approaches to succession planning for their businesses. In some instances, they decide to do nothing, since either they cannot come to grips with retirement psychologically or they cannot envisage anyone running their businesses but themselves. Some entrepreneurs seem to systematically undermine any potential successor to ensure that no one will be able to replace them. This approach can have grave consequences for the business. One study noted that in firms where there was no succession plan or the plan was not shared with the key people, profitability declined after succession took place.[1] This is not surprising, since one can imagine the confusion and uncertainty that would ensue if there were not a clear plan in place. Important contacts with customers and suppliers can be lost if the entrepreneur suddenly dies or becomes incapacitated and there is no one prepared to take over his or her role.

A second option for the entrepreneur nearing retirement is to sell out. This option makes sense for the entrepreneur who wants to get the "sweat equity" out of the business and make a clean break from it. One entrepreneur with this orientation said, "When I quit, I will sell my stock. I'm going to want to get all of my money out of it now because I normally wouldn't trust the person taking over to do it the way that I would want to have it done. I don't see why my retirement and my life savings should be at risk. I'm only going to be part of it if I own it and can control it and run it." Entrepreneurs who decide to sever their ties with the firm for such reasons may find themselves unable to part from it psychologically. One entrepreneur sold his business several times only to buy it back again each time because he could not bear to see it falter under new ownership and management. In some cases, the entrepreneur is retained by the new owners as a consultant for a short time. This consultant role can be very frustrating for the entrepreneur, since the new owners often make changes that are anathema to the entrepreneur, and yet he or she is powerless to change the new policies. However, some entrepreneurs appear to be quite comfortable in the role of consultant.

A third option is to gradually sell out to partners or to take the company public. The advantage of this option is that the entrepreneur can remain in control for an extended period while slowly selling the business to others. The disadvantage is that once the entrepreneur begins to deal with potential new owners, his or her actions are open to the scrutiny of other shareholders. This can be very distasteful to the entrepreneur who treasures secrecy and privacy. It also brings with it the headaches of managing partner relationships.

Managing the Succession Dilemma

In dealing with the succession dilemma, the entrepreneur must keep in mind the two facets of succession — ownership succession and management succession — are tied inextricably together. Entrepreneurs who have successfully passed on their firms' ownership to the next generation argue that ownership should be in the hands of people who can increase the value of the firm.[2] Family members not involved in running the business should receive other kinds of assets, such as nonvoting stock, or should be bought out by those who are involved. Entrepreneurs should leave the controlling interest of the stock in the hands of those who have the entrepreneurs' confidence. This assumes, however, that the entrepreneur has found and developed leaders for the future. It is to this issue that we now turn our attention.

Preparing the Next Generation for Leadership

To prepare for succession in the business, the entrepreneur must choose a successor or successors; train and develop the next generation of leaders; delegate authority and responsibility; set up guidelines and ground rules for the business; establish a timetable for the transition; and develop a new role for themselves. We discuss each of these in turn.

Choosing a Successor

Choosing a successor can be a most difficult task for the entrepreneur. In some cases, an entrepreneur who wants a family member as successor may find that the family member has other ideas. One entrepreneur was quite bitter because his sons did not want to follow in his footsteps: "I have no one to leave all this to. My oldest son dropped out of dental school and now wants to open a restaurant, and my youngest — he's majoring in political science — thinks he might like to be a congressman some day. I have a gold mine to give them and they don't want it. My wife and I would like to take a trip around the world — you know, Hong Kong, Singapore, Bombay. It's time for my sons to step in."[3] One study concluded that only 5 percent of all entrepreneurs will be able to rely on family members to take over their businesses.[4]

Entrepreneurs whose children are working for them in the business have several different options open to them. One survey of family businesses noted the many different kinds of succession plans that were being developed:[5] 35 percent planned to groom one child from an early age to take over; 25 percent planned to let the children compete and choose one or more successors with help from the board of directors; 15 percent planned to let the children compete and choose one or more successors with input from a third party; 15 percent planned to form an executive committee of two or more children; and 10 percent planned to let the children choose their own leader or leaders. Each of these approaches can pose problems. For example, designating one family member at an early age may alienate other potential candidates, and other family members may prove to be more appropriate for the position later on; allowing family members to compete with one another or choose their own leaders may cause serious conflicts in the family; management by committee can prove to be slow and cumbersome.

Succession planning requires the same clarity of expectations and criteria that are required in the hiring and promotion of family members. Family members need to know what kind of background, training, and performance are needed for them to be considered for a top management position. The transition to family successors is most likely to succeed when the entrepreneurs are able to talk openly with their children about these issues. When the children are expected to gain training through schooling and experience through working for another company before joining the business or starting at a relatively low level in the firm and working their way up, the entrepreneur can monitor their performance over time and feel confident that the chosen son or daughter is well prepared to lead the firm in the future.

If no competent family member is available, the entrepreneur must go through a similar process to find and train a nonfamily replacement. This can prove to be a touchy problem if some family members believe that they should be allowed to run the business but the entrepreneur lacks confidence in them. To avoid this problem, the entrepreneur needs to set up clear criteria for hiring and promoting and conduct straightforward performance reviews with family members. If a family member does not demonstrate the level of performance or competence required for a particular position in the firm, the entrepreneur must be able to confront the issue openly and quickly with the family member. Many entrepreneurs prefer to avoid such confrontations with family members, but without such frank discussions, false expectations can be created that will only lead to heartache and conflict in the long run. I have found engaging the help of a third party, such as a nonfamily board member, in making decisions regarding future leadership to be very useful. Third parties can be more objective than the entrepreneur, they can help to reduce the pressure on the entrepreneur, and their judgment can help the entrepreneur to avoid being criticized for playing favorites.

"Headhunters," or executive search firms, can also be engaged to locate potential candidates to succeed the entrepreneur. If this approach is used, the entrepreneur must clearly specify the criteria for the position — years of experience, technical background, conceptual and human skills — and interview candidates thoroughly, perhaps several times. Other board members and key managers should also have input in the selection process. Without such a thorough investigation, the process is likely to result in the kinds of conflicts and unmet expectations that we saw in the case of the entrepreneur Jones and the professional manager Lewis in Chapter Seven.

Training and Development

Once a potential successor or successors are selected, the entrepreneur must set up a training and development program for them. In most cases, the training should involve some sort of formal schooling plus some on-the-job training. The key to a successful training and development program, however, is effective mentoring of future leaders by the entrepreneur and other key managers. Such mentoring involves one-on-one discussions in which the leaders of the business acquaint the future leaders with the subtle nuances associated with running the business, teaching them the tricks of the trade and helping them make contact with key customers, clients, and suppliers. In this way, entrepreneurs can begin to pass on their critical knowledge and skills to the next generation. This, of course, assumes that the entrepreneur is capable of building such a supportive relationship with the next generation of leaders. If the entrepreneur feels jealousy or resentment toward the successors, the entrepreneur might try to undermine them or make their training unbearable. The hoped-for outcome of the mentoring process is an interdependent relationship in which the entrepreneur and the successor rely on each other for help and support, rather than a relationship in which the successors are always dependent on the entrepreneur for direction or the entrepreneur and the successors are always at odds with each other.

An example of a successful interdependent relationship is that between Willard Marriott and his son. Marriott had turned a small root beer stand into a multimillion-dollar conglomerate through a combination of quality service and conservative financing. Marriott avoided debt whenever possible. His son, on the other hand, realized that the company could expand rapidly only through the use of creative financing. While the father was skeptical about his son's ideas, he listened to them; the son, in turn, listened to his father's views about the business and his values. They both learned from each other and benefited in the relationship. By capitalizing on each other's strengths and helping each other, the Marriotts were able to expand their business into a multibillion-dollar empire, and the transition from father to son was a relatively smooth one. Entrepreneurs need to find successors whom they can trust and with whom they can build this type of interdependent relationship, if need be with the help of a consultant or counselor. If this is not possible, they should think seriously about selling out and letting someone else choose the next generation of leadership.

Delegating Authority and Responsibility

One of the most common complaints of successors in entrepreneurial firms is that they have been given a great deal of responsibility but none of the authority needed to carry out their jobs. The need for control often prevents the entrepreneur from delegating authority to future leaders. However, without adequate authority, those future leaders cannot truly be tested on their ability to function effectively as leaders. Thus, entrepreneurs need to improve their skills at delegation if they are to prepare the next generation for leadership. Some guidelines for such delegation are as follows:[6]

1. Clearly identify the project, assignment, or type of work to be performed. Ask how the assignment will help to improve the talents and abilities of the person receiving it. Choose the person who will benefit the most from the assignment and perform it most successfully.
2. Discuss the assignment with the person. Clarify all aspects of the task, including time requirements, and determine the authority needed to carry it out.
3. Make sure that the person doing the task has the necessary resources, such as money, equipment, or additional staff.
4. Provide the training or orientation needed for completing the assignment.
5. Allow the person to move ahead on the task with strong support and encouragement. Do not second-guess the person every step of the way; allow him or her to make mistakes.
6. Set dates to review progress. If there are problems, identify them in these review sessions and help the person make the needed changes.

7. Upon completion of the task, critique the total experience. Ask the person what could have been done to improve the delegating process. Reward the person — praise is often enough — for a job well done.

By following these steps, the entrepreneur can remain involved in the work of the organization while moving away from the day-to-day activities that can be delegated to future leaders.

In delegating authority and responsibility, the entrepreneur needs to show confidence in the ability of the person to whom the assignment was given. If the entrepreneur does not express confidence in potential successors, other managers may not be willing to support them and may encourage the entrepreneur to remain in charge as long as possible. There is nothing quite so devastating to succession planning as the entrepreneur continually denigrating the abilities of potential successors and communicating this lack of confidence to others.

Setting Up Guidelines and Ground Rules: Preparing for Change

Just as they pass on values to their families, entrepreneurs should focus on the values that they would like to leave to their organizations, articulating those values in statements of philosophy and clearly demonstrating them to members of the organization. It is important that the entrepreneur help the members of the organization to understand the overall guiding principles that will likely serve them well in the future, rather than focusing on specific practices that can quickly become obsolete or even counterproductive. For example, the entrepreneur might help members of the organization to understand what it means to provide quality service to customers while allowing them to develop new ways to achieve that goal. As the U.S. Constitution provides a framework for action and articulates general goals, the entrepreneur should frame a kind of "constitution" that outlines guiding principles without putting the organization in a straitjacket so that it is unable to adapt to new conditions.

Succession also provides opportunities to engage in major organizational change. Alan Wilkins of Brigham Young University suggests that there are certain times in an organization's history when it can "repent and reform" and make major changes in the way that it functions.[7] The entrepreneur may want to create a new vision for the future; by articulating this vision and training leaders who share it, the entrepreneur can often use the succession period to initiate major changes. Indeed, the succession period is often the best time to regenerate the entrepreneurial firm.[8] Edgar Schein has noted that founders sometimes promote as future leaders "hybrids"—people who share the entrepreneur's basic values but also bring with them different skills and views of the world.[9] By promoting such people, the entrepreneur can see the organization move in new, progressive directions. While Wilkins believes that those who engage in successful organizational change "honor the past" by celebrating those things that have worked successfully, they also have an eye to the future and recognize that the business must change in certain ways if it is going to survive and thrive. By using the past to propel the firm into the future, the entrepreneur can use the period of succession to initiate changes that might have been resisted in earlier periods and to prepare the organization to meet future challenges.

Establishing a Timetable

To ensure a successful transition in leadership, it is important for the entrepreneur to outline a general timetable for the transition. This can be done with the help of the board of directors. If possible, the timetable should designate who is to take over the leadership positions and over what period of time. This allows the successors to plan for their futures without feeling that they will have to wait forever to get their chance to run the business. Many successors have become frustrated and left a business without future leadership because the entrepreneur refused to develop a clear timetable for a transfer of power.

Ideally, the transition should take place when the organization is doing well. During periods of crisis and uncertainty, people are less trusting and often unwilling to take the kinds of risks that are needed. Thus, waiting until things get bad to make a change in leadership is a poor strategy. It is important for the entrepreneur to be committed to keeping the timetable unless unexpected events require a change in it. One entrepreneur noted that his timetable had essentially been imposed on him by his therapist. This led to significant problems: "My son and I have gone to group therapy and tried to work things out. One of the things that sent me into a tailspin was a famous therapist who came to the conclusion that I should step back in order to help my son flower and prosper. I should start to take it easy in the business. I almost ended up in an institution. I lost contact with people." The timetable and the progress of potential successors should be periodically reviewed by the entrepreneur and the board of directors.

Developing a New Role

As we discussed in Chapter Nine, entrepreneurs preparing for life after an entrepreneurial career need to work out a role in the business that will allow them to continue to make a contribution to the firm even if they have turned over business operations to their successors. In most successful transitions, the entrepreneurs move slowly away from day-to-day operations, rather than removing themselves from the business entirely. For example, some entrepreneurs initially designate their successor as chief operating officer while retaining the titles of chief executive officer and chairman of the board. If the successor functions well in the role of chief operating officer, the entrepreneur might relinquish the title of chief executive officer and remain only as chairman of the board. Over time, the entrepreneur might want to continue to serve on the board but turn over the chair to someone else. In this way, entrepreneurs can continue to help the business by dealing with key strategic, environmental, and competitive issues and meet their own need to stay connected with the business. As one entrepreneur said, "I have to have a place to go where I feel important when I get older."

In preparing for succession, entrepreneurs should play the role of teacher and role model for the next generation rather than spending their time in the more mundane activities that they have enjoyed in the past. To make this transition from doer to teacher is not easy. Entrepreneurs must grapple with psychological barriers to succession, win the support of their families and key managers to make these changes, and set up specific goals and a timetable to make the change. When they have done so, they can feel confident that they have done all that was possible to ensure the continuity of the firm.

Conclusion

In this chapter, we have explored the dilemma of preparing the entrepreneurial firm for a future without the entrepreneur. To do this, we have suggested that the entrepreneur must develop a plan to choose the successors, train and develop them, delegate authority and responsibility, set up guidelines and values for the future, set up a timetable, and develop a new role as a teacher. Given the entrepreneurial personality, developing a succession plan and finding a new role will not be easy. Many entrepreneurs avoid dealing with succession, and the result is a business and a management team that are ill prepared to succeed in the future. Entrepreneurs cannot afford to jeopardize their legacies and therefore need to begin planning for succession before it is too late.

ELEVEN

WHAT SHOULD I LEAVE
TO MY FAMILY?

One of the more complex dilemmas facing late-stage entrepreneurs is the kind of legacy that they leave to their families. As people face retirement and death, they may become interested in the welfare of the next generation and devote their energies to that end, or they may simply become absorbed in their own problems. Thus, the initial dilemma for entrepreneurs is how they will confront this issue with their families: will they attempt to ensure a successful future for their spouses, their children, and other family members, or will they become overwhelmed by their own needs and fail to prepare their families for a future without them? They may also ask themselves, "Should I give a handsome inheritance to my heirs and potentially spoil them, or should I make them earn it in some way?" Whether or not they actively prepare for the future, there are three types of legacies that entrepreneurs can leave to their families: financial assets (or debts), ownership in their companies, and their values. In this chapter, we address each of these three types of assets and discuss some of the problems associated with transferring them to the entrepreneur's family.

Preparing the Family for Retirement

As has been noted, the entrepreneur's family may not encourage the entrepreneur to deal with the issues of retirement and the transfer of assets, ownership, or even values because they want to protect the entrepreneur from facing these painful issues. Moreover, the entrepreneur may have difficulty psychologically coming to grips with retirement. Thus, entrepreneurs need to take the steps noted in Chapter Nine to mobilize themselves and their families to begin to work on this issue. While most entrepreneurs do not feel compelled to plan for retirement, many do feel compelled to do estate planning. However, given entrepreneurs' needs for control and secrecy, they frequently do such planning with their lawyers or other expert counsel but fail to communicate their plans and intentions to family members. Often, the first time that the family knows what planning has been done is when the family lawyer reads the entrepreneur's will. One study of small business owners found that more than 95 percent of them had had no detailed discussions of their estate planning activities with their spouses.[1]

Not knowing what will happen in the event of the entrepreneur's death can result in uncertainty and misunderstandings. For example, the son of one entrepreneur told me that his father had set up an estate plan that would effectively cut him off from receiving much of an inheritance. I asked him how he knew this, and he said that he did not have any detailed knowledge of the estate plan but had picked up bits and pieces of it from his parents. When I asked the father about the estate plan, he described something quite different. I met with father and son to clarify their expectations about the estate plan and asked them why they had not talked about it earlier. The father said that he had not felt that his son needed to know all the details of the plan; the son said that he had been curious but had been embarrassed to ask and had not wanted to anger his father by prying into his affairs. Their relationship had suffered because of the misunderstandings.

Another founder's son reported that even though he was designated as his father's successor in the business, they had had no detailed discussions about what would happen were the father to die. The son had no idea about how the various family holdings would be distributed, how those holdings should be managed, and how the issue of joint family ownership and control of the holdings would be managed. Without such knowledge being shared, the legacy of this founder could be confusion, conflict, and pain for family members. In the case of one family business, a family member said: "We thought there were inequities . . . [and] resented the way it was handled in the will. It wasn't the way he said it was going to be. We had to assume, even though we were hurt, that he just didn't know what he was doing. . . . There just isn't the closeness [in the family] before this all took place. His action divided the family."[2]

Transferring Financial Assets to Family Members

Entrepreneurs take a variety of approaches to the disposition of financial assets, which can range from real estate and family heirlooms to money from life insurance policies. A few entrepreneurs decide to leave none of their assets to family members; in some cases, their assets are swallowed up by debts. While entrepreneurs may not want to leave anything to family members because their families were not supportive of them or they feel that family members should make it on their own, such an approach tends to cause bitter feelings in family members who feel cheated out of their "rightful" inheritance. Entrepreneurs who take this option need to be clear about their motives: Are they trying to punish family members? Are they trying to get family members to accept more responsibility for their own futures? Do they see their actions as a means of retaining control of the family beyond the grave? Whatever the answers to these questions, if the entrepreneur decides to leave nothing to the family, the moral and legal implications of such actions need to be discussed with competent counsel.

Some entrepreneurs, such as Warren Buffet, a successful investment tycoon from Omaha, Nebraska, decide to give family members only a fraction of his total assets. Buffet, whose net worth is estimated to be about $4 billion, has decided to leave only 1 percent of his total assets (still a substantial sum) to his daughter and is giving the rest back to society through various philanthropic organizations.[3] Asked about this arrangement in an interview, Buffet's daughter said that her father has not helped her financially during the past several years; for example, when she had wanted to install a new kitchen in her home, he had made no offer to help, and she had ended up taking out a bank loan. While Buffet's approach seems to have caused some resentment on the part of his daughter, he believes that she needs to find her own way in the world, make her own decisions, and sacrifice to achieve her goals, and that he would not be doing her a favor if he were to give her all the money that she needed.

The option most often employed by the entrepreneurs whom we interviewed is to leave all their assets to be divided by their heirs. This approach can pose its own problems: the heirs may have quite diverse views of what is equitable, or the assets may be used in ways that were not intended by the entrepreneur. For example, I have known of several cases of entrepreneurs who had been divorced and died suddenly leaving all of their assets to their second wives, the children from their first marriage receiving nothing. In some of these cases, when the second wife became the new company president and majority stockholder, she fired the children from the first marriage who were working in the business. The children thus disinherited harbored bitter feelings toward their father because he had not planned for such a contingency.

Conventional Wisdom Regarding Family Inheritance

The entrepreneurs whom we interviewed generally had the following view about those who inherit their estates: Make them earn it! A few felt that they should just give their children an inheritance with no strings attached. Some of these felt guilty because they had not spent enough time with the family, had been divorced, or had committed some other type of "sin" that they felt required compensation. But the vast majority felt that they should set some standards and rules regarding the use of the assets. Some entrepreneurs set a minimum age at which their children could receive their inheritance or specified the way in which it could be used, such as for a college education. Others set up trusts to oversee the proper use of the assets. One entrepreneur seemed to capture this issue of helping his children remain responsible in his approach to estate planning:

> I have a son who works for me, but he really doesn't
> work hard. He's unwilling to make the commitment.

He is a good technician, but at this point in my
life, I'm unwilling to leave the business to him for
this reason: It would destroy him, more than it has
already. My business makes a lot of money, and
if he were to be in a position to get that kind of income with no investment and no personal commitment, it wouldn't do him any good. It would be
the ultimate destruction of him. Maybe not physically, but there would be no growth, no development, no nothing.

It is this view of the world that drives the entrepreneur to find
a way to make the heirs earn their inheritance. In some cases,
however, entrepreneurs are merely fooling themselves. Jealous
of the next generation and wanting to maintain control as long
as possible, they enjoy using the excuse that the heirs are "just
not ready yet," when they really do not want their heirs to take
over any of their assets. If such is the case, the entrepreneur
is in a position to do great damage to the family.

Transferring Ownership to the Next Generation

An important category of assets that might be transferred to
the family is the entrepreneur's stock. In most cases, the entrepreneur sets up a buy-sell agreement with partners to ensure
perpetuation of the business. The purchase of stock under the
agreement is generally funded by insurance policies set up for
that purpose. Without such an agreement, the disposition of
the stock and company assets can be tied up in legal wrangling
for years, which can cripple the business. Families who have
gone through the death of an entrepreneur often advise that a
majority of the stock, at least the voting stock, be bequeathed
to family members who will be making decisions regarding the
business and other kinds of assets be left to those who are not
interested in being a part of the firm.

Entrepreneurs must be aware of the family dynamics that
are likely to occur as a result of how stock ownership and decision-
making authority are distributed. One son of an entrepreneur,
whom I will call Fred, described his experience this way:

I think that the mistake that my father made was that he said [to the children]: "You're equal owners, you should share responsibility." What he should have said was, "When I go, Fred takes over." I tried, at first, to live this idea that you are all equal owners. But there were six people involved and ten different relationships. It worked all right for six months until one of my brothers decided that he had too many problems with his wife. She kept talking about things going on in the business, and she didn't understand the business. This was making him too anxious, and he asked if meetings could be held without her. There were also other problems. As long as Dad was there as the cement and everything was theoretical, and there were no problems to deal with that would keep people awake at night, it worked fine. But later on [after Dad's death], rivalries began. Finally, I said to each of them, "I'm your father from now on," and everything has been fine since. I guess that the rest of the family, except for one member, became more comfortable when I took over. One member that wasn't more comfortable sold her stock.[4]

The way that the stock is distributed can also result in people who are incompatible having to work together as partners. As one founder's son explained:

Unfortunately, in my father's situation, there was no will, and I found myself—I won't say in partnership, but involved with a stepmother that I barely knew, that had no knowledge of the company whatsoever. And she dragged her feet for five years, just thinking that she was going to put the bite to me. It was long and involved. This inheritance situation is a very, very tender spot. Eventually, we hammered out an agreement. It didn't work out very well. I was so overly generous that it was a painful situation. Oh, I'm courteous and so forth

seeing my stepmother at Christmastime, but there
is no conversation the rest of the year.[5]

Rather than transferring stock directly to family members,
some entrepreneurs decide to turn it into financial assets to be
passed on to their families by selling it to company employees.
Employee stock ownership programs (ESOPs) have become increasingly popular as a way of turning over the business to those
who have been loyal and are committed to seeing the business
succeed. This is a particularly good option if the entrepreneur's
family is not interested in owning the business. Joseph Nederlander, the founder and chair of Ticket World, Inc., decided to
give equity to the six men who had helped him build the business.
Inc. magazine quotes Nederlander as follows: "If I have a stroke
and die . . . I don't want to have one of these guys coming in
here and finding he doesn't have a job. How do you reward a
young guy for loyalty? They get so good they can go other places.
I hear them calling their wives at 9 o'clock to say they're missing dinner. They're giving their leisure time. . . . How do you
say thanks to people like that?"[6]

Unintended Consequences of Transferring Ownership

As entrepreneurs begin estate planning, they may feel that for
tax purposes they should begin to transfer stock to family members while they are are still quite young. While this can turn
out to be advantageous if the founder should die unexpectedly,
it can also cause some unexpected problems. This was true in
the case of John and Georgia White (names disguised), founders
of a large retail chain. As Georgia puts it:

> There are definitely a few things that John and I
> would change if we could do it all over again. I
> would like to go back in our history. As we devel-
> oped the company, John and I traveled a great deal
> together visiting various stores, helping to ensure
> their continued success. We were working out of
> a very small town, which is very difficult to fly in

and out of, and so we bought our own jet airplane. But then we worried about being killed while we were traveling together, leaving our business in jeopardy and our children with huge inheritance taxes. We had a very severe tax load at this time. It was a 70 percent income tax bracket because we were a closely held company. We were paying close to 85 percent of our money in tax dollars to Uncle Sam. Paying those taxes was an area that caused John great concern. How do you grow a business with that kind of a tax burden? Why should we risk millions of dollars, when Uncle Sam took it all with no risk involved? We were not accumulating any money, but we kept on reinvesting our money and taking more risks. Even after eight years, we really didn't have any money. John was working day and night with attorneys and accountants trying to keep up with our taxes and grow our business. At this time, we were advised by our CPAs to form a corporation with our children, giving each a one-fifth share of 49 percent of our business. They were very young, and they were to have nonvoting stock. But if anything were to happen to John and me, the inheritance tax would not destroy the company. Before our children were thirty years old, we sold the company in a leveraged buyout. We did this for several reasons: to stabilize our financial position, to help the company grow, and to get away from the Mom-and-Pop business image. The number one change that we would make today, had we known that we were going to sell the company, would be to not give our children 49 percent of our business in stock. Our children would first have to earn their own money, get an education, go into careers of their own choice, buy their first homes, struggle to buy their furniture, have direction, and accomplish goals. To actually know the thrill of what it is to achieve success on their own. We feel that this is an area that we as their parents totally lost control of and that we have done a big disservice to our children, and it is a big concern to us. Of course, they would be shocked at hearing me say this. They are thrilled to have this wonderful opportunity to have new houses, to go golfing every day, to be able to do whatever they want. But they received too much money too soon, and it could really be a curse to them in the future. Its not being handled properly is the biggest worry John and I have. They will never know or understand the true value of achievement.

Leaving Values to the Next Generation

Besides tangible assets, the founder can leave the family a legacy of values. This is often the most lasting legacy that entrepreneurs can leave to their families. However, if the entrepreneur has not spent time inculcating values in the family by the later stages of the career, it may be difficult to change well-ingrained behavior patterns. One way that entrepreneurs can transfer values and beliefs is by writing a life history, outlining key events and lessons learned over the years. My father, a noted academic, wrote his own personal history while serving as dean of the business school at Brigham Young University. I have found it fascinating to read of the important events in his life and his views of the world. Sprinkled in with the description of his life are certain words of advice for our family. After he has passed away, this history will become an even more important document to my family, for it will be the main source of information about his life.

Entrepreneurs could also list their values in a short document to be shared with the family. Thomas Watson of IBM did this in a short book containing the significant features of his own philosophy. Or the entrepreneur could use family councils, family reunions, or asset management boards to express his or her feelings and beliefs. In any event, entrepreneurs need to develop a strategy to share their values with their family in both word and deed. While the family may not agree with those values or fully accept them, creating a dialogue between generations to discuss what is important for the future can be helpful for both the family and the business.

Again, Willard Marriott provides a useful example. The night before Marriott promoted his son Bill to the office of executive vice president was a restless one for him. He knew that this appointment would eventually lead to Bill's appointment as president of the company. He wanted Bill to know what he was feeling and what he felt were important values or "guideposts" to live by. At four o'clock in the morning, he began writing the following letter:

> Dear Bill,
>
> I am mighty proud of you. Years of preparation, work and study have shown results.
>
> A leader should have character, be an example in all things. This is his greatest influence. In this you are admirable. You have not taken advantage of your position as my son. You remain humble.
>
> You have proved you can manage people and get them to work for you. You have made a profit — your thinker works. You are developing more patience and understanding with people, more maturity.
>
> It is not often that a father has a son who can step into his shoes and wear them on the basis of his own accomplishments and ability. Being the operating manager of a business on which probably 30,000 people depend for a livelihood is a frightening responsibility, but I have the greatest confidence you will build a team that will insure the continued success of a business that has been born through years of toil and devotion by many wonderful people. I have written down a few guideposts — all born out of my experience and ones I wish I could have followed more closely.
>
> Love and best wishes.
> Sincerely,
> [signed] Dad

Marriott wrote his fifteen "guideposts" on separate sheets of stationery:

1. Keep physically fit, mentally and spiritually strong.
2. Guard your habits—bad ones will destroy you.
3. Pray about every difficult problem.
4. Study and follow professional management principles. Apply them logically and practically to your organization.
5. People are No. 1—their development, loyalty, interests, team spirit. Develop managers in every area. This is your prime responsibility.
6. Decisions: Men grow making decisions and assuming responsibility for them.
   a. Make crystal clear what decision each manager is responsible for and what decisions you reserve for yourself.
   b. Have all the facts and counsel necessary— then decide and stick to it.
7. Criticism: Don't criticize people but make a fair appraisal of their qualifications with their supervisor only (or someone assigned to do this). Remember, anything you say about someone may (and usually does) get back to them. There are few secrets.
8. See the good in people and try to develop those qualities.
9. Inefficiency: If it cannot be overcome and an employee is obviously incapable of the job, find a job he can do or terminate *now*. Don't wait.
10. Manage your time.
    a. Short conversations—to the point.
    b. Make every minute on the job count.
    c. Work fewer hours—some of us waste half our time.
11. Delegate and hold accountable for results.

12. Details:
    a. Let your staff take care of them.
    b. Save your energy for planning, thinking, working with department heads, promoting new ideas.
13. Ideas and competition:
    a. Ideas keep the business alive.
    b. Know what your competitors are doing and planning.
    c. Encourage all management to think about better ways and give suggestions on anything that will improve business.
14. Don't try to do an employee's job for him — counsel and suggest.
15. Think objectively and keep a sense of humor. Make the business fun for you and others.[7]

These guideposts have become a central feature of Bill's management philosophy, as well as the overall philosophy of the Marriott Corporation. It is likely that Marriott had talked in general about these principles with his son, but putting them down on paper helped to crystallize them in his own mind and allowed him to share them more concretely with his son and others. Such an approach to sharing values can succeed if entrepreneurs are willing to spend the time to articulate their values and write them down for posterity.

Preparing the Family for Succession

Preparing the family for the transfer of financial assets, ownership, or values requires the entrepreneur to attempt to create the kinds of conditions that will facilitate the transition. I have found that five conditions are present in those families where such transfers are relatively smooth.[8]

Consistent Views of Equity

The family's views about what is fair and equitable have a great deal to do with how the family handles the transfer of assets.

In Chapter Eight, we described the case of the Williams family, where the father left all the stock to his sons and nothing to his daughters. Both sons and daughters felt that this was inequitable, but they had no process for resolving the inequities, and this has led to much pain and conflict.

Having consistent views of equity in the family does not mean that each family member will receive an equal share in the estate. Some family members might be compensated more because they spend more time in the business, have taken greater risks, or have greater needs. Regardless of what criteria are used, the family needs to discuss what should be considered equitable treatment and to clarify expectations regarding the entrepreneur's estate. Without coming to some general understanding of what is equitable, the family will likely experience a great deal of turmoil after the death of the entrepreneur.

Planning for Contingencies

Many of the problems described in this book occurred because the entrepreneur failed to plan for the unexpected. Some entrepreneurs were unable to anticipate what an unexpected death, a transfer of ownership, or the creation of a new set of partners would mean for their families. For example, Georgia White had not foreseen the possibility that she would have to sell her business while her children were still young, and this has led to a great deal of anxiety for her. Unfortunately, the unexpected happens all too often, and therefore the entrepreneur needs to carefully plan for such events.

Mechanisms to Manage Conflict

The transfer of assets and the transition of leadership to the next generation entail inevitable conflicts. Transition is a time of uncertainty. New roles begin to be created, and power shifts among family members. Thus, conflicts should be seen as a natural consequence of this transition period. To succeed as a family during these periods requires the development of mechanisms and skills to resolve such conflicts. For families that lack the necessary skills, the conflicts are likely to be debilitating, and selling the business may be the best option. For other families, an asset management board or a family council may be necessary to create a dialogue to discuss these issues. A mediator, family counselor, or consultant might also need to be called in to resolve some of these issues if the family reaches an impasse. It is essential to open the lines of communication to resolve these sensitive issues, and third parties may help to facilitate the flow of information.

Superordinate Goals

To work through these delicate issues, entrepreneurs and their families need some overarching goals to help them to focus their efforts. In some families, each family member is out for his or her own interests, regardless of the impact on other family members. Obviously, such conduct is detrimental to resolving the transfer dilemma.

Family members need to see a higher purpose or goal to which they can subordinate their own self-interest. For example, some families have the goal of continuing to manage the family business and will do anything to see that that goal is achieved. Others want to maintain family harmony and solidarity and therefore cooperate with each other to maintain good relationships. Thus, in some cases selling the business might be the best option if it would contribute to family harmony. Other families achieve their goals by setting up family foundations to engage in philanthropy.[9] By using family assets to improve society, entrepreneurs and their families can achieve a sense of mission and accomplishment as well as receiving accolades from the public for their work.

Trust

Underlying all the previous issues is the issue of trust. I have found that if there is basic trust between the entrepreneur and the family, most problems can be resolved. If people believe that others are acting in good faith, they are willing to endure some inequities and hardships in the short run and to give others the benefit of the doubt without always questioning their motives. When the family operates in a climate of trust, it is much easier to develop consistent views of equity, engage in contingency planning, resolve conflicts, and develop common goals.

Trust results from open communication and acting consistently with what is said. This is often difficult for entrepreneurs, who are not inclined to be open and sometimes do things that are quite inconsistent with their stated views. If trust is lacking in the family, the issue must be confronted openly and steps taken to resolve it, which typically means creating forums for open communication, negotiating new relationships, and following through with agreements. In most cases where trust has been lost, the entrepreneur will need the assistance of a third party who is trusted by the family.

Conclusion

In this chapter, we have described some of the dilemmas that entrepreneurs face as they attempt to transfer assets, ownership, and values to their families. After building a successful enterprise, entrepreneurs would not want to ruin their legacy through poor estate planning. To avoid this, entrepreneurs must share thoughts and feelings. They must get input from family members regarding their desires. They must also get input from a variety of experts on estate planning, such as accountants, lawyers, board members, and sometimes family counselors as well. To set up an estate plan that looks only at the tax issues can be shortsighted. While entrepreneurs' gut reaction to sharing such feelings and information may be negative, they must overcome such feelings to help their own families work through the transition issues. This does not mean that entrepreneurs must share everything, but they do need to share important information regarding the estate plan with key family members and be willing to modify that plan to meet the family's needs.

PART FOUR

DEVELOPING A SUCCESSFUL ENTREPRENEURIAL CAREER

TWELVE

WHO CAN HELP
THE ENTREPRENEUR?
STRATEGIES FOR FAMILY,
CO-WORKERS,
AND CONSULTANTS

The previous chapters have looked at the dilemmas of an entrepreneurial career primarily from the entrepreneur's point of view. We have examined the kinds of personal, family, and business dilemmas that entrepreneurs face, their approaches to dealing with those dilemmas, and a variety of options available to them. In this chapter, we explore how others who are part of the entrepreneurial experience — the entrepreneur's family, co-workers, and consultants — can be more effective in helping the entrepreneur cope with these dilemmas. In my experience in consulting with entrepreneurs, the family's response to the entrepreneur's career, the kind of support entrepreneurs receive from co-workers, and the advice and counsel from consultants all combine to either help or hinder entrepreneurs as they attempt to cope with their career dilemmas.

Strategies for Families

The issues that entrepreneurs' families face in attempting to help them differ widely over the stages of the entrepreneurial career. In this section, we outline strategies that can be useful at each of the different stages.

209

Early Career Strategies

Early in the career, the entrepreneur's relationship with his or her spouse is central. This is a time of great uncertainty and pressure, and the spouse needs to encourage the entrepreneur to share his or her thoughts and feelings. Entrepreneurs too often suffer in silence because they are unwilling to appear vulnerable and share their fears and aspirations. Moreover, those seeking an entrepreneurial career frequently experience an "identity crisis" as they struggle to find out whether they have what it takes to succeed as an entrepreneur. To help entrepreneurs cope with the stresses of managing early career dilemmas, their spouses should be sounding boards for them and develop good listening skills. Given that the entrepreneur's life-style is quite hectic, the couple might set up certain times each week to just visit with one another, go out on a date, or enjoy a recreational activity to relieve some tension and "share the dream."

These times together can achieve two important purposes: reducing tension by allowing the entrepreneur and his or her spouse to let off steam and express their feelings (the spouse may also be working full-time and experiencing a lot of stress as well) and improving their relationship by allowing them to share goals, solve problems, and understand each other's point of view. Since entrepreneurs often feel that they are always on call, I suggest that several times a year, the entrepreneur and the spouse should get away from the office, the telephone calls, and the decisions to work on these issues by themselves. All too often, I find that the telephone is the biggest enemy of the spouse who wants to spend some time with the entrepreneur to work on improving their relationship.

Unfortunately, some husband-wife discussions can result in an unresolved fight. For example, if the wife wants her entrepreneur husband to spend more time with the family, but he believes that he is already spending too much time in this way, a discussion of these issues may hurt rather than help the relationship. This is particularly true if the husband and wife have not learned to problem solve together. If the issues cannot be easily resolved and a discussion could lead to a serious rift in the relationship, a counselor should be called in to help mediate the dispute.

To help the entrepreneur manage the stress of early career, the spouse must develop mechanisms to handle stress, particularly the financial pressures that accompany the starting of a new business. The spouse must be able to effectively juggle finances from month to month and exercise patience with the entrepreneurial life-style. The spouse might also show some interest in and support of the business venture so that it becomes a common concern rather than a wedge that drives the couple apart.

Work and family trade-offs are difficult to manage. The spouse of an entrepreneur may have to assume a great deal of the burden of caring for the children; if both are working outside the home, additional help will need to be found. However, to help the entrepreneur recognize the trade-offs involved, the spouse must be able to communicate clear expectations regarding the entrepreneur's responsibility to the family and keep the entrepreneur informed of problems that require attention. A study done several years ago in Great Britain found that while many working women were quite dissatisfied with their marriages, others seemed to be quite satisfied. The key factor determining satisfaction seemed to be the husband's willingness to accommodate the wife's career. Wives whose husbands were understanding and supportive and willing to share in the burdens of child rearing and household duties were much happier with their lives and careers than other wives were.[1] Similarly, in the entrepreneurial couple, the spouse and the entrepreneur must build a partnership wherein each accommodates the other's needs and meets the needs of the family as well. If the entrepreneur does not meet obligations at home, the spouse may become resentful about the lack of support. A number of late career entrepreneurs that we interviewed reported that they had neglected their families and realized that such neglect had led to some poor family relationships. While it is difficult to say exactly how much time an entrepreneur should spend at home, there needs to be an open discussion with the spouse of the work-family trade-offs, in both the short and the long run.

Midcareer Strategies

In midcareer, in addition to the areas discussed above, the spouse often needs to help the children who may be thinking about working with the entrepreneur to make good career decisions and develop a good relationship with the entrepreneur. Research has shown that a family's feelings about the father's occupation (and, by extension, the mother's occupation as well) can determine how satisfied the father is with his work.[2] If the family has negative feelings about the entrepreneur's career, this can serve as an additional obstacle for the entrepreneur to overcome. Thus, even if they have reservations about the career, spouses of entrepreneurs should be careful not to characterize the entrepreneur's career in a way that alienates the children from the entrepreneur.

It is important to develop a forum for the family to clarify expectations and express feelings. To prevent the conflicts and misunderstandings that often arise when the entrepreneur decides to employ family members, the entrepreneur's spouse and children should encourage the use of family councils to share what is happening in the business and how the entrepreneur is feeling, to discuss what the entrepreneur could do to help the family deal with various issues, and to explore what the family could do to be more helpful to the entrepreneur. In such a forum, family members can develop better communication and help one another deal with the dilemmas that confront the family and the entrepreneur. However, if family members do not trust one another, have deficient conflict resolution skills, or reach an impasse, they may need to turn to a counselor or therapist to help them resolve their problems.

Late Career Family Strategies

In late career, the issues of retirement, estate planning, and succession take center stage. To be helpful to the entrepreneur, the family must understand the terrible psychological toll that dealing with these issues takes on the average entrepreneur. The family should encourage the entrepreneur to set up an asset management board and other advisory groups to help with estate planning and succession planning. The use of competent consultants in the areas of estate and succession planning should also be encouraged. The family should then actively participate when possible in making the difficult decisions required as they plan to disengage from the career. In this way, the family can help to build a support system and provide a sounding board for the entrepreneur.

Since serious problems can develop for the families of entrepreneurs who are unable to overcome personal fears and thus fail to plan for succession, the family must be active in encouraging the entrepreneur to share information and plans. Unfortunately, some entrepreneurial families become what might be called "enablers," who allow the entrepreneur to avoid the responsibility for estate and succession planning. As the families of alcoholics sometimes cover up for their failings and thus enable them to continue drinking, the entrepreneurial family can succumb to the pain expressed by the entrepreneur regarding retirement and thus encourage the entrepreneur to avoid confronting the problems. If little progress is being made regarding estate and succession planning, the family must confront the entrepreneur; if the family is unable or unwilling to confront the entrepreneur or there are serious disagreements and a breakdown in communication, they also might encourage the use of personal or family counselors.

In summary, for family members to effectively help the entrepreneur cope with the various career dilemmas, they might use the following guidelines:

- Keep the lines of communication open. Find the time to talk together about concerns and express feelings.
- Clarify expectations about work and family responsibilities.
- Be flexible. The entrepreneurial career can take unexpected twists and turns. The spouse may need to provide stability for the family in the midst of chaos and uncertainty.
- Use family councils and asset management boards as forums to express concerns and solve problems.
- Encourage the use of consultants and counselors when needed.

- Recognize how difficult some of these dilemmas are for the entrepreneur. Be patient and understanding.
- Do not be an "enabler." Confront the entrepreneur regarding agreements and expectations that are not met. Get outside help if needed.

Even with the best of intentions and help from competent counsel, the family may not be able to help the entrepreneur. For example, entrepreneurs with deep insecurities and feelings of mistrust may simply not listen to family members. The spouse of one entrepreneur tried for years to get her husband to get counseling for himself and for the family. Family fights were commonplace, and the entrepreneur was generally at the center of the conflict. Whenever the business and family were in crisis, the entrepreneur would seek help for a time but then discontinue counseling when the counselors began to ask him to make significant changes in his behavior or the crisis had passed. The wife finally concluded that her husband would not change and therefore contemplated her options: separation, divorce, or continuing to make the best of the situation. She decided that the best option for herself and her family was to continue to stay in the marriage and to seek counseling herself to help her cope with her husband's erratic behavior.

Strategies for Co-Workers

Since most entrepreneurs are rather authoritarian and autocratic, those employed by them are generally in dependent positions and subject to the whims of the entrepreneur. While some people enjoy working in an entrepreneurial environment, others feel trapped and exploited. In this section, we discuss seven strategies to help those working for entrepreneurs help themselves as well as their bosses:

1. Develop a power base from which to influence the entrepreneur.
2. Develop a clear understanding of the entrepreneurial mindset and the problems that entrepreneurs face.

3. Challenge the entrepreneur. Do not be afraid to ask questions.
4. Recognize the entrepreneur's strengths and help carry the entrepreneur's burdens.
5. Encourage the entrepreneur to think strategically and avoid micromanagement.
6. Encourage the use of boards, committees, and consultants to share information and make decisions.
7. Help the entrepreneur develop a plan for succession.

Developing a Power Base

One of the keys to developing a successful relationship with entrepreneurs is to create a power base from which to influence them. Entrepreneurs—and authority figures in general—respond to others who have resources that they want and need, particularly if those resources are scarce. Four of the most common power bases that can be used in an entrepreneurial firm are *information* regarding operations, marketing, key customers, suppliers, and so on; *expertise* in areas such as finance, marketing, manufacturing, law, or research and development; *connections* with key suppliers, clients, shareholders, or those with other resources; and *charisma* and the power of persuasion (a strong personality, however, might prove threatening to the entrepreneur, so the use of this power base could backfire).

Subordinates should consider carefully how they might be able to build their power base. They might ask themselves: Can I get access to important information? Can I develop a needed skill? Can I develop good relations with key resource holders? Can I improve my ability to persuade the entrepreneur to adopt my ideas? Those who work with entrepreneurs without a base of power to operate from often feel frustrated since they seldom see their ideas adopted and have little influence. One power base that such people can develop is having another job opportunity available. People with other options may be more willing to take risks and speak openly rather than keeping quiet and submitting to the dictates of the entrepreneur.

Entrepreneurs benefit by having co-workers who have information, skills, and expertise that can help the business grow and to whom they can turn for help and advice. If entrepreneurs feel that those who work for them have little to offer, they will be unwilling to confide in them and seek their help. Thus, both subordinates and the entrepreneur can benefit by developing interaction patterns based on mutual influence.

Understanding the Entrepreneurial Mind-Set

On more than one occasion, I have heard entrepreneurs complain that their subordinates "don't think like entrepreneurs." Entrepreneurs who feel that their subordinates are not looking out for their interests are unwilling to trust and confide in them.

To develop a better understanding of the issues facing entrepreneurs, I suggest the following types of activities: (1) Read autobiographies and biographies of entrepreneurs that discuss their feelings, hopes, dreams, and problems. (2) Ask the entrepreneur to tell his or her story to you or to a group of employees. Get the entrepreneur to discuss his or her current concerns as well as concerns for the future. I have found that most entrepreneurs are eager to tell their own histories to anyone willing to listen. (3) Envision yourself as an entrepreneur or imagine that you were in the founder's shoes. What concerns would you now have? What actions might you take? What help would you need? By answering these kinds of questions, co-workers can be better able to respond effectively to the entrepreneur's current concerns and anticipate future problems.

Challenging the Entrepreneur

Those who work with entrepreneurs are most effective when they have built a power base and understand the entrepreneur well enough to challenge his or her ideas and actions. Because of the loneliness and isolation that entrepreneurs often feel, they can end up managing in a vacuum without the help of good advice and criticism. Moreover, when subordinates feel threatened by the entrepreneur — as they often do — they are reluctant to challenge the entrepreneur. Of course, some entrepreneurs are so insecure that they meet any challenge with hostility, and employees of such entrepreneurs who would like to remain employed should probably keep quiet. However, if the entrepreneur is leading the company off course, this also makes the subordinate's job insecure. I have interviewed many employees in entrepreneurial firms who are quite forceful in expressing their convictions when I talk with them privately but turn docile and submissive when dealing with the entrepreneur.

One way that co-workers could help to create a climate that encourages debate and challenge is to encourage the entrepreneur to set up a "management review committee" to review and critique key strategy and policy decisions. This at the very least creates a forum for debate and discussion. However, if there is still reluctance to confront issues, the use of a consultant to help co-workers confront the entrepreneur in a relatively safe environment may be the best option available. It might also be helpful to play the role of devil's advocate rather than confronting the entrepreneur directly. For example, when hearing an idea from the entrepreneur, a subordinate might say, "Have we thought through all the consequences of that idea? Let me just play the role of devil's advocate and examine the possible consequences of that course of action." This strategy allows the co-worker to confront the idea without confronting the entrepreneur directly. Co-workers must be willing to accept some risk in confronting the entrepreneur, but the payoff in better communication, better decisions, and a more effective organization is generally worth that risk.

Recognizing the Entrepreneur's Strengths
and Helping to Carry the Burdens

Most of the entrepreneurs that we interviewed discussed how heavy some of their burdens were to carry, and they often wanted to find others — family, friends, co-workers, or consultants — who could help them lighten their load. Entrepreneurs also appreciate being praised and acknowledged for their accomplishments. They are often the focal point for criticism and need support and encouragement to offset the complaints that they receive. Co-workers who can recognize entrepreneurs' strengths and help to ease their burdens by doing some of the onerous detail work, filling in so the entrepreneur can take a vacation, locating key resources, being a peacemaker in the midst of conflict, or providing information and expertise to develop a succession plan can become an invaluable resource.

To employ this strategy, one must carefully decipher messages behind what the entrepreneur is saying and anticipate potential problems and concerns. Then, in a frank discussion with the entrepreneur, the employee might discuss what burdens might be delegated so that the entrepreneur is kept informed of progress while being relieved of certain tasks.

Encouraging the Entrepreneur to Think Strategically

One of the biggest problems that can confront a growing entrepreneurial firm is a leader who continues to micromanage by making all decisions, both major and minor. This can be disastrous for the organization and for the development and self-confidence of future leaders. As a firm grows, problems posed by the organization's external environment, such as government regulation, new competition, changes in consumer tastes, and new technology, can make it extremely difficult for even a highly successful firm to maintain its competitive edge. While the entrepreneur may feel more comfortable working on internal issues and problems, the success of most organizations is largely dependent on top management's ability to handle these external problems.

Employees in entrepreneurial firms must encourage their leaders to spend most of their time dealing with environmental concerns. Entrepreneurs need to be encouraged to fulfill their leadership roles by focusing on big-picture problems. Their reputations and stature in the business community allow them to make the kinds of connections and have the kinds of influence that few others can. Yet if they do not use their influence, many opportunities may be lost, and the organization may suffer. I have found that the best way to get the entrepreneur to think strategically is for senior managers and board members to articulate the entrepreneur's role and regularly encourage the entrepreneur to focus on the problems posed by the external environment. Asking the entrepreneur to report at board meetings on how particular external problems are being studied and solved will encourage the entrepreneur to focus on external problems and create a strategy for dealing with them. For the entrepreneur to feel comfortable in this role, employees must demonstrate the competence, consistent performance, and integrity required for them to handle most of the internal problems, such as manufacturing and engineering, while the entrepreneur addresses the external issues.

Encouraging the Use of Boards, Committees, and Consultants

While boards, committees, and consultants can be useful in helping entrepreneurs to cope with career dilemmas, many entrepreneurs find the use of groups cumbersome and dislike airing their "dirty laundry" before strangers. Few of the entrepreneurs with whom I have worked have experienced success in working with consultants and even fewer in working with groups. Thus, I would encourage those trying to get the entrepreneur to use these vehicles to solve problems, to start slowly and create group situations in which the entrepreneur can feel comfortable. For example, they might encourage the entrepreneur to hold brown-bag lunches or "sensing meetings" with top management or other employees to share his or her ideas and vision for the future. Most entrepreneurs are quite willing to discuss important issues in a forum where they are the center of attention and clearly in control. Once the entrepreneur begins to feel more comfortable in such a group setting, it is just one step further to regularly schedule such meetings. Over time, the employees might suggest that the entrepreneur create a formal committee to debate key issues. As more information is generally needed by a committee or a board in a growing, complex organization, the natural tendency will be to turn to consultants or board members to help the committee deal with its problems.

By starting slowly and promoting "small wins" whereby the entrepreneur can see the benefits of using a group or outside consultant, employees in the entrepreneurial firm can have more input over time in the decision-making process and can help prevent "entrepreneurial myopia" by encouraging the entrepreneur to present ideas in a forum where they can be scrutinized, debated, and modified if necessary.

Helping the Entrepreneur Plan for Succession

To help the entrepreneur to deal with the problems associated with succession planning discussed in Chapters Nine through Eleven, employees need to be aware of the internal and external forces affecting the entrepreneur. Before proceeding to help the entrepreneur examine the succession question, employees might try to determine where the entrepreneur is psychologically: Is the entrepreneur in the denial stage? Is he or she angry? Has he or she come to terms with the inevitability of succession? Timing is very important in helping the entrepreneur through this period; succession planning is much easier if the entrepreneur is past the denial and anger stages. However, if he or she is not, employees may need to listen to, support, and show empathy for the entrepreneur while encouraging the entrepreneur to at least begin the process of estate planning and identification of potential successors.

If the entrepreneur's health is deteriorating or his or her capacity to govern is impaired, action needs to be taken quickly. Since employees who suggest succession planning are often branded as disloyal, the first step is generally to locate an outside consultant who specializes in succession planning to make an unbiased assessment of the situation and recommend steps be taken. Eventually, employees must help the entrepreneur confront the issue of succession, not only for the sake of their own careers and the organization's future but for the well-being of the entrepreneur and the entrepreneur's family.

Summary

Co-workers can do much to help entrepreneurs deal with their career dilemmas. To be helpful requires one to be in a position to help. Thus, developing a strategy to empower oneself is the first step. Once the entrepreneur recognizes that employees have something to offer and have a power base, the entrepreneur is more likely to listen to them and take their advice and suggestions. Moreover, when working from a base of power, employees are more likely to take the kinds of risks associated with helping the entrepreneur confront some of his or her weaknesses and negative tendencies and develop ways to overcome them.

Strategies for Consultants

Numerous books have been written about how consultants can carry out their functions, so I will make no attempt to present an overall framework for consulting.[3] However, in working with entrepreneurs in a consulting role, I have found that there are several areas where consultants can get themselves into trouble. I have learned, often the hard way, of the pitfalls that can befall those consulting with entrepreneurs. I have found the following areas to be the most troublesome.

Contracting with Entrepreneurs

Setting the initial consulting contract can be an area of difficulty for those consulting with entrepreneurs. Many entrepreneurs have not had much experience in working with consultants, nor are they often in a position to compensate consultants at their usual rates. Thus, the consultant must both be clear and creative when contracting with an entrepreneur (compensation schemes may include stock or deferred payments).

The first question to be answered in contracting is: Who is the client? Of course, the entrepreneur will assume that he or she is the client, which is true in many cases. However, I have found that entrepreneurs have preferred solutions to their problem that may hurt some people—family members, employees, or other stakeholders. Thus, I try to be clear to entrepreneurs that while I am working for them, I will not recommend a course of action that I believe will not be in the best interests of themselves, their families, company employees, or other affected parties. In fact, once I have diagnosed the situation, I often recommend that the entrepreneur him- or herself needs to change in some way rather than putting the onus for change on someone else. Developing this understanding is not easy, but I have found it essential.

Developing a Trusting Relationship

In all consulting situations, the consultant must develop a trusting relationship with the client. However, the level of trust needed depends largely on the depth of the consultant's intervention. For example, for a consultant helping a client with operational problems such as setting up an accounting or computer system, trust generally need be minimal, since the type of intervention involved does not require the client to change dramatically. However, if the situation requires that the client be asked to reexamine relationships with family, subordinates, and partners, a great deal of trust is required between the consultant and the entrepreneur, since such a change effort may have great impact on the entrepreneur's psyche and relationships and hence be quite threatening.

For the entrepreneur to develop enough trust in the consultant to be willing to encounter new and possibly painful experiences, the consultant should spend a great deal of time in one-on-one interactions with the entrepreneur, both during periods of work and during periods of relaxation and reflection. The consultant should first attempt to help the entrepreneur work through small dilemmas to build trust before tackling the more difficult career dilemmas. This approach requires the consultant and the entrepreneur to engage in a long-term relationship. I have found that it often takes a year or so of working together before the relationship is such that the consultant and the entrepreneur can begin working on the more significant problems. If the entrepreneur wants a quick fix — as many of them do — I generally find it difficult to be helpful.

Looking Deeper Than the Presenting Problem

Entrepreneurs (and people in general) tend to frame their problems in their own terms and fail to see the entire picture. For example, one entrepreneur whom I was called in to assist reported that his major problem was that his successor was not enthusiastic about the succession plan that he had proposed. He was partially right. As I explored this issue with the successor, I found not only that he definitely disliked the succession plan but more fundamentally that there was a basic communication problem between him and the founder. Thus, the problem that needed to be worked on was not the succession plan but the underlying dynamics of communication that were the source of the conflict. The consultant must dig deep to understand what is behind the overt problems facing the entrepreneur.

Diagnosing with the Entrepreneur

While several models for diagnosing organizational problems have been developed over the years,[4] I have found that the model one chooses is not as important as developing a process to get the entrepreneur involved in the diagnosis. In entrepreneurial firms, the founders are the locus of power and control, and thus any action taken must be taken with their knowledge and blessing. This requires that they be involved in the process. While they might not collect data as part of a diagnosis, they should be actively involved in deciphering the meaning of the data.

Consultants also need to share their theories of diagnosis, intervention, and change with their entrepreneur clients. When entrepreneurs understand the theory and method in practical terms, they generally develop more trust in the consultant and are more willing to give the consultant latitude to work on problems. This also allows the entrepreneur to make more informed choices and assess the quality and effectiveness of the consultation.

Protecting Anonymity

As a fledgling consultant to various organizations, both large and small, I generally tried to protect the anonymity of the people that I interviewed, feeling that they would be more candid and open if they knew that their responses would be kept anonymous and reported only in the aggregate. However, I have found that in relatively small entrepreneurial firms—and even in some large ones—the entrepreneur can generally figure out who said what, regardless of the way the data are presented. In a family business, it is difficult if not impossible for the consultant to protect the anonymity of family members. There are few anonymous "oldest sons" in a family business. Furthermore, if the data are to be helpful and problems are to be solved, those reporting the data will generally need to acknowledge their views and discuss them with the entrepreneur.

For these reasons, I now tell those that I interview that while I may not directly attribute their remarks to them, they will likely be identified by the entrepreneur and others, and so they should not assume that they will be anonymous. However, if they have something to say off the record that could help me in working with the entrepreneur or the company, I tell them that I will not report those remarks in any form to the entrepreneur or others. While some appear uncomfortable even speaking off the record, I have found that many are willing to share their thoughts and feelings with me and to allow me to share them with others. Thus, I feel that I lose very little by taking this approach. Moreover, I feel that I am more honest when I inform those I interview that their remarks may be identified—and they seem to perceive me as more honest as well.

Using the Entrepreneur to Initiate Change

Since entrepreneurs are the catalysts for change in their organizations, the consultant must help them to effectively initiate change. Unfortunately, as we have seen, many entrepreneurs use inappropriate change strategies. They may fail to adequately diagnose the problems, or they may use only a power strategy to initiate change rather than building support for their plans. I believe that consultants are most effective when they serve in the role of coach or mediator to help the entrepreneur implement the change strategy, offering the entrepreneur new models and theories, providing the impetus to create forums to discuss problems and initiate action, and helping the entrepreneur to manage process problems that arise as he or she attempts to work through issues with various groups and individuals.

Most entrepreneurs want to take the lead in a change effort. No matter how misguided this may be, they feel that they need to assume the leadership role and make sure that everyone knows that they are in charge. Consultants who try to share the spotlight with the entrepreneur tend to create confusion among the employees regarding just whose plan is being implemented, and this can undermine the change process. I have found that it is more useful for the consultant to stay in the background, reinforcing the entrepreneur's leadership role but coaching the entrepreneur so that he or she can create positive change in the organization without undermining employees' morale and commitment.

Follow-Up and Evaluation

One of the major sins that consultants can commit is failing to develop strategies to follow up and evaluate the impact of a change effort. The dilemmas that have been discussed in this book are not ones that can be resolved quickly. They require a great deal of thought, preparation, and action over many years, and a number of stumbling blocks will be encountered along the way. Therefore, the consultant and the entrepreneur must establish a set of signposts or targets to determine how successful the change effort has been and a timetable to determine when evaluations should take place.

Entrepreneurs seem to run hot and cold: they may be excited about a project one day and feel that it is worthless the next. Such vacillation can easily undermine any change effort and can be extremely unnerving to employees. Thus, before any change effort is undertaken, the wise consultant will map out the potential consequences for the entrepreneur and the organization and insist on following up to ensure that the entrepreneur is following through on his or her commitment and to determine whether the changes have been effective or new initiatives are needed. In the change programs that I am involved with, I usually try to hold progress meetings with the entrepreneur every three or four months after the change effort has begun. After a year, the change effort should be thoroughly evaluated. At that time, the entrepreneur and consultant can set up guidelines to continue to evaluate progress or decide to terminate the change program if it has achieved its goals.

Getting Additional Help

The dilemmas facing an entrepreneur — family issues, legal issues, business issues, tax issues, personal issues — are extremely complex. Indeed, I have worked with some entrepreneurs who have simultaneously employed family therapists, lawyers, accountants, business consultants, and psychiatrists to help them deal with their problems. I have found that if they are not careful, consultants can overstep the bounds of their experience and expertise and give advice that might be damaging. For example, business consultants may be tempted to tell the entrepreneur how to solve their family problems, or family therapists may have ideas about how to improve the business. In either case, the consultant, while having good intentions, may be giving half-baked advice that ultimately ends up misleading the entrepreneur. In many cases, the use of a team of consultants with different types of expertise may be the best approach to helping an entrepreneur, rather than relying on one individual with a limited perspective.

Summary

Consulting with entrepreneurs requires a sensitivity to certain issues. I suggest the following guidelines for consultants working with entrepreneurs:

1. Develop a clear contract defining the client-consultant relationship.
2. Build a strong trusting relationship over time so that the entrepreneur will have enough confidence in the consultant to make difficult changes.
3. Look deeper than the presenting problem — the entrepreneur might mislead the consultant.
4. Diagnose the problems with the entrepreneur to gain understanding and commitment.

5. Recognize that you may not be able to protect the anonymity of those you interview and attempt to use this fact to your advantage to get people to be more open in sharing their problems with others.
6. Let the entrepreneur initiate the change effort. The consultant should reinforce the entrepreneur's leadership role.
7. Follow up and evaluate any change effort. Without such follow-up and evaluation, most change efforts will fail or have only modest success.
8. Get additional help if needed. Do not give advice in areas where you do not have the necessary expertise or experience.

In the end, do not be surprised if you fail as a consultant to an entrepreneur. Entrepreneurs can be unpredictable, and their lives and situations are complex. However, I have found that if I can get an entrepreneur to change his or her behavior, dramatic changes and improvements can occur almost overnight. For this reason, I find helping entrepreneurs to be exciting and worthwhile, although it is certainly disappointing and discouraging at times.

Conclusion

In this chapter, we have discussed how family members, co-workers, and consultants might help entrepreneurs navigate the rocks and shoals of an entrepreneurial career. Such support often determines whether the entrepreneur succeeds or fails. A supportive family, understanding co-workers, and insightful consultants can all combine to make the dilemmas seem less overwhelming and can allow entrepreneurs to experiment with new ideas and behaviors that can help them chart a successful course.

THIRTEEN

CAN I MEET
THE CHALLENGE
OF AN
ENTREPRENEURIAL
CAREER?

Over the course of this book, we have explored the dilemmas that are encountered at each stage of the entrepreneurial career. In early career, entrepreneurs develop their career identities, attempt to balance the demands of work and family, and struggle to find resources to build their businesses, often with the help (and the headaches) of partners or other investors. We have seen how entrepreneurs in midcareer can feel very lonely and isolated in their roles. They must also determine whether to involve family or professional managers in the business. And in a growing business, the entrepreneur struggles to maintain control over operations. Finally, in late career, entrepreneurs struggle with their feelings about retirement, death, and succession. Estate and tax planning become even more important as entrepreneurs attempt to ensure the financial well-being of their families. Moreover, they must find, develop, and mentor successors for their businesses in order to protect the legacies that they have built over the years.

From the research and case examples that have been presented in this book, one can see how difficult some of these dilemmas are for the entrepreneur and how easy it is for the ill-prepared entrepreneur to stumble. In this final chapter, I summarize the attributes that seem to characterize entrepreneurs

228

that handle these dilemmas well and outline a general approach to developing those attributes. Finally, I discuss the issues that will become even more important for entrepreneurs in the twenty-first century.

Attributes Affecting Success

The case studies and interviews that provided the background material for this book indicate some common attributes among entrepreneurs who are successful in coping with their career dilemmas. There also seem to be some common behavior patterns associated with entrepreneurs who have had great difficulty meeting the challenges of an entrepreneurial career. I have identified four positive attributes and four negative attributes (which are, to some degree, the opposite of the positive attributes):

Positive Attributes	*Negative Attributes*
Collaboration	Authoritarianism
Cosmopolitanism	Provincialism
Trust	Distrust
Proactiveness	Reactiveness

It is important to note that when I speak of career success, I mean that the entrepreneur is able to handle with some success the personal, family, and business dilemmas that he or she encounters over the span of the career. Looking at only one point in time can give a misleading picture of the career success of an entrepreneur. Some entrepreneurs seem to be quite successful early in their careers even though they have many of the negative attributes listed above. However, I have found that unless entrepreneurs are able to develop at least some of the positive attributes over time, they usually fail at later stages of their careers. For example, entrepreneurs who successfully handle the early-stage issues of balancing work and family, gaining insight into personal problems, and meeting the challenges of a business can still be considered failures if they cannot face dealing with retirement and therefore fail to prepare their businesses and families for a future without them. We will now discuss each of these attributes in greater detail.

Collaboration Versus Authoritarianism

At each stage of the career, entrepreneurs generally find themselves needing to rely on the expertise, resources, or experience of others. Early on in the career, they need to build resource networks, consult family members regarding work and family demands, and develop a good working relationship with partners or other investors. Over time, the entrepreneur will need to become skilled at building a team to run the various facets of the business and create forums such as asset management boards, family councils, and management committees to tackle dilemmas. To accomplish these things requires the entrepreneur to have a *collaborative* orientation. This does not mean that the entrepreneur should allow all employees or family members to participate in decision making, nor does it mean that the entrepreneur must give up control. It does mean that entrepreneurs must be able to recognize when help is needed, use their influence and contacts to get that help, and take advantage of a group setting to help them solve many of their dilemmas. In contrast, many of the entrepreneurs who fail have great difficulty collaborating with others. They have an *authoritarian* orientation. They lead by directing, typically acting alone and failing to consult others.

David McClelland has an apt way of categorizing these two types of entrepreneurs. McClelland believes that there are basically two types of power orientations: personal power and social power.[1] Those who have a personal power orientation enjoy wielding power for their own benefit, often at the expense of others. They get satisfaction from being totally in control. Those with a social power orientation, while they enjoy using power, do so for the benefit of those around them, their families and their organizations. Entrepreneurs with an authoritarian orientation seem to enjoy the personal power of the position and may use that power for personal aggrandizement, with some negative results for those around them, while entrepreneurs with

needs to exercise power for the benefit of their families or organizations are likely to be more collaborative. For example, Roger
Peay and I found that entrepreneurs with high social power needs
prepared their organizations for succession by sharing information, planning, and mentoring successors much more effectively
than did entrepreneurs with high needs for personal power.[2]
If entrepreneurs could live in a vacuum, then collaboration
would not be necessary. However, given the nature of an entrepreneurial career and the demands for collaboration, the more
successful entrepreneurs are those who are able to get others
to help them cope with the career dilemmas that they face.

Cosmopolitanism Versus Provincialism

Entrepreneurs who tend to be successful in their careers are in
a "learning mode" throughout their lives. They are willing to
explore new ideas, issues, and approaches to managing their
businesses, their families, and their personal lives. While still
relying on a set of core values that have helped them succeed,
cosmopolitan entrepreneurs listen to different points of view and
recognize that others may have opinions of value. The entrepreneur who is open to new ideas is comfortable in managing
conflict and is therefore willing to create a variety of forums
where issues can be debated. Indeed, such an entrepreneur might
attempt to encourage conflict rather than discourage differences
of opinion. Kenneth Olsen, founder of Digital Equipment Corporation, is known throughout the company for encouraging
people to "beat on ideas" and challenge themselves and each other
to do whatever is necessary to find the appropriate solution to
a problem. One of the attributes that contributes to Olsen's cosmopolitan orientation is his humility. He recognizes that in a
complex marketplace, no one has the corner on all truth. He
realizes that he does not have all the answers but that if debate
is stimulated, the answers to the company's problems can eventually be found.

    Entrepreneurs with *provincial* attitudes feel that what has
worked well in the past will work well in the future. They tend
to avoid experimenting with new approaches to problems, since

they are uncomfortable with new ideas and situations where they are not in complete control. They also tend to filter data, hearing only what they want to hear, and feel threatened if someone comes up with an idea that is not their own. Given this orientation, provincial entrepreneurs surround themselves with "yes-men." They force their ideas on others and want compliance rather than a thoughtful review of their ideas. Underlying this provincial orientation may be an overactive ego. Pride in one's accomplishments is certainly warranted, but when entrepreneurs' egos become so inflated that they view themselves as infallible, they are often ready for a precipitous fall.

Trust Versus Distrust

Another attribute that seems to characterize successful entrepreneurs is their ability to *trust* others. While entrepreneurs should certainly have a healthy skepticism and should not trust people indiscriminately, they should be able to build trusting relationships with the important people in their lives. Entrepreneurs who can build trust are able to manage many of the career dilemmas much more easily than those who are not able to create such a relationship. They can more easily delegate responsibility to others, they can collaborate more effectively with family members and professional managers, and they are more willing to be open in their communications and share their plans with others. Showing trust in their subordinates enables them to mentor successors effectively and to enhance the self-confidence and self-esteem of those who will lead the business and the family in the future. To trust others requires entrepreneurs to be self-assured and to have confidence in their own abilities.

Entrepreneurs who have a basic *distrust* of others and cannot build trust are always questioning the others' motives. Thus, they tend to believe that they must do it all and closely supervise those who work for them. They tend to be very secretive, rarely sharing their thoughts and plans, and to exercise influence through power strategies or through rumor and innuendo rather than being open about the reasons behind their actions. Such an approach tends to undermine the confidence and self-esteem of those around them and makes them also become distrusting and secretive. In such a climate of distrust, it is difficult if not impossible to build a successful organization. As the time comes for a transfer of power to the next generation, conflict and uncertainty plague company employees and members of the entrepreneur's family.

Proactiveness Versus Reactiveness

A final dimension that we will consider is a *proactive* versus a *reactive* orientation. Those with a proactive orientation learn from the past. They are able to reflect on their own behaviors — their strengths and their weaknesses — and take positive steps to change. Proactive entrepreneurs are future-oriented. They can anticipate changes in the marketplace, their businesses, their families, and themselves and take actions to prevent problems or solve them as they arise. Proactive entrepreneurs not only keep abreast of day-to-day operations but take time to think strategically about the future of their businesses.

Reactive entrepreneurs always seem to be putting out fires. They have little time to reflect on their experiences and make course corrections. They fail to learn from past mistakes. They are often good at solving here-and-now operational problems but fail to plan for future contingencies. With this type of orientation, the entrepreneurial career becomes a kind of frantic race, with all kinds of twists and turns in the road, providing little relief for the overburdened and stress-riddled entrepreneur. Without a vision and a clear plan for the future, the reactive entrepreneur seems always to be moving from one crisis to the next.

Developing the Attributes of Career Success

The attributes discussed above appear to be an integral part of the core personalities of entrepreneurs and thus are not easily changed. They seem to spring from early childhood and family experiences that leave an indelible impression on the entrepreneur. As an entrepreneur meets with career successes, such traits are reinforced, even though the negative traits are likely to have adverse consequences in the future. The self-confidence that can prove so helpful to entrepreneurs can also make it difficult for them to carefully examine themselves and be willing to change.

Few of the entrepreneurs whom I have studied seemed to have made significant changes from the negative attributes to the more positive ones. Those who did often had done so only after a significant event in their lives such as a nearly fatal accident, a serious illness, or the death of someone close to them. In moments of intense frustration when working with entrepreneurs, I have often fantasized about how helpful it would be to give a few of them a near-death experience in order to stimulate them to change. (Unfortunately, I have yet to find an ethical way to carry out such a plan.)

It is difficult to tell an entrepreneur to "be more collaborative" or "stop being distrusting," for such statements are either too vague or too threatening and thus have little impact on the entrepreneur. I have found that entrepreneurs can begin to work on turning these negative attributes into positive ones by focusing on solving the major problems that face them. In attempting to solve these problems, they generally come to realize that their previous way of approaching problems is not very useful and become more willing to reexamine their assumptions about the world. For those entrepreneurs interested in changing their behavior patterns and resolving their career dilemmas, I suggest a number of guidelines: (1) develop a "felt need" to change; (2) seek social support for the change; (3) enlist the help of qualified counselors and consultants as needed; (4) set specific, attainable change goals; and (5) evaluate progress on a regular basis.[3]

Developing a Felt Need to Change

In the absence of an uncontrollable event, such as a near-death experience, that can get entrepreneurs to feel a need to change, I have found that entrepreneurs are often willing to change if they recognize that what they are doing is creating problems for themselves or others; are able to make the needed change; and feel that the change will enhance their self-esteem. Entrepreneurs are generally quite practical people and are willing to explore new approaches to problems if they can see a direct payoff from them. However, if they are to explore new ideas, they must come to an awareness that something is not right. To enhance such awareness, they should develop a set of quantitative and qualitative measures to determine organizational, family, and personal effectiveness. These might include "hard" organizational measures on such factors as productivity and profitability and "soft" measures such as "level of conflict in the family" or "personal stress." By monitoring these measures and by continually getting information from family members and co-workers through interviews, sensing meetings, or even questionnaires, the entrepreneur may become aware of a discrepancy between expectations and results and begin to feel a need to change. As noted in Chapter Twelve, direct confrontation on key issues by family, co-workers, or partners can also create a need for change in the entrepreneur.

Entrepreneurs will resist changing if they feel that change will be difficult or will cause them to lose power and prestige. Thus, entrepreneurs may need to seek help to gain the skills required for change and develop an understanding of how such a change will enhance their self-image. For example, a common problem for some entrepreneurs is their lack of understanding of how computers might help them in their work. Even though they realize that a computer might be useful, they resist implementing computer systems because they do not want to reveal their ignorance. In addition, they fear that implementing such a system might make it more difficult for them to keep financial information confidential. To overcome this problem, entrepreneurs should gain knowledge and skills for using computers before the notion of implementing a computer system is introduced. Entrepreneurs should also understand that there are ways of safeguarding important information and, more important, that being able to gain access to such information quickly will enable them to have more control and make better decisions.

Seeking Social Support for the Change

Several years ago, Gene Dalton of Brigham Young University conducted a study of how organizations such as Alcoholics Anonymous and Weight Watchers get their members to change their behavior.[4] Dalton discovered that one of the key ingredients in a successful change effort is support from people who are highly respected by the person attempting to change. If family members, a boss, a clergyperson, or co-workers support the change efforts, the change is more likely to be successful and to persist.

As we have seen, entrepreneurs' families, employees, and partners may not always be supportive of their efforts to plan for succession or engage in activities that would take them away from the business. This lack of support undermines entrepreneurs' efforts to change. Thus, before beginning any change effort, entrepreneurs need to communicate their goals to those whose support is needed to help them change their behavior. Once this is done, those supporting the entrepreneurs need to actively encourage them to achieve those goals.

Enlisting the Help of Consultants and Counselors

Many change goals require entrepreneurs to gain new skills and information. For example, they may need to improve their communications skills, increase their understanding of strategic planning, or acquire technical information to help them develop an estate plan. To do this may require the help of experts — accountants, lawyers, psychologists, family therapists.

The consultant or counselor can help entrepreneurs select the type of information, training, or experiences that will be needed to help them change. This is generally a function of the kinds of problems that the entrepreneur faces. Personal and relationship problems generally take more time to solve and require more effort and consultation than do day-to-day operations problems. For example, entrepreneurs and their families may need to be involved in a long-term counseling relationship if the problems are deep and difficult to solve quickly. On the other hand, they may be able to get all the legal help they need from their lawyers in one afternoon. Even if the entrepreneur feels well in control of the problems, it could still be useful to have a sounding board of experts to bounce ideas off of and to periodically get input from regarding progress in achieving certain personal, family, or organizational goals.

Finding the right consultant is not an easy task for the entrepreneur. Below are some general guidelines to follow when looking for one.

Identify the Type of Consultant Needed. This requires the entrepreneur to articulate whether the problem is personal, family-related, business-related, or some combination. For example, do not call in a business consultant if the real problems are related to the dynamics of the family.

Engage in a Broad Search for the Right Consultant. This requires the entrepreneur to gather data about possible consultants from such resources as the small business development centers located across the United States, professional associations such as the Family Firm Institute, industry associations, and local networks such as chambers of commerce. Entrepreneurs should use these resources as well as their own networks to identify potential consultants.

Get References. After identifying several potential candidates, contact each of them, explain the general nature of the problem that you are confronting, ask them their fee schedule, and ask them for the names of entrepreneurs with whom they have worked in the past. Call these entrepreneurs to find out how effective the consultants are.

Ask for a Presentation. Ask the consultants who seem to fit your needs to make a presentation to yourself and others whose support may be needed. Determine whether they are addressing your needs and are clear about their theory and method of consulting. Ask them pointed questions to test their knowledge and skill.

Choose a Consultant with Whom You Feel Comfortable. In any consultant-client relationship, the client must trust and have faith in the consultant. Thus, rather than choosing a consultant merely on the basis of reputation or presentation, entrepreneurs should choose someone with whom they feel they can work and have a comfortable relationship.

Be Creative in Negotiating Fees. The founder of a new business is not likely to have great resources to pay large consulting fees, so payment in company stock, the use of company products or resources, or a percentage of the profits may be the only options available to a struggling entrepreneur. Generally, you do get what you pay for, so the entrepreneur needs to be creative to afford good consulting help.

Set Specific, Attainable Goals

Change efforts often fail because people do not set specific goals for themselves. A person who wants to lose weight must set a goal of following a certain diet and losing a certain amount of weight each day or week. A smoker who wants to quit must set up a specific timetable for quitting altogether or cutting down on the number of cigarettes smoked per day. The goals must be realistic. The person who is one hundred pounds overweight is likely to be discouraged if he or she sets a goal of losing the entire one hundred pounds in one month — and if such a goal were achieved, severe health problems would likely result.

Like people who want to lose weight or quit smoking, entrepreneurs who want to change must also develop specific goals — setting up an effective board of directors, improving the resource network, creating a family council, developing an organization chart with job descriptions, or creating an estate and succession plan. For each goal, they should outline a specific set of activities and a timetable for accomplishing them. Some entrepreneurs never get around to doing succession planning because they fail to set up a timetable. They recognize the need for a plan but are unwilling to set specific dates and times to accomplish the various tasks involved in such planning. Thus, they continually frustrate themselves and others by their procrastination.

Evaluate Progress Regularly

Once the entrepreneur has felt the need to change, has gained support and expertise, and has set specific goals, the next step is to implement the change plan and track progress. Entrepreneurs should meet periodically with those supporting the change effort to review progress and set new goals if needed. As they review their progress toward specific goals, they should also begin to ask themselves questions that focus on the attributes of success: Am I able to collaborate with others and use groups effectively? Do I listen more and dictate less? Do I take other's opinions into account more readily? Do I seek new approaches to solving problems? Am I building trust with my family and those I work with? Do I share my ideas and plans with others? Do I delegate responsibilities when possible? Do I actively seek to solve problems before they arise? How good am I at anticipating the future needs of myself, my business, and my family? A regular assessment of progress toward developing a more effective set of assumptions for confronting the problems of an entrepreneurial career, including the mundane day-to-day problems, will help entrepreneurs to achieve their goals and make course corrections when necessary.

What's Next? Entrepreneurship in the Twenty-First Century

The nature of the world's global economy will continue to encourage entrepreneurial activity well into the next century. New markets will continue to expand in such areas as Eastern Europe, Latin America, the Middle East, Africa, and China, and this will create opportunities for entrepreneurs with vision. Entrepreneurs with ideas for new products and new technologies will continue to shape the international marketplace. As large organizations are forced to shed their bureaucratic ways and become more flexible to stay competitive, we are likely to see them sponsoring employees with entrepreneurial tendencies in starting new businesses under the corporate umbrella and entering into a variety of joint ventures with entrepreneurs. Thus, the future is bright for those who have the ability and determination to succeed as entrepreneurs.

Despite these opportunities to enjoy the benefits of an entrepreneurial career, the dilemmas and problems that have been discussed in previous chapters are likely to continue and may become even more difficult to overcome. Entrepreneurs just launching their careers may find it even more difficult to find the needed resources — particularly capital and personnel — to help them succeed in what will be an increasingly complex and competitive environment. More financial partners and joint venture arrangements may be needed to ensure the success of a new venture, thus increasing the difficulty and complexity of managing partnership relationships. Furthermore, the time and energy required to develop new markets and technologies will put an additional strain on the entrepreneur's family life, thus increasing the likelihood of marital discord, estrangement from one's children, and divorce.

Entrepreneurs in midcareer may find the complexities of managing a growing business almost overwhelming in the twenty-first century. Team building, delegating, and finding competent professionals will continue to be important. The entrepreneur will continue to need to develop ways to cope with the pressures of the job and avoid feelings of loneliness and isolation. Developing a control system that allows the entrepreneur to oversee operations will become more critical as entrepreneurial organizations span the globe. Working with family members will still remain a thorn in the side of many entrepreneurs.

Late career issues of retirement, estate planning, and succession will also have to be dealt with by entrepreneurs in the next century. Given that entrepreneurs are likely to live longer in the twenty-first century, we might find many of them running their organizations well into their eighties or even nineties. This would have significant implications for their successors, particularly if they are the children of the entrepreneurs, since many will not want to wait until they are sixty years old to take over the business. Thus, entrepreneurs will need to be creative in devising ways to allow the next generation of leaders to develop themselves and have an influence on the business while maintaining a meaningful role for themselves well into their later years. New tax laws and estate planning options will require entrepreneurs to be well informed to protect their families' assets.

Conclusion

What will be needed in the future will be "enlightened entrepreneurs" who not only have a vision for their respective businesses but also have a good understanding of themselves and their families' needs. They must be able to reflect on and learn from the past, and they must be willing to explore new ways of managing their worlds. Interpersonal communications skills, the ability to build a team, and the ability to handle conflict are a few of the core skills that will be required for an entrepreneur to succeed in the future. The attributes of success discussed in this chapter will become even more critical in the twenty-first century.

Virtually none of the entrepreneurs whom we studied would trade their careers for another—they had built successful businesses, developed new products, created new jobs. However, many had still not achieved career success and personal satisfaction, for they were still struggling with some of the dilemmas that have been discussed in this book. Indeed, they will not know whether they have succeeded until they can look back on their careers and review how successfully they handled all the dilemmas that they faced. It is my hope that they will gain the necessary wisdom and skills to help them resolve these dilemmas as they go through the entrepreneurial experience.

RESOURCE

INTERVIEW QUESTIONS

These questions reflect the issues that were explored in our in-depth interviews with entrepreneurs. We also attempted to answer these questions while analyzing the case histories of entrepreneurs.

Entrepreneurial Identity

What was your experience prior to starting your own business?

What were the conditions that led you to go into business for yourself?

What were the issues that you considered when deciding on an entrepreneurial career? Which of these gave you the greatest concern? How did you resolve these issues?

How did you decide on what field you would enter when starting on your own?

What role did your spouse and family play in your becoming an entrepreneur?

What training or experience did you have that led you to believe that you could make it as an entrepreneur? Was that experience actually as relevant to the venture as you expected when you started?

What do you see as the best and worst reasons for becoming an entrepreneur?

What do you see as the most important skills or attributes contributing to entrepreneurial success?

If a friend came to you seeking advice about whether to start a business or pursue more traditional employment, what advice would you give him or her?

Obtaining Resources

What resources are necessary when starting a business? Which are essential, and which could you do without in a crunch?

242

How did you raise start-up capital? Would you use the same means if you were starting today?

Did you take any action regarding start-up financing that you or others might consider unique?

Many entrepreneurs are unwilling to deal with venture capitalists, others view them as a necessary evil, and still others are very comfortable with venture capital arrangements. What are your feelings about using outside venture capital — the pros, the cons, the trade-offs?

Did you have partners, technical advisers, or managerial people on whom you relied in the early stages? If so, how did you go about identifying people to fill these roles?

How did you go about finding employees who you believed could really contribute to your business? How did you compensate and reward them?

Were there ever times when your efforts required exceptional demands of your employees (payroll crunches, long hours, and so on)?

In the early days, how did you go about identifying and developing markets for your product or service? How would you do it if you were starting over?

Having networks and appropriate support systems seems to be important in the early days of a business. What networks did you have in the financial world or in the industry? How did you develop those relationships?

What was the most serious business challenge you faced as you launched your business, and how did you deal with it? Would you handle it the same way now? What would you do to avoid the cause of this problem?

Organizing the Business

How would you recommend that a new venture be organized in terms of structure, information and accounting systems, rewards, and so on?

How important is it for an entrepreneur to have a business plan and an organization that promotes that plan? How do you go about getting alignment between the business plan and the organization?

Describe the organization of your business when you started out. How has it changed over the years? What would you change in this regard if you were starting again?

What is the governance structure of your business (type of organization, such as proprietorship or corporation; composition of the board; and so on)?

What is the distribution of ownership of your company? How did you determine who should have equity? How much equity are you willing to part with?

What is the decision-making process relative to partners, employees, directors, outside advisers?

If you have a partner or partners, how do you manage the partnership? How are responsibilities divided among you?

Do you have a buy-sell agreement? Can you give an example of how you and your partner have resolved differences in the past?

Family Issues: Personal Aspects

How has your choice of an entrepreneurial career affected your relationships with your spouse and children?

Having an entrepreneur in the family can be quite stressful. What has been your experience in this regard, and what have you done to make it easier for your family?

What has been your greatest challenge in balancing your career and your family obligations? How did you manage it?

Was there a time in your family's development when being an entrepreneur was particularly difficult?

Was there a time in your company's development when it was particularly difficult to be effectively involved in your family's activities?

Family Issues: Business Aspects

What roles do family members now play in the business?

What arrangements have you made for the entry of family members into the business?

Do you hope or expect that one of your children will succeed
you in leadership of the company? If so, what are you doing
to groom him or her for leadership? Have you established
a succession plan? Is that plan known to management?

Do family members now hold any stock in the company? If so,
how did you determine the distribution of stock? What are
the conditions of owning stock? How is the stock vested?

Do you have any special arrangements, such as family board
members or a family advisory board, that help to protect family interests in the company?

Team Building and Delegation

Entrepreneurs are usually the center of their organizations, often
handling a large part of daily operations. What actions have
you taken to concentrate your efforts on the big issues and
leave some of the other responsibilities to others in the organization?

What have you done to build a management team that is capable of sharing the responsibility?

How do you get your management team to delegate effectively?

What do you believe are the most important issues regarding
team building and delegation?

Formalizing Business Operations

How important is it to you that business practices are formalized or rationalized?

In which areas of the business is it most necessary to implement
formal procedures and controls?

As your business has grown, what business practices have you
introduced, and how have you done so?

How do you effectively balance the necessary controls of sound
business with the flexibility that so often gives smaller, less
formal businesses their competitive edge?

What are your feelings about professionalizing management?
Have you brought in outsiders, developed your own people,
and so on? What has been your experience in this regard?

Sharing the Vision: Socialization

Most entrepreneurs have a fairly clear vision of what they want
to make of their company. How do you instill that vision in
your employees (for example, speeches, awards, newsletter)?
What do you look for in new hires? How do you screen them?
Do your new hires go through any special training to bring them
up to speed?
What would you do with an employee who did not seem to catch
the vision and accept the values that you are trying to promote in your organization?

Managing Change

Anticipating and adjusting to a changing business environment
are among the great challenges of the owner-manager. What
are some of the changes that you have had to make in your
company, and how have you managed them?
Do you have a particular process for introducing changes? What
is that process?
Have you attempted to implement any changes that just did not
take hold? In retrospect, what do you think kept these changes
from being successfully implemented?

Coping with the Responsibilities of Wealth

Founding a successful venture often results in a considerable
financial windfall for the entrepreneur. Have you experienced
any unexpected responsibilities pertaining to this?
Has your financial position had any implications for how you
raised or are raising your children? What is your philosophy
toward your family and money?
Is it important to you that your wealth be preserved and passed
on to family or others? Do you have any mechanisms in place
(for example, trust funds) to promote this end?
Do you currently contribute to any charitable causes? What are
your preferences in taking on charitable obligations? Do you
have a philosophy about how much your wealth should be
used to benefit community, industry, church, and so on?

Succession Planning and Retirement

Do you expect that your business will outlast your active involvement? How do you foresee your exit from the company taking place (sell-out, successor, and so on)?

Do you have a succession plan in place? Who is likely to succeed you? Does your management team and/or board know your plan?

How are you preparing your organization for the time when you will take a less active role in operations?

What will you do if and when you decide to withdraw from activity in the company?

Will you ever retire?

Do you have friends or associates who have retired from entrepreneurial activity? How did they manage the transition?

NOTES

Preface

1. Dyer, W. G., Jr. "Culture in Organizations: A Case Study and Analysis." Working paper 1279–82, Sloan School of Management, Massachusetts Institute of Technology, Feb. 1982; Dyer, W. G., Jr., and Page, R. A., Jr. "The Politics of Innovation." *Knowledge in Society*, 1988, *1*(2), 23–41; Dyer, W. G., Jr., and Lucero, D. "Crystalazer (A)(B)(C)." Unpublished case study, Brigham Young University, 1988; Meek, C., Woodworth, W. W., and Dyer, W. G., Jr. *Managing by the Numbers: Absentee Owners and the Decline of American Industry*. Reading, Mass.: Addison-Wesley, 1988.

Introduction

1. Birch, D. L. "The Truth About Start-Ups." *INC.*, Jan. 1988, p. 14.
2. Meek, C., Woodworth, W., and Dyer, W. G., Jr. *Managing by the Numbers: Absentee Owners and the Decline of American Industry*. Reading, Mass.: Addison-Wesley, 1988.
3. Bird, B. J. *Entrepreneurial Behavior*. Glenview, Ill.: Scott, Foresman, 1989.
4. Bird, *Entrepreneurial Behavior*.
5. Goffman, E. "The Moral Career of the Mental Patient." In E. Goffman, *Asylums*. New York: Anchor Books, 1961, p. 127.

6. Schein, E. H. *Career Dynamics: Matching Individual and Organizational Needs.* Reading, Mass.: Addison-Wesley, 1978.

7. Goffman, "The Moral Career of the Mental Patient," p. 127.

8. Arthur, M. B., Hall, D. T., and Lawrence, B. S. (eds.). *Handbook of Career Theory.* Cambridge, England: Cambridge University Press, 1989.

9. Kotkin, J. "The Reluctant Entrepreneurs." *INC.,* Sept. 1986, pp. 81–86.

10. Birley, S. "Female Entrepreneurs: Are They Really Different?" *Journal of Small Business Management,* 1989, *27*(1), 37.

Chapter One

1. Kilby, P. "Hunting the Heffalump." In P. Kilby (ed.), *Entrepreneurship and Economic Development.* New York: Free Press, 1971.

2. See Schumpeter, J. A. *The Theory of Economic Development.* New York: Oxford University Press, 1961.

3. Dalton, G. W., and Holdaway, F. "Preliminary Findings — Entrepreneur Study." Working paper, Brigham Young University, 1989.

4. Stevenson, H. H. "General Management and Entrepreneurship." Working paper, Harvard University, 1987.

5. Cunniff, J. "Entrepreneurs Survive by Ignoring Realities." *Salt Lake City Tribune,* Feb. 7, 1988, p. F7.

6. Ronstadt, R. "Does Entrepreneurial Career Path Really Matter?" In K. H. Vesper (ed.), *Frontiers of Entrepreneurship Research.* Babson Park, Mass.: Babson College, 1982, pp. 540–567.

7. Ronstadt, "Does Entrepreneurial Career Path Really Matter?" p. 542.

8. O'Brien, R. *Marriott: The J. Willard Marriott Story.* Salt Lake City, Utah: Deseret Book, 1987.

9. See Kets de Vries, M.F.R. "The Entrepreneurial Personality: A Person at the Crossroads." *Journal of Management Studies,* 1977, *14,* 34–57; Kets de Vries, M.F.R. "The Dark Side of Entrepreneurship." *Harvard Business Review,* Nov.–Dec. 1985, pp. 160–167.

10. Kets de Vries, "The Entrepreneurial Personality," pp. 35–36.
11. Kets de Vries, "The Entrepreneurial Personality," p. 51.
12. Lynn, R. "Personality Characteristics of a Group of Entrepreneurs." *Occupational Psychology,* 1969, *43,* 151–152.
13. Boyd, D. P., and Gumpert, D. E. "The Effects of Stress on Early Age Entrepreneurs." In J. A. Hornaday, J. A. Timmons, and K. H. Vesper (eds.), *Frontiers of Entrepreneurship Research.* Babson Park, Mass.: Babson College, 1983, pp. 180–191.
14. Cooper, A. C. *The Founding of Technologically Based Firms.* Milwaukee, Wis.: Center for Venture Management, 1971.
15. Roberts, E. B. "The Personality and Motivations of Technological Entrepreneurs." *Journal of Engineering and Technology Management,* 1989, *6*(1), 5–23.
16. McClelland, D. E. *The Achieving Society.* New York: Van Nostrand Reinhold, 1961.
17. Kotkin, J. "The Reluctant Entrepreneurs." *INC.,* Sept. 1986, pp. 81–86.
18. Schein, E. H. *Career Anchors: Discovering Your Real Values.* San Diego, Calif.: University Associates, 1990.
19. Case, J. "The Origins of Entrepreneurship." *INC.,* June 1989, pp. 51, 52.

Chapter Two

1. Timmons, J. A. *New Venture Creation.* Homewood, Ill.: Irwin, 1990.
2. Stevenson, L. "Toward Understanding Young Founders." In N. C. Churchill, J. A. Hornaday, B. A. Kirchhoff, O. J. Krasner, and K. H. Vesper (eds.), *Frontiers of Entrepreneurship Research.* Babson Park, Mass.: Babson College, 1987, pp. 275–288.
3. Clarke, D. G., Dalton, G. W., Dyer, G. W., Jr., and Wilkins, A. L. "High Tech Business in Utah Valley." Multidisciplinary study for the Utah Technology Finance Corporation, 1989.
4. South, S. E. "Competitive Advantage: The Cornerstone of Strategic Thinking." *Journal of Business Strategy,* 1981, *1*(4), 15–25.

5. Clarke, Dalton, Dyer, and Wilkins, "High Tech Business in Utah Valley."

6. MacPhee, W. *Rare Breed: The Entrepreneur, an American Culture.* Chicago: Probus, 1987, pp. 193–194.

7. MacPhee, *Rare Breed,* p. 189.

8. Kuratko, D. F., and Cirtin, A. "Developing a Business Plan for Your Clients." *National Public Accountant,* Jan. 1990, pp. 25–26.

9. Ward, J. L., personal communication, 1991.

10. Kotkin, J. "The Reluctant Entrepreneurs." *INC.,* Sept. 1986, pp. 81–86.

11. Clarke, Dalton, Dyer, and Wilkins, "High Tech Business in Utah Valley."

12. Aldrich, H., Rosen, B., and Woodward, W. "The Impact of Social Networks on Business Founding and Profit: A Longitudinal Study." In R. Ronstadt, J. A. Hornaday, R. Peterson, and K. H. Vesper (eds.), *Frontiers of Entrepreneurship Research.* Babson Park, Mass.: Babson College, 1986, pp. 154–168.

13. Birley,S. "The Role of Networks in the Entrepreneurial Process." In J. A. Hornaday, E. B. Shils, J. A. Timmons, and K. H. Vesper (eds.), *Frontiers of Entrepreneurship Research.* Babson Park, Mass.: Babson College, 1985, pp. 325–337.

14. Case, J. "The Origins of Entrepreneurship." *INC.,* June 1989, p. 51.

15. Chambers, B. R., Hart, S. L., and Denison, D. R. "Founding Team Experience and New Firm Performance." In B. A. Kirchhoff, W. A. Long, W. E. McMullan, K. H. Vesper, and W. E. Wetzel, Jr. (eds.), *Frontiers of Entrepreneurship Research.* Babson Park, Mass.: Babson College, 1988, pp. 106–118.

16. Egge, K. A., and Simer, F. J. "An Analysis of the Advice Given by Recent Entrepreneurs to Prospective Entrepreneurs." In B. A. Kirchhoff, W. A. Long, W. E. McMullan, K. H. Vesper, and W. E. Wetzel, Jr. (eds.), *Frontiers of Entrepreneurship Research.* Babson Park, Mass.: Babson College, 1988, pp. 119–133.

17. Hyatt, J. "Rewriting the Book on Entrepreneurship." *INC.,* Aug. 1989, pp. 86–93.
18. Hyatt, "Rewriting the Book on Entrepreneurship," p. 88.

Chapter Three

1. Welles, E. O. "BLOWUP: The Saga of a Partnership Gone Bad." *Inc.,* May 1989, p. 63.
2. Welles, "BLOWUP," p. 78.
3. Moore, H. L. "Breaking Up Is Hard to Do." *Dun and Bradstreet Reports,* July–Aug. 1988, pp. 38–41.
4. Moore, "Breaking Up Is Hard to Do," p. 40.
5. Moore, "Breaking Up Is Hard to Do," p. 40.
6. Connelly, M. "The Price for Venture Capital May Be Founder's Departure." *Wall Street Journal,* June 24, 1985, p. 21.
7. For a more detailed account, see Dyer, W. G., Jr. "Ownership Structure as a Context for the Development and Change of Organizational Cultures." Working paper, Brigham Young University, 1990.
8. Blackman, I. L. "Pro's and Con's of S Corporations." *National Petroleum News,* Nov. 1988, p. 72; Brewerton, J. L., and Rifkin, S. G. "The S-Corp: Is It the Best Structure for Your Company?" *Colorado Business Magazine,* May 1988, pp. 85–86; Joyner, J. "Subchapter 'S' Election: The Pros and Cons." *National Underwriter Life & Health-Financial Services,* Jan. 11, 1988, pp. 21–25; Rutman, G. "Should You Go Corporate?" *Nation's Business,* May 1990, pp. 46–48.
9. Blotnick, S. "Two for the Money." *Forbes,* Feb. 23, 1987, p. 166.
10. Dyer, W. G., Jr. *Cultural Change in Family Firms: Anticipating and Managing Business and Family Transitions.* San Francisco: Jossey-Bass, 1986.
11. Dyer, *Cultural Change in Family Firms,* p. 38.
12. Ward, J. L., and Handy, J. L. "A Survey of Board Practices." *Family Business Review,* 1988, *1*(3), 289–308.
13. Jonovic, D. J. "Outside Review in a Wider Context: An Alternative to the Classic Board." *Family Business Review,* 1989, *2*(2), 125–140.

14. Ward and Handy, "A Survey of Board Practices," pp. 289–308.
15. Lang, N. "3-Man Teams Help Partners Settle Disputes." *Sporting Goods Business,* Feb. 1987, pp. 12–13; O'Toole, P. "Choosing a Perfect Partner." *Savvy,* Jan. 1982, pp. 61–72; Stoffman, D. "Parting Ways." *Canadian Business,* Sept. 1987, pp. 157–161.
16. Lang, "3-Man Teams Help Partners Settle Disputes," p. 12.

Chapter Four

1. Ronstadt, R. "Ex-Entrepreneurs and Their Decision to Start an Entrepreneurial Career." In J. A. Hornaday, F. Tarpley, Jr., J. A. Timmons, and K. A. Vesper (eds.), *Frontiers of Entrepreneurial Research.* Babson Park, Mass.: Babson College, 1987, pp. 437–460.
2. Boyd, D. P., and Gumpert, D. E. "The Effects of Stress on Early Age Entrepreneurs." In J. A. Hornaday, J. A. Timmons, and K. H. Vesper (eds.), *Frontiers of Entrepreneurship Research.* Babson Park, Mass.: Babson College, 1983, pp. 180–191.
3. Thomas, B. *Walt Disney: An American Original.* New York: Pocket Books, 1976.
4. Boyd and Gumpert, "The Effects of Stress on Early Age Entrepreneurs."
5. MacPhee, W. *Rare Breed: The Entrepreneur, an American Culture.* Chicago: Probus, 1987, p. 199.
6. MacPhee, *Rare Breed,* p. 64.
7. Stinnett and DeFrain, *The Secrets of Strong Families.* Boston: Little, Brown, 1985.
8. Stinnett and DeFrain, *The Secrets of Strong Families,* p. 14.
9. Brenner, M. *House of Dreams.* New York: Random House, 1988.
10. Boyd and Gumpert, "The Effects of Stress on Early Age Entrepreneurs."
11. Blum, R. H., and Associates. *Horatio Alger's Children: The Role of the Family in the Origin and Prevention of Drug Risk.* San Francisco: Jossey-Bass, 1972.

12. Stinnett and DeFrain, *The Secrets of Strong Families,* p. 101.
13. Peck, M. S. *The Road Less Traveled: The Psychology of Spiritual Growth.* New York: Simon & Schuster, 1978.
14. Hansen, D. "Personal and Positional Influence in Formal Groups: Propositions and Theory for Research on Family Vulnerability to Stress." *Social Forces,* 1965, *44,* pp. 202–210.
15. Dyer, W. G., and Kunz, P. H. *Effective Mormon Families: How They See Themselves.* Salt Lake City, Utah: Deseret Book, 1986, p. 198.
16. Whetten, D. A., and Cameron, K. S. *Developing Management Skills.* Glenview, Ill.: Scott, Foresman, 1984.

Chapter Five

1. Boyd, D. P., and Gumpert, D. E. "The Loneliness of the Start-Up Entrepreneur." In J. A. Hornaday, F. Tarpley, Jr., J. A. Timmons, and K. H. Vesper (eds.), *Frontiers of Entrepreneurship Research.* Babson Park, Mass.: Babson College, 1984, pp. 478–487.
2. MacPhee, W. *Rare Breed: The Entrepreneur, an American Culture.* Chicago: Probus, 1987, p. 210.
3. MacPhee, *Rare Breed,* p. 210.
4. Cray, E. *Levi's.* Boston: Houghton Mifflin, 1978, p. 185.
5. Bernstein, P. W. "Atari and the Video-Game Explosion." *Fortune,* July 27, 1981, pp. 40–46.
6. "From Atari to Androbot." *Newsweek,* Nov. 15, 1982, p. 123.
7. MacPhee, *Rare Breed,* p. 211.
8. MacPhee, *Rare Breed,* p. 211.
9. Beckhard, R., and Harris, R. T. *Organizational Transitions: Managing Complex Change.* Reading, Mass.: Addison-Wesley, 1977.
10. Block, P. *The Empowered Manager: Positive Political Skills at Work.* San Francisco: Jossey-Bass, 1987.
11. Dyer, W. G., and Dyer, W. G., Jr. "Organization Development: System Change or Culture Change?" *Personnel,* Feb. 1986, pp. 14–22.
12. Littman, J. *Once upon a Time in Computerland.* Los Angeles: Price, Stern, Sloan, 1987.

13. Kanai, T. "Entrepreneurial Networking: A Comparative Analysis of Networking Organizations and Their Participants in an Entrepreneurial Community." Unpublished doctoral dissertation, Sloan School of Management, Massachusetts Institute of Technology, 1989, p. 137.
14. Kanai, "Entrepreneurial Networking," p. 191.

Chapter Six

1. Perrow, C. *Complex Organizations: A Critical Essay.* (2nd ed.) Glenview, Ill.: Scott, Foresman, 1979.
2. House, R. "A 1976 Theory of Charismatic Leadership." In J. G. Hunt and L. L. Larson (eds.), *Leadership: The Cutting Edge.* Carbondale: Southern Illinois Press, 1977, p. 194.
3. Wilkins, A. L., and Ouchi, W. G. "Efficient Cultures: Exploring the Relationship Between Culture and Organizational Performance." *Administrative Science Quarterly,* 1983, *28,* 468–481.
4. Gustin, L. R. *Billy Durant: Creator of General Motors.* Grand Rapids, Mich.: Eardman, 1973.
5. Lawrence, P. R., and Lorsch, J. W. *Organization and Environment: Managing Differentiation and Integration.* Homewood, Ill.: Irwin, 1967.
6. Galbraith, J. R. *Organization Design.* Reading, Mass.: Addison-Wesley, 1977.
7. MacPhee, W. *Rare Breed: The Entrepreneur, an American Culture.* Chicago: Probus, 1987, p. 97.
8. Hackman, J. R. "Designing Work for Individuals and for Groups." In J. R. Hackman, E. E. Lawler, and L. W. Porter (eds.), *Perspectives on Behavior in Organizations.* New York: McGraw-Hill, 1977, pp. 242–256.
9. Allyn, S. C. *My Half Century with NCR.* New York: McGraw-Hill, 1967, pp. 146–147.

Chapter Seven

1. Crowther, S. *John H. Patterson: Pioneer in Industrial Welfare.* New York: Doubleday, 1929, p. 29.

2. Hayes, R. H., and Abernathy, W. J. "Managing Our Way to Economic Decline." *Harvard Business Review*, 1980, *58*, 66–77; Chandler, A. D., Jr. *The Visible Hand.* Cambridge, Mass.: Harvard University Press, 1977; Meek, C., Woodworth, W. W., and Dyer, W. G., Jr. *Managing by the Numbers: Absentee Owners and the Decline in American Industry.* Reading, Mass.: Addison-Wesley, 1988.

3. See Schein, E. H. "Organizational Socialization and the Profession of Management." *Industrial Management Review*, 1968, *9*, 80–88.

4. Meek, Woodworth, and Dyer, *Managing by the Numbers.*

5. Meek, Woodworth, and Dyer, *Managing by the Numbers;* Hayes and Abernathy, "Managing Our Way to Economic Decline."

6. See Lansberg, I. "Managing Human Resources in Family Firms: The Problem of Institutional Overlap." *Organizational Dynamics*, 1983, *12(1)*, 39–46.

7. Schein, E. H. "The Role of the Founder in Creating Organizational Cultures." *Organizational Dynamics*, 1983, *12* (1), 13–28.

8. Meek, Woodworth, and Dyer, *Managing by the Numbers.*

9. Van Maanen, J., and Schein, E. H. "Toward a Theory of Organizational Socialization." In B. Staw (ed.), *Research in Organizational Behavior.* Vol. 1. Greenwich, Conn.: JAI Press, 1979.

10. White, R. N. "The Organizational Context of Professional Socialization: A Case Study of Two Business Schools." Paper presented at the annual meeting of the American Sociological Association, Chicago, 1977.

11. Schein, E. H. "The First Job Dilemma: An Appraisal of Why College Graduates Change Jobs and What Can Be Done About It." In J. B. Ritchie and P. H. Thompson (eds.), *Organization and People.* St. Paul, Minn.: West, 1976.

12. Dyer, W. G., and Nyman, M. "Succession in a Small Company." Unpublished case study, Brigham Young University, 1987.

13. Dyer, W. G., Jr. *Cultural Change in Family Firms: Anticipating and Managing Business and Family Transitions.* San Francisco: Jossey-Bass, 1986.

14. Dyer, *Cultural Change in Family Firms.*
15. Dyer, *Cultural Change in Family Firms.*
16. Warner, W. L., and Low, J. O. *The Social System of the Modern Factory.* New Haven, Conn.: Yale University Press, 1947.
17. Meek, Woodworth, and Dyer, *Managing by the Numbers.*
18. Dyer, *Cultural Change in Family Firms.*

Chapter Eight

1. Toy, S. "A New Generation Takes the Wheel at U-Haul." *Businessweek,* Mar. 28, 1988, p. 57.
2. "U-Haul Meeting Erupts into a Family Fistfight." *Deseret News,* Mar. 6, 1989, p. D5.
3. Rosenblatt, P. C., de Mik, L., Anderson, R. M., and Johnson, P. A. *The Family in Business: Understanding and Dealing with the Challenges Entrepreneurial Families Face.* San Francisco: Jossey-Bass, 1985, p. 82.
4. Dyer, W. G., Jr. *Cultural Change in Family Firms: Anticipating and Managing Business and Family Transactions.* San Francisco: Jossey-Bass, 1986; Dyer, W. G. "A Comparison of Family and Business Systems." Conference notes, Brigham Young University Family Business Conference, 1988.
5. Beckhard, R., and Dyer, W. G., Jr. "Challenges and Issues in Managing Family Firms." Working paper 1188–81, Sloan School of Management, Massachusetts Institute of Technology, 1981.
6. Rosenblatt, de Mik, Anderson, and Johnson, *The Family in Business,* p. 21.
7. Beckhard, R., and Dyer, W. G., Jr. "Managing Continuity in the Family-Owned Business." *Organizational Dynamics,* Summer 1983, pp. 5–12.
8. Rosenblatt, de Mik, Anderson, and Johnson, *The Family in Business,* pp. 236–237.

Chapter Nine

1. Cray, E. *Levi's.* Boston: Houghton Mifflin, 1978.
2. Duffy, P. B., and Stevenson, H. H. "Entrepreneurship and Self Employment: Understanding the Distinctions." In J. A. Hornaday, F. Tarpley, Jr., J. A. Timmons, and

K. A. Vesper (eds.), *Frontiers of Entrepreneurship Research.* Babson Park, Mass.: Babson College, 1984, pp. 461–477.
3. Beckhard, R., and Dyer, W. G., Jr. "SMR Forum: Managing Change in the Family Firm—Issues and Strategies." *Sloan Management Review,* 1983, *24*(3), 60–61.
4. Kübler-Ross, E. *On Death and Dying.* New York: Macmillan, 1969.
5. Erikson, E. H. *Identity and the Life Cycle.* New York: International Universities Press, 1959.
6. Schein, E. H. *Career Dynamics: Matching Individual and Organizational Needs.* Reading, Mass.: Addison-Wesley, 1978.
7. Lansberg, I. "The Succession Conspiracy." *Family Business Review,* 1988, *1*(2), pp. 119–143.
8. Lansberg, "The Succession Conspiracy."
9. Meek, C., Woodworth, W., and Dyer, W. G., Jr. *Managing by the Numbers: Absentee Owners and the Decline of American Industry.* Reading, Mass.: Addison-Wesley, 1988.

Chapter Ten

1. Trow, D. B. "Executive Succession in Small Companies." *Administrative Science Quarterly,* Sept. 1961, pp. 228–239.
2. Paisner, M. "Myths About Succession." *INC.,* Oct. 1986, pp. 146–147.
3. Blotnick, S. "The Case of the Reluctant Heirs." *Forbes,* July 16, 1984, p. 180.
4. Blotnick, "The Case of the Reluctant Heirs."
5. Brown, B. "Succession Strategies for Family Firms." *Wall Street Journal,* Aug. 4, 1988, p. 19.
6. Dyer, W. G. *Contemporary Issues in Management and Organizational Development.* Reading, Mass.: Addison-Wesley, 1983.
7. Wilkins, A. L. *Developing Corporate Character: How to Successfully Change an Organization Without Destroying It.* San Francisco: Jossey-Bass, 1989.
8. Poza, E. J. *Smart Growth: Critical Choices for Business Continuity and Prosperity.* San Francisco: Jossey-Bass, 1989.
9. Schein, E. H. "The Role of the Founder in Creating Organizational Culture." *Organizational Dynamics,* 1983, *12*(1), 13–28.

Chapter Eleven

1. Lewis, M. B. "Surviving Quarterback of the Estate Planning Team." *Trusts and Estates,* Oct. 1978, p. 694.
2. Rosenblatt, P. C., de Mik, L., Anderson, R. M., and Johnson, P. A. *The Family in Business: Understanding and Dealing with the Challenges Entrepreneurial Families Face.* San Francisco: Jossey-Bass, 1985, p. 192.
3. "Adam Smith's Money World," PBS Broadcast, Sept. 29, 1990.
4. Dyer, W. G., Jr. *Cultural Change in Family Firms: Anticipating and Managing Business and Family Transitions.* San Francisco: Jossey-Bass, 1986, pp. 82–83.
5. Rosenblatt, de Mik, Anderson, and Johnson, *The Family in Business,* pp. 192–193.
6. Posner, B. G. "In Search of Equity." *INC.,* 1985, *7*(4), p. 55.
7. O'Brien, R. *Marriott.* Salt Lake City, Utah: Deseret Book, 1987, pp. 265–267.
8. Dyer, *Cultural Change in Family Firms.*
9. See *Family Business Review,* 1990, *3*(4), for several articles regarding family foundations.

Chapter Twelve

1. Bailyn, L. "Career and Family Orientations of Husbands and Wives in Relation to Marital Happiness." *Human Relations,* 1970, *23*(2), 97–113.
2. Dyer, W. G. "Family Reactions to the Father's Job." In A. Shostak and W. Gomberg (eds.), *Blue-Collar World: Studies of the American Worker.* Englewood Cliffs, N.J.: Prentice-Hall, 1964, pp. 86–92.
3. See Nevis, E. C. *Organizational Consulting: A Gestalt Approach.* New York: Garner Press, 1987.
4. See Cummings, T. G., and Huse, E. F. *Organization Development and Change.* St. Paul, Minn.: West, 1989; Kotter, J. P. *Organizational Dynamics: Diagnosis and Intervention.* Reading, Mass.: Addison-Wesley, 1978.

Chapter Thirteen

1. McClelland, D. C. "The Two Faces of Power." *Journal of International Affairs,* 1970, *24,* 29–47.
2. Peay, R. J., and Dyer, W. G., Jr. "Power Orientations of Entrepreneurs and Succession Planning." *Journal of Small Business Management,* 1989, *27*(1), 47–52.
3. See Dalton, G. W. "Influence and Organizational Change." In J. B. Ritchie and P. Thompson (eds.), *Organization and People* (1st ed.) St. Paul, Minn.: West, 1976, pp. 363–387.
4. Dalton, "Influence and Organizational Change," pp. 363–387.

INDEX

262